THE GREEK CHRONICLES

PART II

SUPPLEMENTS

TO

VETUS TESTAMENTUM

EDITED BY

THE BOARD OF THE QUARTERLY

VOLUME XXVII

LEIDEN
E. J. BRILL
1974

THE GREEK CHRONICLES

THE RELATION OF THE SEPTUAGINT OF I AND II CHRONICLES
TO THE MASSORETIC TEXT

BY

LESLIE C. ALLEN

PART II

TEXTUAL CRITICISM

LEIDEN
E. J. BRILL
1974

ISBN 90 04 03933 3

PRINTED IN BELGIUM

Dedicated to the memory of
W. P. M. Walters (Peter Katz)

CONTENTS

FOREWORD

This book is the sequel to the work already published, *The Greek Chronicles*, part I : *The Translator's Craft* (Supplements to Vetus Testamentum, vol. XXV), the bibliography of which was intended to cover this second volume. The two parts essentially hang together. In the first were explained presuppositions which govern many of the conclusions of the present volume, while in the second are supplied explanations for which the patient reader of the first has had to wait.

The whole study, which has grown out of a London University Ph. D thesis, represents a trek across a large literary and textual island with the aid of such scholarly maps as are available. The first volume reported a landing on the broken coastline of the extant Greek manuscript tradition, and forays into the hinterland of translation technique which lies behind the mountainous terrain of recensional activity. Now for the second half of the journey. On the other side of our island lies the level shore of the Masoretic Text, but many a path has to be hacked through the jungles of Greek and Hebrew corruption before contact with it may be made. On the way a comprehensive survey is drawn up showing territory stretching from one end of the island to the other for the critical use of future explorers.

I welcome this opportunity to record anew my gratitude to the British Academy, the Managers of the Hort Memorial Fund, the Trustees of the Bethune-Baker Fund and the Board of Governors of the London Bible College for financial aid towards the publication of this research.

The illustrations in chapter v, section 9, have been reproduced from "The Development of the Jewish Scripts" by F. M. Cross, Jr., in *The Bible and the Ancient Near East*, by kind permission of the publishers, Routledge and Kegan Paul, Ltd.

London Bible College   LESLIE C. ALLEN

ABBREVIATIONS

AJSL	*American Journal of Semitic Languages and Literatures*
Arm	Armenian Version
Boh	Bohairic Version
CBQ	*Catholic Biblical Quarterly*
ET	*Expository Times*
Eth	Ethiopic Version
Gk	Greek
Heb	Hebrew
HTR	*Harvard Theological Review*
HUCA	*Hebrew Union College Annual*
ICC	*International Critical Commentary*
IEJ	*Israel Exploration Journal*
JAOS	*Journal of the American Oriental Society*
JBL	*Journal of Biblical Literature*
JNES	*Journal of Near Eastern Studies*
Jos	*Josephus*
JQR	*Jewish Quarterly Review*
JSS	*Journal of Semitic Studies*
JTS	*Journal of Theological Studies*
La	Old Latin Version
LXX	Septuagint, Septuaginta
ms., mss.	manuscript(s)
MT	Massoretic Text, according to *Biblia Hebraica*[3]
NTS	*New Testament Studies*
OT	Old Testament
OTS	Oudtestamentische Studiën
PSBA	*Proceedings of the Society of Biblical Archaeology*
Pesh	Peshitta, cited according to Lee's edition and Barnes' *Apparatus Criticus*
RB	*Revue Biblique*
SBOT	*Sacred Books of the Old Testament*
Syh	Syro-Hexaplar Version
Targ	Targum, cited according to Sperber's edition
TLZ	*Theologische Literaturzeitung*
TQ	*Theologische Quartalschrift*
TR	*Theologische Rundschau*
TZ	*Theologische Zeitschrift*
VT	*Vetus Testamentum*
Vulg	Vulgate
ZAW	*Zeitschrift für die alttestamentische Wissenschaft*

The following abbreviations are used for OT and Apocryphal books. Where different the LXX is bracketed.

Gen Exod Lev Num Deut Jos Jud Sam (Rg) Ki (Rg) Isa Jer Ezek Hos Jon Hab Zeph Zech Mal Psa Prov Lam Eccles Esth Dan Neh (Esdr) Chron (Par and Esdr) Ecclus Macc.

CHAPTER ONE

GREEK TEXTUAL CHANGES

When a reading in Par ostensibly differs from MT, it is clearly important to locate at what stage divergence came about. In very many cases the root of the difference is imbedded within the Gk tradition and the Gk text can be reasonably emended, often with the aid of the textforms other than G, as Rehm noted,[1] to a reading identical with or close to MT. G embodies the oldest textform of Par but in a corrupt condition. This is the case especially where forms of names are concerned. Ziegler cites with approval Fischer:[2] "Die vielen und vielfachen Abweichungen der LXX von MT in der Eigennamen beruhen grösstenteils auf innergriechischer Korruption".[3] The treatment of names in this chapter depends upon the principles of transliteration set out by Wutz, Kahle and Ziegler.[4]

Only cases of inner-Gk corruption which have a possible bearing upon the pointed MT are handled in this chapter : many variants, such as those involving a perfect or an aorist tense, are immaterial for the present purpose. Instances which not only involve Gk corruption but actually go back to a *Vorlage* different from MT will be considered mainly in later chapters. Most of the possible sources of error are dealt with in standard works of Gk textual criticism.[5] The influence of adjacent columns, mentioned in Part I, ch. viii,[6] will be found to be an important factor here too.

Corrections of G which are to be found in Rahlfs' *Septuaginta* are marked "Ra.". His edition, in which no explanation of corruptions is generally given, tends to be a medley of the different textforms, mainly of G O R. In many cases his readings represent correct restoration of

---

[1] *Textkritische Untersuchungen zu den Parallelstellen der Samuel-Königsbücher und der Chronik*, p. 13.

[2] *Beiträge zur Jeremias-LXX*, p. 61.

[3] *Das Alphabet der LXX Vorlage im Pentateuch*, p. 13.

[4] Wutz, *Die Transkriptionen von der LXX bis zu Hieronymus*, pp. 64ff.; Fischer, *op. cit.*, pp. 1ff.; Kahle, *Cairo Geniza*², pp. 164ff.; Ziegler, *op. cit.* p. 60f.

[5] E.g., Greenlee, *Introduction to NT Textual Criticism*, pp. 63ff.

[6] p. 146.

the text of G, but unfortunately his text frequently incorporates material derived from the later, edited revisions of O L R.

The instances set out in each category are not necessarily complete. Some cases overlap and are only mentioned in one section. Others have already been mentioned in ch. viii or will be covered in later chapters.

Corruptions of the G group as a whole are to be discussed in this chapter. The discussion will also extend to cases where B has a corrupt reading while another member or other members of the group are free from the particular corruption in view. This latter area is covered on two counts. First, B is so often cited in editions, etc., and the fact that its readings are not characteristic of the group is overlooked or not realised. Secondly, when the group consists only of B c₂, as so often, it is difficult to decide in many cases whether c₂ has a revised text or not. If the present writer has at times erred in his judgment that c₂ preserves the correct text, rather than restores it, often along with other groups, these instances are not excluded, and little harm is done.

1. Substitution

(i) *Assimilation*

It was observed in Part. I, ch. ix that parallel passages in Sam-Ki/Rg exerted a powerful force of attraction upon Par both in its Gk form and in the underlying Heb. In fact, conformity to other elements is the strongest corrupting factor in the textual history of Par. Within a word consonants or syllables at times influence another part. In a sentence or passage one expression can exercise a moulding influence over a neighbouring one. Similar passages or phrases elsewhere in the book or even in other books can have a levelling effect.

(a) *Internal assimilation*

Parts of words in G have been influenced by other parts as follows. The second Gk form is the corrected one.

I 11.46 אלנעם : $E\lambda\lambda\alpha\alpha\mu$ (- $\lambda\alpha\mu$ S^{vid}) G : $E\lambda\nu\alpha\alpha\mu$ O R (Ra.).

12.5/4 יוזבד : $I\omega\zeta\alpha\beta\alpha\beta$ S (-$\beta\alpha\nu$ c₂ by phonetic error, $I\omega\alpha\zeta$- B by assimilation to $I\omega\alpha\nu\alpha\nu$) : $I\omega\zeta\alpha\beta\alpha\delta$ O L (Ra.).

II 17.8 טוב אדוניה : $T\omega\beta\alpha\delta\omega\beta\epsilon\iota\alpha$ B (-$\omega\beta\alpha$ c₂) : $T\omega\beta\alpha\delta\omega\nu\iota\alpha$ A a.

24.26 יהוזבד : $Z\omega\zeta\alpha\beta\epsilon\delta$ G : $I\omega\zeta\alpha\beta\epsilon\delta$ O L R (Ra.).

(b) *Local assimilation*

The influence of the context is evident in many cases. Names will be considered first. The second Gk form is the magnet to which the first has been attracted; the third one is the corrected form.

I 1.35 יעוש‎ : $I\epsilon ov\lambda$ G O : $P\alpha\gamma ov\eta\lambda$: $I\epsilon ovs$*.

v. 40 מנחת‎ : $M\alpha\chi\alpha v\alpha\mu$ G : $\Sigma\omega\lambda\alpha\mu$: $M\alpha v\alpha\chi\alpha\theta$ O R (Ra.). Metathesis has played a part in the corruption.

v. 49f. בעל חנן‎ : $B\alpha\lambda\alpha\epsilon vv\omega\rho$ G : $A\chi\alpha\beta\omega\rho$: $B\alpha\alpha\lambda\epsilon vv\omega v$* cf. $B\alpha\lambda\alpha\epsilon vv\omega v$ O.

v. 51 תמנע‎ : $\Theta\alpha\iota\mu\alpha v$ G : Θ. v. 53 : $\Theta\alpha\mu\alpha v\alpha$ O (Ra.).

2.14 רדי‎ : $Z\alpha\delta\delta\alpha\iota$ G : $M\alpha\zeta\alpha\rho$, $Z\alpha\phi\omega\epsilon\iota v$ 1.53f. in the previous column (12 lines away in BM) : $P\alpha\delta\delta\alpha\iota$ O (Ra.).

v. 23 ארם‎ : $A\rho\rho\alpha v$ G : A. v. 10 in the previous column (13 lines away in BM) : $A\rho\alpha\mu$ O L R (Ra.).

v. 25 רם‎ : $P\alpha v$ G : $B\alpha v\alpha\iota\alpha$: $P\alpha\mu$ O L R (Ra.).

ibid. אצם‎ : $A\sigma\alpha v$ G : $A\rho\alpha v$ O[1] : $A\sigma o\mu$ O L R (Ra.).

v. 29 אחבן‎ : $A\chi\alpha\beta\alpha\rho$ G : $I\alpha\sigma\alpha\rho$ v. 18 in the previous column (12 lines away in BM) : $A\chi\alpha\beta\alpha v$*.

v. 33 פלת‎ : $\Theta\alpha\lambda\epsilon\theta$ G : $I\omega v\alpha\theta\alpha v$: $\Phi\alpha\lambda\epsilon\theta$ O R (Ra.).

v. 48 תרחנה‎ : $\Theta\alpha\rho\alpha\mu$ G : $A\chi\epsilon\iota v\alpha\alpha\mu$ 3.1 in the next column (10 lines away in BM) : $\Theta\alpha\rho\alpha\alpha v\alpha$ L.

v. 50 שובל‎ : $\Sigma\omega\beta\alpha\rho$ G a n : $K\alpha\rho\iota\alpha\theta\iota\alpha\rho\epsilon\iota\mu$: $\Sigma\omega\beta\alpha\lambda$ O R (Ra.), as in v. 52.

v. 51 חרף‎ : $A\rho\epsilon\iota\mu$ G y : $K\alpha\rho\iota\alpha\theta\iota\alpha\rho\epsilon\iota\mu$ v. 50 : $A\rho\epsilon\iota\phi$*, as in II Esdr 17.24; 20.19 for חריף‎. BH falsely posits חרם‎.

3.5 שמעא‎ : $\Sigma\alpha\mu\alpha v$ G : $\Sigma\omega\beta\alpha v$: $\Sigma\alpha\mu\alpha\alpha$ O L R (Ra.).

ibid. שובב‎ : $\Sigma\omega\beta\alpha v$ G : $N\alpha\theta\alpha v$: $\Sigma\omega\beta\alpha\beta$ O L R (Ra.).

3.7 נפג‎ : $N\alpha\phi\alpha\theta$ B (-σ c₂) : $\Sigma\alpha\phi\alpha\theta$ v. 22 in the next column (13 lines away in BM) : $N\alpha\phi\alpha\gamma$* (Ra.). In the parallel 14.6 the name was changed to suit ($N\alpha\phi\alpha\tau$ S, c₂ omits).

v. 12 יותם‎ : $I\omega\alpha\theta\alpha v$ B N g n (-$\omega v\alpha$- c₂) : $M\alpha v\alpha\sigma\sigma\eta s$ v. 13, $I\omega\alpha v\alpha v$ v. 15 : $I\omega\theta\alpha\mu$ b R.

v. 18 יקמיה‎ : $I\epsilon\kappa\epsilon v\iota\alpha$ G O : $I\epsilon\chi ov\iota\alpha$ v. 17 : $I\epsilon\kappa\epsilon\mu\iota\alpha$ L R (Ra.).

v. 19 שלמית‎ : $\Sigma\alpha\lambda\omega\mu\epsilon\theta\epsilon\iota$ B O (-$\alpha\theta$- c₂) : $\Delta\epsilon v\epsilon\theta\epsilon\iota$ v. 18 : $\Sigma\alpha\lambda\omega\mu\iota\theta$ L (Ra.).

4.6 אחזם‎ : $\Omega\chi\alpha\iota\alpha$ B ($A\chi$- c₂) : $\Sigma\alpha\rho\alpha\iota\alpha$ v. 14 in the next column (10 lines away in BM) : $\Omega\chi\alpha\zeta\alpha\mu$ O (Ra.).

---

[1] See part I, p. 154.

ibid. אחשתרי : *Ασηραν* G : *Θαιμαν* : *Ασθηραι** cf. *Ασθηρα* A N h. *Θ* was lost after C.

v. 12 תחנה : *Θαιμαν* B (-εμ- c₂) : *Θ.* v. 6 : *Θανα* O R (Ra.).

v. 16 תיריא : *Ζαιρα* G : *Ζαιφα* A i : *Θαιρια** cf. *Αιθρια* b.

v. 17 אשתמע : *Εσθαιμων* G : *Μαιων* : *Εσθαμω* R, as in 6.42/57.

v. 18 בתיה : *Γελια* B (*Γελθια* c₂) from *Γεδια** : *Γεδωρ* : *Βεθια* e m. BH unnecessarily suggests a *Vorlage* עליה.

v. 20 זוחת² : *Ζωαβ* G : *Μωαβ* v. 22 : *Ζωαθ* O R (Ra.).

v. 21 מרשה : *Μαιχα* G : *Ληχα* : *Μαρισα* R.

v. 22 יואש : *Ιωαδα* G : *Λααδα* O v. 21 : *Ιωας* O L R (Ra.).

v. 37/36 שפעי : *Σαφαλ* B (c₂ omits) : *Ασοσαλ* : *Σαφαι* R.

5.5 ראיה : *Ρηχα* G O : *Ηχα* : *Ρααια** ?, as originally in 4.2.

v. 6 תלגת פלנאסר : *Θαλγαβανασαρ* G : *Βαναια* v. 4 : *Θαλγαθφαλνασαρ** cf. *Θαγλ.* O.

v. 7 יעיאל : *Ιωηλ* G O L R : *Ι.* vv. 4, 7, 8 : *Ιειηλ**.

v. 13 יורי : *Ιωρεε* B O (-σε c₂) : *Σεβεε* : *Ιωρει**.

v. 14 ירוח : *Ιουρει* B (*Ουρει* c₂)¹ : *Ουρει* : *Ιρουα** ?

v. 16 גלעד : *Γαλααμ* G : *Ζαβουχαμ* v. 14 : *Γαλααδ* O L R (Ra.).

v. 26 פול : *Φαλωκ* m c₂ (-χ B) : *Σαδωκ* 6.12 in the next column (12 lines away in BM) : *Φωλ** ?

ibid. גוזן : *Χωζαρ* B (*Χωραρ* c₂) : *Χαβωρ* : *Γωζαν* O R (Ra.).

v. 32f./6.6f. מריות : *Μαρειηλ* G : *Οζειηλ* 6.18 in the next column (10 lines away in BM) : *Μαριωθ* L R. The same form is found in 6.37/52.

6.6/21 יואה : *Ιωαβ* B (-μ c₂) : *Αμειναδαβ* v. 22 : *Ιωαχ* O (Ra.).

v. 9/24 תחת : *Κααθ* B (*Καλθ* c₂) : *Κ.* v. 22 : *Θααθ* O L R (Ra.), as in v. 37.

v. 54/69 גת־רמון : *Γεθωρων* G : *Βαιθωρων* v. 68 (Albright, "List of Levitic Cities", p. 68) : *Γεθρεμμων* O L (Ra.).

v. 65/80 מחנים : *Μααναιθ* G : *Γεεμαιθ* c₂ (*Γεμεεθ* B) in 7.8 in the next column (13 lines away in BM) : *Μααναιμ* O R (Ra., Albright, p. 65).

v. 66/81 יעזיר : *Γαζερ* G : *Γ.* v. 67 (Albright, p. 73) : *Ιαζηρ* O L R (Ra.).

7.10 כנענה : *Χανααν* G L : *Ζαιθαν* : *Χανανα* O R (Ra.), as originally in II 18.10,23.

v. 13 בלהה : *Βαλαμ* G : *Ουλαμ* v. 17 : *Βαλαα** (Ra.) cf. *Βαλλα* O.

v. 15 עלפחד : *Σαπφααδ* G : *Σαπφειν* *: *Σαλπααδ* A L (Ra.).

---

¹ The Gk forms stand in place of יחדו which was transposed with ירוח : see p. 64.

v. 33 יפלט‎[1,2] : *Αφαληκ* G (*Ιαφαηλ* B in second case, assimilated to *Ιμαβαηλ*) : *Βαισηκι* : *Ιαφαλητ* O (Ra.). *Iota* was lost by haplography.

8.12 אונו‎ : *Ωναν* B (*Εν-* c2), earlier *Ωνα* R before receiving a case ending : *Ωλα* 7.39 in the previous column (12 lines away in BM) : *Ωνω* O (Ra.).

v. 13 אילון‎ : *Αιλαμ* G O R : *A.* v. 24 : *Αιλων**, as originally in II 28.18.

v. 14 שׁשׁק‎ : *Σωκηλ* G : *Μειχαηλ* v. 16 : *Σωσηκ* A N (Ra.), cf. v. 25. The assimilation took place after the original form had suffered metathesis to *Σωκης**.

v. 18 אלפעל‎ : *Ελχααδ* G : *Μελχηλ* v. 35 in the next column (13 lines away in BM) : *Ελφααλ* O R (Ra.).

v. 21 עדיה‎ : *Αβια* G : *Αβιουδ* v. 3 in the preceding column (12 lines away in BM) : *Αδια**.

v. 25 שׁשׁק‎ : *Σωιηκ* B (*Σωηηκ* c2) : *Φελιηλ* : *Σωσηκ* O R (Ra.).

v. 36 עזמות‎ : *Σαλμω* G : *Σαλαιμαθ* : *Ασμωθ* L (Ra.). *Θ* was lost.

v. 38 עזריקם‎ : *Εζρεικαι* B* (*Εζρει* c2) : *καί* : *Εζρικαμ* O L R (Ra.).

v. 39 עשׁק‎ : *Ασηλ* B (-*Εσ* c2 R) : *Εσηλ* v. 38 : *Ασεκ* L ?

9.17 אחימן‎ : *Αιμαμ* B (*Αιλ-* c2) : *Ταμμαμ* : *Αιμαν* O L (Ra.).

v. 44 עזריקם‎ : *Εσδρεικαν* B (*Εζρ-* S h c2) : *Αναν* : *Εσδρικαμ* i (Ra.).

11.12,29 אחוחי‎ : *Αχωνει* G (*Αρχ-* B in v. 12, assimilated to *άρχοντες* v. 10; *Αναχωνει* S* in v. 29, assimilated to *Αναθωθει* v. 28) : *Αχαμανει* v. 11 : *Αχωχι* O R (Ra.) in v. 12.

v. 30 מהרי‎ : *Νεερε* G (-*αι* c2) : *Νετωφατει* : *Μοοραι* O (Ra.). There is no need to posit נהרי‎ with BH. In the parallel II Rg 23.28 *Νοερε* KR (*Μααρναν* L, assimilated to *Ελιμαν*) is probably assimilated to Par.

v. 41 זבד‎ : *Ζαβετ* G : *Χεττει* : *Ζαβεδ* m.

12.21/20 יוזבד‎ : *Τωζαβαθ* G : *αὐτῷ* : *Ιωζαβαδ* O L R (Ra.).

v. 28/27 יהוידע‎ : *Τωαδαε* S c2 (-*ας* B) : *τῷ Ααρων* : *Ιωδαε* O[mss].

13.6 קרית יערים‎ : *πόλιν Δαυιδ* G O R : *π. Δ.* v. 13 in the next column (11 lines away in BM) : *Καριαθιαρειμ* L[1].

14.11 בעל פרצים‎[1] : *Φααλφαθισειμ* B (*Φαλ-* c2, *Φαλααδφαθισει* S) : *Ναφαθ* v. 6 : *Βααλφαρισειμ**. The first *Φ* is by internal assimilation.

15.18 עני‎ : *Ιωηλ* G (*Ελιωηλ* B, anticipating *Ελιαβ*) : *I.* v. 17 : *Ωνι** (Rothstein, Ra.), as in v. 20. Dittography of *iota* encouraged the assimilation.

19.16 שׁופך‎ : *Σωφαρ* B N, *Εσωφαρ* S* (*Σωφακ* c2 = L R) : *άρχ-*,

---

[1] See part I, p. 165.

$A\delta\rho\alpha\alpha\zeta\alpha\rho$: $\Sigma\omega\phi\alpha\chi$ O (Ra.). Rehm, p. 58, thinks in terms of a ר/כ error.

25.19 חשביה : $A\rho\iota\alpha$ B ($\Sigma\alpha\rho\iota\alpha$ i c₂) : $A\zeta\alpha\rho\iota\alpha$: $A\sigma\alpha\beta\iota\alpha$ O L (Ra.). ʌc was lost between c and A.

v. 31 רוממתי עזר : $Po\mu\epsilon\lambda\chi\epsilon\iota\omega\theta$ Bᵃᵇ ᵛⁱᵈ c₂ ($Po\mu\epsilon\lambda\chi\epsilon\iota$ B*) : $M\epsilon\lambda\chi\epsilon\iota\alpha$ 26.14 (16 lines away in BM) : $Po\mu\epsilon\mu\theta\iota\omega\delta$* (Ra.). עוד was read; there was a δ/θ error.

26.4 יואח : $I\omega\alpha\theta$ G : $I\omega\zeta\alpha\beta\alpha\theta$: $I\omega\alpha\chi$*, as originally in 6.6/21; II 29.12. Ziegler sees here a χ/θ error,[1] but this explanation is hardly adequate.

v. 24 שבאל : $I\omega\eta\lambda$: I. v. 22 : $\Sigma\omega\beta\alpha\eta\lambda$*, then dittography of iota, cf. $I\omega\beta\alpha\eta\lambda$ 24.20.

27.10 חלץ : $X\epsilon\sigma\lambda\epsilon\varsigma$ G : -εc six times in v. 9f. : $X\epsilon\lambda\lambda\eta\varsigma$ O L R (Ra.). II 11.6 בית-לחם : $B\alpha\iota\theta\sigma\epsilon\epsilon\mu$ B* A n ($B\epsilon\epsilon\theta$- c₂) : $B\alpha\iota\theta\sigma\sigma\upsilon\rho\alpha$ v. 7 : $B\alpha\iota\theta\lambda\epsilon\epsilon\mu$ Bᵃᵇ a (Ra.).

v. 18 אליאב : $E\lambda\iota\alpha\nu$ G : $A\beta\alpha\iota\alpha\nu$: $E\lambda\iota\alpha\beta$ O L R (Ra.).

v. 19 זהם : $Po\omicron\lambda\lambda\alpha\mu$ G : $Po\beta o\alpha\mu$ v. 18 : $Z\alpha\alpha\mu$ L R, probably via $Z\alpha\lambda\alpha\mu$ O.

14.8/9 מרשה : $M\alpha\rho\iota\sigma\eta\lambda$ G : $\mathring{\eta}\lambda\theta\epsilon\nu$: $M\alpha\rho\iota\sigma\eta\varsigma$*, as in v. 10; 20.37.

22.5 רמות : $P\alpha\mu\alpha$ G : P. v. 6 : $P\alpha\mu\omega\theta$ R, as in 18.2ff. רמה would be impossible in the context. רמת (BH) is less likely.

23.1 ירחם : $I\omega\rho\alpha\mu$ G O L R : I. 22.7 in the preceding column (13 lines away in BM) : $I\rho\alpha\alpha\mu$*, as in I 8.27; 9.8,12.

ibid. אלישפט : $E\lambda\epsilon\iota\sigma\alpha\phi\alpha\nu$ B b R (-$\phi\alpha$ c₂ e₂) : 'Αζαρίαν, Μασάιαν : $E\lambda\iota\sigma\alpha\phi\alpha\tau$ O. ן– (BH) must be ruled out.

27.1 צדוק : $\Sigma\alpha\delta\omega\rho$ B h (-$\omega\iota$ c₂) : $\theta\upsilon\gamma\acute{\alpha}\tau\eta\rho$: $\Sigma\alpha\delta\omega\kappa$ O R (Ra.).

29.12 עזריהו¹,² : $Z\alpha\chi\alpha\rho\acute{\iota}o\upsilon$ G O R, $Z\alpha\chi\alpha\rho\acute{\iota}\alpha\varsigma$ G m n : $Z\alpha\chi\alpha\rho\iota\alpha$ v. 1 (15, 16 lines away in BM) : 'Αζαρίου L, 'Αζαρίας O L R. An underlying זכריה (Curtis, BH) is less likely : the two names are frequently confused in the LXX.

ibid. זמה : $Z\epsilon\mu\mu\alpha\theta$: $M\alpha\alpha\theta$, $M\alpha\theta\theta\alpha\nu\acute{\iota}\alpha\varsigma$ v. 13 : $Z\epsilon\mu\mu\alpha$ L R.

ibid. עדן : $I\omega\delta\alpha\nu$ G A c : $I\omega\alpha\chi\alpha$: $I\alpha\delta\alpha\nu$ f j (l = ע). According to Kittel, SBOT, the form was originally $\Omega\delta\alpha\nu$* and iota came in by dittography. In 31.15 $O\delta o\mu$ ($I\alpha\delta\alpha\nu$ L) appears.

31.13 אליאל : $I\epsilon\epsilon\iota\eta\lambda$ G : $I\epsilon\iota\eta\lambda$ O L R : $E\lambda\iota\eta\lambda$ O L R (Ra.). The corruption was encouraged by dittography of iota.

35.9 יעיאל : $I\omega\eta\lambda$ G : $I\omega\zeta\alpha\beta\alpha\delta$: $I\epsilon\iota\eta\lambda$ O L R (Ra.).

---

[1] Op. cit., p. 4f.

In all these cases the group reading of G has been corrupted by assimilation to adjacent forms. Below are set out instances where B has been so affected, but the original reading has been preserved intact or fairly so by (an)other member(s) of the group.

I 1.42 יעקן : $Ωναν$ B (-$αμ$ c₂) : $Ωναν$ v. 40 : $Ιωκαν$ h (Ra.). *Iota* was lost after $καί$.

2.34 ששׁן[1,2] : $Σωσαμ$ B : $Ραμεηλ$ v. 33 : $Σωσαν$ c₂ O R (Ra.). as in vv. 31,35.

v. 51 בית־גדד : $Βαιθγαιδων$ B ($Γαι$- c₂) : $Σαλωμων, Λαμμων$: $Βαιθγαιδωρ$ h = $Βαιθγεδωρ$ O (Ra.).

4.8 עגוב : $Εννων$ B : $Σεννων$ v. 7 : $Ενωβ$ c₂ O R (Ra.).

v. 20 זוחת[1] : $Ζωαν$ B : $Αναν$ * : $Ζωαθ$ c₂ (Ra.).

5.16 בשׁן : $Βασαμ$ B : $Ζαβουχαμ$ v. 14 : $Βασαν$ c₂ O L R (Ra.).

v. 24 יחדיאל : $Ιελειηλ$ B : $Ελειηλ$: $Ιεδιηλ$ c₂ O L (Ra.).

6.65/80 ראמות : $Ραμμων$ B : $Εσεβων$ v. 81 : $Ραμωθ$ c₂ O R (Ra.).

7.17 בדן : $Βαδαμ$ B : $Ουλαμ$ v. 16 : $Βαδαν$ c₂ O R (Ra.).

11.31 איתי : $Αιρει$ B : $Ουρει$ v. 32 : $Αιθει$ S c₂ (Ra.).

v. 34 הררי : $Αραχει$ B* ($Αχρει$ c₂[vid]) : $Αχειμ$ v. 35 : $Αραρει$ B[ab] O R (Ra.), cf. $Ραρει$ S.

19.18 שׁופך : $Σαφαθ$ (-$ατ$ c₂) : $Γολιαθ$ 20.5 in the next column (13 lines away in BM), then internal assimilation : $Σωφαχ$* (Grabe, Ra.), cf. v. 16 and $Σοφαχ$ h.

II 23.1 עדיהו : $Αζεια$ B* : $'Αζαρίαν$: $Αδεια$ B[ab] c₂.

Other types of word besides proper nouns have been corrupted by attraction to other words nearby. Forms of $υίός$, for instance, appear to have suffered such inner-Gk corruption at times.

I 5.14 בן[1] : $υίοί$ G R : $υίοί$ earlier : $υίοῦ$ O L (Ra.), as needed in the context.

26.1 לקרחים : $υίοί$ G R $Κορεειμ$ G : $υίοί$ in the oft repeated formula in 25.9-31 : $υίοῖς$ O (Ra.).[1]

v. 2 בנים : $υίοῦ$ G : $Ζαχαρίου$: $υίοί$ O L R (Ra.).

The error has been perpetrated in B only, of the G group, as follows:

I 4.15 ובניו : $καὶ$ $υίοῦ$ B : $υίοῦ$ two words later : $κ.$ $υίοί$ c₂ O L R (Ra.). The genitive makes no sense.

5.18 בני : $υίοῦ$ B N f m n : series of $υίοῦ$ v. 14f. : $υίοί$ c₂ O L R (Ra.).

25.10 בניו : $υίὸς$ $αὐτοῦ$ B : $τρίτος$: $υίοί$ a. c₂ O R (Ra.).

---

[1] For $Κορεειμ$ see Part I, p. 150.

Forms of αὐτός are often confused through the proximity of different case-endings.

I 7.21 והרגום : καὶ ἀπέκτειναν αὐτόν G z : αὐτοῦ earlier : ...αὐτούς O L (Ra.) via αὐτοῦ R. The error in z is probably independent of G. αὐτῶν in v. 21f. strongly suggests an original plural here. Rothstein and BH wrongly posit והרגוהו.

v. 22 אחיו : ἀδελφοὶ αὐτῶν G : αὐτῶν six words before : ...αὐτοῦ O L R (Ra.), as required in the context.

10.3 וימצאהו : καὶ εὖρον αὐτούς G : αὐτοῦ vv. 2,4 : ...αὐτόν O L R (Ra.) via αὐτοῦ*. The next verb ἐπόνεσεν S O R was then made plural in B c₂.

v. 10 כליו : τὰ σκεύη αὐτῶν G : αὐτῶν four words later : ...αὐτοῦ O L R (Ra.), as τὴν κεφαλὴν αὐτοῦ shows.

II 26.14 להם : αὐτούς G L : ὑπεναντίους : αὐτοῖς O R (Ra.).

II Ki.24.2/36.5b בו : ἐπ᾽ αὐτοῦ G A : ἀπ᾽ αὐτοῦ v. 5a : ἐπ᾽ αὐτούς Bᵃᵇ O L R (Ra.).[1]

Similar errors are found in B.

I 15.9 אחיו : οἱ ἀδελφοὶ αὐτῶν B z : ἄρχων : ...αὐτοῦ S c₂ O L R (Ra.), as required in the context.

16.41 עמהם : μετ᾽ αὐτοῦ B O : τοῦ ... τοῦ v. 40 : μετ᾽ αὐτῶν S c₂ L R (Ra.).

II 20.33 אבתיהם : τῶν πατέρων αὐτοῦ B e g e₂ : τοῦ πατρὸς αὐτοῦ v. 32 : ...αὐτῶν c₂ O b R (Ra.).

Forms of the definite article and of αὐτός are sometimes confused.[2]

II 19.2 אל־המלך : αὐτῷ Βασιλεύ(ς) G O L R . τῷ βασιλεῖ*.

27.3 (עפל)ה : αὐτοῦ G, cf. αὐτῆς R : τοῦ O L (Ra.).

33.14 (עפל)ל : εἰς αὐτόν G, cf. αὐτό Oᵐˢˢ, αὐτήν R: εἰς τό oᵐᵍ, cf. εἰς τόν Oᵐˢˢ L.

Confusion of forms of ἡμεῖς and ὑμεῖς are at times due not merely to itacism but to local assimilation.

II 13.12 עליכם ... אבתיכם : ἐφ᾽ ἡμᾶς G m ... τῶν πατέρων ἡμῶν G O R : ἡμῶν earlier : ... ὑμᾶς O L R (Ra.) ... ὑμῶν L.

29.9 אבותינו ... ובנינו ובנותינו ונשינו : οἱ πατέρες ὑμῶν B O ... ὑμῶν G O L ... ὑμῶν G O L ... ὑμῶν G O L: ὑμεῖς ... ὑμῶν v. 8 : ἡμῶν c₂ L R, R, R, R. Despite אבותיכם in one Ken. ms., assimilated to

---

[1] See Part I, p. 116.

[2] Cf. too Part I, pp. 150, 200 note 1.

בעיניכם v. 8, the error is probably Gk here. Curtis suggested that the change was deliberate : Hezekiah's own family did not suffer.

30.9 אלהיכם : ὁ θεὸς ἡμῶν G O L R : ἐλεήμων : ... ὑμῶν e. ἐπιστρέψωμεν G O (L) R for תשובו is an inner-Gk adaptation of ἐπιστρέψητε f j after the earlier error. But ἀφ'ὑμῶν for מכם intervenes in B f h j. This must at an earlier stage have been ἀφ' ἡμῶν c₂ O L R (Ra.), assimilated to ἡμῶν.

32.11 יצילנו : σώσει ὑμᾶς G O L : ὑμᾶς twice in this verse, σῶσαι ὑμᾶς v. 14 : σ. ἡμᾶς R (Ra.).

Sometimes an error of this kind in B has not been perpetrated elsewhere in the group.

I 12.18/17 אבותינו : τῶν πατέρων ὑμῶν B c₂ Omss. : ὑμᾶς : ... ἡμῶν S Omss. L R (Ra.).

28.8 בניכם : τοῖς υἱοῖς ἡμῶν B : ἡμῶν earlier : ... ὑμῶν c₂ O L R (Ra.).

II 10.11,14 עלכם : τὸν ζυγὸν ἡμῶν B f e₂*, B e₂ : τ. ζ. ἡμ. v. 10 : ...ὑμῶν c₂ O b R (Ra.).

19.10 מאחיכם : τῶν ἀδελφῶν ἡμῶν B A e g e₂ : ἡμῶν 20.6 in the next column (13 lines away in BM) : ... ὑμῶν c₂ O b R (Ra.).

Verb endings in - εν, - ον and the like are frequently confused through the influence of a verb or other word nearby.

II 8.18 ויבאו ... ויקחו : καὶ ᾤχετο G ... καὶ ἔλαβεν G c e : ᾤχετο (= הלך) v. 17 : ᾤχοντο ... ἔλαβον O L R (Ra.). The second verb was adapted after the first was corrupted.

20.3 ויקרא : καὶ ἐκήρυξαν G O : νηστείαν : κ. ἐκήρυξεν L R (Ra.). There is no reason for a plural.

v.21 ואמרים : καὶ ἔλεγεν G A : the singular verbs earlier : κ. ἔλεγον O L R (Ra).

v. 36 ויעשׂו : καὶ ἐποίησεν G O L R : four verbs ending in - εν vv. 35, 37 : κ. ἐποίησαν f j.

21.11 ויזן : καὶ ἐξεπόρνευσαν G : κ. ἐξεπόρνευσας v. 13 : κ. ἐξεπόρνευσεν O L R (Ra.).

24.11 ויערו : καὶ ἐξεκένωσεν G t : the preceding singular verb before a composite subject : κ. ἐξεκένωσαν B^ab O L R (Ra.). The plural verb four words later (n c₂ make it singular) points to an original plural here.

25.27 וישלחו ... וימיתהו : καὶ ἀπέστειλεν G N^a? d* f j y* ...

ἐθανάτωσεν B j : ἔφυγεν, κατόπισθεν : κ. ἀπέστειλαν O L R (Ra.)
... ἐθανάτωσαν c₂ O L R (Ra.). After the first verb was mechanically
assimilated, the second verb was adapted in B j only.

28.5 ויכו¹ : καὶ ἐπάταξεν G O L R : ἐν following : κ. ἐπάταξαν*, as
expected before the following plural verb. For the error compare v. 17
ἐπάταξαν ἐν : - ξεν ἐν d p c₂.

29.15 ויאספו : καὶ συνήγαγεν G b : κ. συν. v. 20 in the next column
(11 lines away in BM) : κ. συνήγαγον O e₂ R (Ra.). The plural is
necessary in the context.

30.6 וישב : καὶ ἐπιστρέψατε G : ἐπ. earlier (= שובו) : κ. ἐπιστρέψει
O L R (Ra.).

v. 19 לדרוש : ἐκζητούσης G : κατευθυνούσης : ἐκζητῆσαι O L R
(Ra.).

32.3 ויעזרוהו : καὶ συνεπίσχυσεν αὐτῷ G : the verbs ending in -εν in
vv. 2-4 : κ. συνεπίσχυσαν ... O L R (Ra.). The singular is impossible
in the context.

v. 20 ויזעקו : καὶ ἐβόησεν G : κ. ἐβόησεν v. 18 : κ. ἐβόησαν O L R
(Ra.), as required in the context.

33.10 הקשיבו : ἐπήκουσεν G a : the singular verbs before and after :
ἐπήκουσαν O R (Ra.). This could conceivably be a case of haplography
of waw, but αὐτούς in v. 11 suggests an original plural in Par.

34.17 ויתנוהו : καὶ ἔδωκεν G : κ. ἔδ. (= ויתן) v. 15 : κ. ἔδωκαν O L
(Ra.).

35.24 וירכיבהו : καὶ ἀνεβίβασεν αὐτόν G : κατέστησεν 36.4 in the
next column (13 lines away in BM) : κ. ἀνεβίβασαν ... O L R (Ra.).
A singular is out of place in the context.

Similar errors in B, not reproduced elsewhere in the group, are as
follows :

II 10.3 ויקראו ... וישלחו : κ. ἀπέστειλεν κ. ἐκάλεσεν B h : the singular verbs before and after : κ. ἀπέστειλαν κ. ἐκάλεσαν c₂ O L R (Ra.).

22.8 וימצא : καὶ εὗρον B : οἶκον : κ. εὗρεν c₂ O L R (Ra.).

25.13 ויבזו ... ויכו : καὶ ἐπάταξεν B a e h e₂ ... καὶ ἐσκύλευσεν B :
ἐν after ἐπάτ. : κ. ἐπάταξαν c₂ O b R (Ra.) ... κ. ἐσκύλευσαν c₂
O L R (Ra.). After the first mechanical change the second verb was
adapted.

There are a large number of miscellaneous corruptions influenced
by elements in the context.

I 7.29 באלה : ἐν ταύτῃ G : αὐτῆς : ἐν ταύταις O L R (Ra.) via ταύτης* ?

9.33 פטירים (בלשכת) : διατεταγμέναι G O : ἐφημερίαι B c₂ O R, for which S rightly has ἐφημερίᾳ : διατεταγμένοι Sᵃ L R (BH). The phrase does not go back to a different unknown *Vorlage*, as Rothstein claims, but is a paraphrase. "Set apart in the Temple chambers" is interpreted, not unreasonably, as "on duty in a Levitical course". It is interesting to note that διατάσσειν occurs in Par elsewhere only at II 5.11, again in a free rendering : διατεταγμένοι G O L R for לשמור.

18.8 (מבחרי[1]) : ἐκ τῶν ἐκλεκτῶν πολέμων B S h : πολεμ- twice in v. 10 : ... πόλεων c₂ O L R (Wutz, p. 33 ; Ra.). c₂ has probably been revised. Wutz compares 26.27 ; Isa 14.21 for the error. Here assimilation is clearly the cause.

20.3 (ערי-) לכל : τοῖς παισίν G R : παῖδες 21.3 (13 whole lines away in BM) : τ. πᾶσιν f g n (Ra.). Cf. 22.17 for a similar error, as Ra. notes, and also II 6.14 παισίν : *omnibus* Arm. There is no need to read ταῖς πόλεσιν with Schleusner.[2]

21.6 נתעב (read as נבעת) : κατίσχυσεν (λόγος ...) G : λόγος ... κατίσχυσεν* (=חזק) v. 4 (the second suggestion of Schleusner, vol. ii, p. 239) : κατέσπευσεν* (= נבעת v. 30). The operative phrase is now missing in B, but it probably stood there in this form before the whole clause was lost by parablepsis (c₂'s partial filling of the lacuna can hardly be original). For κατέσπ. compare κατετάχυνεν L, κατετάχησεν R, which may well be replacements of the original with a synonym : cf. II 24.5 σπεύσατε : ταχύνατε L. Compare too μηδὲν μελλησάντα in Jos., *Ant.* vii. 318. The translator took the Heb to mean that David's orders did not allow Joab enough time to complete the work.

v. 11 קבל : ἔκλεξαι G O L R: ἔκλ. v. 10 : ἔκδεξαι n (Rehm, p. 51). As Rehm notes, the error had already occurred when ἔκλ. σεαυτῷ was taken over into II Rg. 24.13.

22.17 כל : παισίν G A m : ταῖς ἡμέραις v. 9 (12-13 lines away in BM) : πᾶσιν O R (Ra.).

24.31 ראשי : ἄρχων τῶν G Oᵐˢˢ : τῶν and other - ων syllables : ἀρχόντων A N* c h Arm (Ra.).

26.27 המלחמות : τῶν πόλεων G O L R : δυνάμεως v. 26 : τ. πολέμων A* (Wutz, p. 33, Ra.).

---

[1] See Part I, p. 195.

[2] *Lexicon*, ii, p. 627. See Part I, p. 117.

29.23 וַיִּצְלַח : καὶ εὐδοκήθη G O L R : εὐδοκῆσαι v. 3 : κ. εὐοδώθη*
(Thackeray, *Grammar*, p. 268; Wutz, p. 34; Goettsberger). This is in
fact the standard equivalent in Par. Thackeray compared the LXX variant in A at Isa. 54.17 Goettsberger, without referring to Thackeray,
also cites variants in Jer 2.37; 14.10. It needs to be added that the
corruption is here due to a reminiscence of the verb in v.3.

II 1.16 הסוסים : τῶν ἱππέων G R : τ. ἱπ. (= הפרשים) v. 14 (Ra.) :
τ. ἵππων O L (Ra.). Rehm, p. 42, compares III Rg. 10.32 and finds
here parallel assimilation. But the error may easily be independent :
cf. ἱππέων in Rg. v. 29. If it is a case of parallel assimilation, it is
probably *from* Par : cf. the borrowing of v. 31 from II Par. 1.15.

3.8 רתבו : τὸ μῆκος G R : μ. earlier : τὸ εὖρος O L (Ra.), as rendered
in 4.1; 6.13.

v. 11 כרוב : χερουβειν G : χ. earlier : χερουβ O L R (Ra.).

v. 15 הבית : τοῦ τοίχου G : τ. τ. τοῦ οἴκου v. 11f. : τοῦ οἴκου
O L R (Ra.).

6.16 בתורתי : ἐν τῷ ὀνόματί μου G : τῷ ὀν. v. 10 in the previous
column (12 lines away in BM) : ... νόμῳ ... O L R (Ra.). Ziegler lists
a number of places where the words are confused, but omits this one.[1]
BH wrongly presupposes בשמי.

v. 41 חסידיך : (ἱερεῖς ...) οἱ υἱοί σου G O : ἱερεῖς ... οἱ υἱοί 7.2f. :
οἱ ὅσιοί σου L R = *sancti* La (Wutz, p. 34; Katz, *TLZ* lxi, col. 269;
Rudolph).

7.11 הבא על : ὅσα ἐποίησεν ἐν G : ἐποίησεν vv. 7-10, ποιῆσαι later
in the verse : ὅ. ἐπῆλθεν* supported by *supervenerant* La. O L R
correct to ἠθέλησεν according to the parallel III Rg 9.1 for חפץ or to
II Par 8.6 for חשק. The emended equivalent is found also at 20.9;
22.1; 32.23. ἐπί follows in those cases, but the dative here is good Gk
for the special sense here employed "come into one's mind".

9.28 לשלמה : τῶν Σ. G : τῶν earlier : τῷ Σ. O L R (Ra.). Cf. 1.16
τῷ : τῶν A for the same reason.

13.6 וימרד על : καὶ ἀνέστη ἀπό G : ἀνέστη earlier : κ. ἀπέστη
O L R (Ra.). Cf. ἀποστῆναι ἀπό for מעל ב in 26.18 G O L R, etc.

v. 7 ויתאמצו : καὶ ἀνέστη G : ἀνέστη v.6 : κ. ἀντέστη O R.[2] Cf.
התחזק : ἀντέστη G O R at the end of the verse.

16.13 בשנת ארבעים ואחת : ἐν τῷ ἐνάτῳ καὶ τριακοστῷ ἔτει (Bab)[3]

---

[1] *Op. cit.*, p. 45.

[2] For the singular in the *Vorlage* see p. 151.

[3] For parablepsis in B* see p. 50f.

c₂ O L : the same phrase in v. 12 : ἐν τῷ ἑνὶ καὶ τεσσερακοστῷ ἔτει*. Cf. ἐν τῷ τεσσ. κ. ἑνὶ ἔτει A, an unusual order according to Thackeray.[1]

21.18 לחלי : μαλακίαν B (c₂) a f h j : κοιλίαν : μαλακία O R (Ra.). c₂ omits by homoeoteleuton of -ίαν.

24.5 מהרו : ἐπίστευσαν G O : ἐπισκευάσαι v. 12 in the next column (13 lines away in BM) : ἔσπευσαν R (Wutz, p. 16; Ra.). Note the same equivalent just before.

v. 6 והקהל : ὅτι ἐξεκ(κ)λησίασεν G Omss e₂ R : ὅτι v. 7 : ὅτε ... Omss (Ra.).

v. 18 באשמתם : ἐν τῇ ἡμέρᾳ G O L (in doublet) R : Ιερουσαλημ ἐν : ἐν τῇ ἁμαρτίᾳ* (Schleusner, ii, p. 21; Rudolph). Cf. 28.13 for the rendering. After the sequence ημε probably τημερτίᾳ* was read, which was "corrected" to the present error. Peccato La preserves the original form, as Rudolph notes. BH wrongly posits (ההוא) ביום.

28.10 אשמות : μαρτυρῆσαι G O R : ὑμῖν μεθ' : ἁμαρτῆσαι* (Schleusner, ii, p. 410; Wutz, p. 33; Rudolph). This equivalent appears in v. 13. After the sequence νμ, (ὑμῶν) μαρτῆσαι* was probably written, and then "corrected" to the present form. For confusion of the two verbs compare in the New Testament John 5.39 αἱ μαρτυροῦσαι : ἁμαρτανοῦσαι D.

29.7 לאלהי (בקדש) : (ἐν τῷ ἁγίῳ) θεῷ G (O L R) : ἁγίῳ : θεοῦ*. ἁγίῳ was wrongly regarded as an adjective. It was intended in a substantival sense "holy place, i.e., nave".[2]

30.25 ביהודה (היושבים) : (οἱ κατοικοῦντες) ἀπὸ Ιουδα G : εἰσελθέντες ἀπό : ἐν I. O L R (Ra.). This could theoretically be a ב/מ error, but the Gk reads most unnaturally.

32.18 ליראם : τοῦ βοηθῆσαι αὐτοῖς G O R : ἐβόησεν : τοῦ φοβῆσαι αὐτούς L (Ra.). Wutz, p. 31, suggested πτοηθῆσαι (sic); cf. Schleusner, vol. i, p. 463 "orta ex πτοῆσαι".

v. 19 אלהי עמי : θῡ Σαλωμων G : Ιερουσαλημ : θεοὺς λαῶν O R (BM, Ra.) probably via ΘΕΟΥϹΑΛΗΜΩΝ*.

34.22 שומר הבגדים : φυλάσσουσαν τὰς ἐντολάς G O L (in doublet) R : φυλασσειν τὰς ἐντολάς v. 31: lower down in the next column (18 lines away in BM) : ... στολάς (Schleusner, ii, p. 375f., following Montfaucon -c/є-, Wutz, p. 22, Ra.). Rehm, p. 61 posits הַפְּקוּדִים, for

---

[1] Grammar, p. 189.

[2] Gehman, VT iv, p. 345.

which Orlinsky rightly takes him to task.[1] The present writer has seen
no previous reference to the influence of v. 31.

v. 30 הנמצא (...ספר) : τοὺς εὑρεθέντας G L R : τ. εὑρ. v. 32f. : τοῦ
εὑρεθέντος O (Ra.).

35.7 עזים : ἀγίων G : ἄγια v. 13 in the next column (12 lines away in
BM) and ἄγια O R v. 6 : αἰγῶν O L R (BM, Ra.).

v. 15 עבדתם : τῆς λειτουργίας ἀγίων G O (R) : ἄγια v. 13 : ... αὐτῶν
L (Wutz, p. 18). For the confusion cf. Isa 54.5 αὐτός for ἄγιος* (Grabe,
Wutz, p. 18); Ecclus. 48.12 αὐτοῦ B S : ἀγίου A.

II Ki 23.26/35.19c הכעסים : τὰ προστάγματα G : πρόσταγμα
v. 25 in the next column (14 lines away in BM) : τὰ παροργίσματα
O L R (Ra.).

v. 21 מלחמתי : πόλεμον πολεμῆσαι G : πόλεμον : π. ποιῆσαι O L R
(Ra.).[2] For the error compare 26.13 ποιοῦντες πόλεμον : πολεμοῦντες
π. h. The phrase ποιεῖν πόλεμον is common in Par : I 5.10,19; 22.8;
II 26.11. BH wrongly posits להלחם.

II Ki 24.3/36.5c להסיר : τοῦ ἀποστῆναι αὐτόν G L : πλήν, ἦν : τ.
ἀποστῆσαι ... O (Ra.).

In some places an error of a similar kind in B has not been perpetrated elsewhere in the group.

I. 3.14 אמון : Αμνων B* : A. v. 1 in the preceding column (11 lines
away in BM) : Αμως Bab c2 O R, the standard form, as in II 33.20, etc.

9.19 הספים : τὰς φυλακάς B O L : φυλάσσοντες : τ. πύλας c2 R
(Schleusner, iii, p. 412; Ziegler, Beiträge, p. 34). Cf. v. 22 ספים : πύλαις
G O R. Schleusner explained as due to the phrase φυλάσσειν φυλακάς
in 23.32; II 13.11; 23.6. He usefully compared II 34.9 φυλάσσοντες
τὴν πύλην : φυλ. τὴν φυλακήν R.

12.8/7 מן־הגדור : (Ρααμ) καὶ οἱ τοῦ Γ. B : Σοβοκαμ καὶ οἱ v. 7/6 :
υἱοὶ τοῦ Γ. S c2 O L R (Ra.).[3]

14.15 בראשי : αὐτῶν ἄκρων B : αὐτῶν v. 14 : τῶν ἄκρων S c2 (Ra.)[4]

26.1 לשערים : τῶν φυλῶν B : φυλάσσοντες v. 10, higher up in the
next column (9 lines away in BM) : τ. πύλων c2 O L R (Ra.). Cf. 27.16
φυλῶν : πύλων b.

II 1.13 ירושלם : τῆς ἐν Ιερ. B : τῆς ἐν Γαβαων : εἰς Ιερ. c2 O L R
(Ra.).

---

[1] *JBL* lviii, p. 398.

[2] For the infinitival rendering see Part I, p. 126.

[3] See p. 88.

[4] For the avoidance of the preposition see Part I, p. 44.

10.18 רחבעם : (καὶ ὁ βασιλεὺς) Ιεροβοαμ B : ἐβασίλευσεν ... Ιεροβοαμ v. 17 : Ροβοαμ c₂ O L R (Ra.).

14.6/7 עודנו : ἐνώπιον (...κυριεύσομεν) B : ἐνώπιον κυρίου v. 1/2, v. 12/13 (12 lines away in BM) : ἐν ᾧ c₂ O L R (Benzinger, Ra.). Schleusner, vol. i, p. 792; ii, p. 341, following L. Bos, wrongly considered that B was a corruption of ἐν ᾧ ἡ γῆ ἐνώπιον ἡμῶν*.

20.17 יהודה : ἰδού B : ἰδού v. 16 : Ιουδα c₂ O L R (Ra.). Cf. 24.27 ἰδού : Ιουδα A 971. Wutz, p. 30, explains as metathesis.

25.13 מלכת : τοῦ μὴ εὐρεθῆναι B : εὗρεν v. 5 in the previous column (14 lines away in BM) : ...πορευθῆναι c₂ O L R (Ra.). For the opposite error compare 34.32 εὑρεθέντας : πορευθέντας R under the influence of πορευθῆναι v. 31.

28.5 מלך : (χειρὸς) βασιλέων B m : χεῖρας βασιλέων : βασιλέως c₂ O L R (Ra.).

(c) *The influence of similar places elsewhere in Par*

II 25.15 נביא ... ויחר אף : καὶ ἐγένετο ὀργὴ G O L R ...προφήτας G O L : these words in 24.18f. In view of the plural noun καὶ εἶπαν B m (cf. εἶπον O) appears for ויאמר. The singular references in v. 16 suggest that the assimilation is late and Gk. Rogers, p. 33, thought that the changes were made by the translator to tone down an anthropopathism and to enhance the impact of the prophecy.

29.16 לפנימה : ἕως (εἰς) G N m, influenced not only by βασιλέως in v. 15, but also by the phrase ἕως εἰς 17.12; 31.1,10. It was originally ἔσω O L R (Wutz, p. 30, Ra.), as in v. 18 G O L R.

(d) *The influence of similar places outside Par*

There is one case in B :

II 30.8 ערפכם : (μὴ σκληρύνητε) τὰς καρδίας ὑμῶν B N g* : a reminiscence of Psa 95/94.8 : originally τοὺς τραχήλους ὑμ. c₂ O L R (Ra.).

(ii) *Confusion of letters*

Similarity of consonants in the GK scripts caused much confusion in the mss. of the G groups. Many apparent cases are in fact better explained as due to local assimilation, but there remains a large number where palaeographical or phonetic similarity seems to be the sole cause.

(a) *Λ-shaped letters*

A, Δ, Λ, M are a notorious group of interchanging letters in the uncial script. The second Gk form is the correct one.

I 1.47f./51 שלמה : $\Sigma\alpha\mu\alpha\alpha$ G O L R : $\Sigma\alpha\lambda\mu\alpha$* (Podechard, *RB* xiii, p. 384).

2.37 אפלל[1,2] : $A\phi\alpha\mu\eta\lambda$ B[b] c₂ (-$\eta\delta$ B*), G : $A\phi\alpha\lambda\eta\lambda$* (Ra.).

v. 49 גבעא : $\Gamma\alpha\iota\beta\alpha\lambda$ G N : $\Gamma\alpha\iota\beta\alpha\alpha$ A i (Ra.) = $\Gamma\epsilon\beta\alpha\alpha$ a g m.

v. 53 האשתאלי : $\upsilon\iota o\grave{\iota}$ $E\sigma\theta\alpha\alpha\mu$ (-$\lambda\alpha\mu$ c₂) G : ... $E\sigma\theta\alpha\alpha\lambda$*.

3.2 תלמי : $\Theta o\alpha\mu\alpha\iota$ B ($\Theta o\mu o\iota$ c₂) : $\Theta o\lambda\mu\alpha\iota$ R (Ra.).

4.3 ידבש : $I\alpha\beta\alpha\varsigma$ G : $I\delta\beta\alpha\varsigma$*.

v. 15 אלה[2] : $A\delta\alpha$ G : $A\lambda\alpha$ O (Ra.).

v. 19 נחם : $N\alpha\chi\epsilon\theta$ (= $N\alpha\chi\epsilon\delta$* phonetically) B, $N\alpha\chi\epsilon\lambda$ c₂ : $N\alpha\chi\epsilon\mu$ O (Ra.).

v. 29 בעצם : $B o o\sigma\alpha\lambda$ G : $B o\alpha\sigma o\mu$ O (Ra.).

v. 37 אלון : $A\mu\mu\omega\nu$ B ($\Lambda\alpha\mu\mu\omega\nu$ in v. 36 c₂) : $A\lambda\lambda\omega\nu$ O R (Ra.).

v. 42 פלטיה : $\Phi\alpha\lambda\alpha\epsilon\tau\tau\epsilon\iota\alpha$ B (-$\epsilon\nu\tau\iota\alpha$ c₂) : $\Phi\alpha\lambda\lambda\epsilon\tau\tau\iota\alpha$ h i.

5.14 אביחיל : $A\beta\epsilon\iota\chi\alpha\iota\alpha$ G O[mss] : $A\beta\iota\chi\alpha\iota\lambda$* (Ra.) cf. -$\chi\alpha\eta\lambda$ c e g.

6.59/74 משל : $M\alpha\alpha\sigma\alpha$ G : $M\alpha\sigma\alpha\lambda$ O (Ra.). There is no cause to re-construct the form with Albright as $M\alpha\sigma\alpha\alpha\lambda$ = Jos 21.30 LXX for משאל Jos MT.[1]

7.1 פואה : $\Phi o\upsilon\delta$ ($\Phi o\upsilon\tau$ B by phonetic error) G R : $\Phi o\upsilon\alpha$ O L (Ta.).

v. 7 בלע : $B\alpha\delta\epsilon\epsilon$ (-$\delta\epsilon$ c₂) : $B\alpha\lambda\epsilon\epsilon$ b' or $B\alpha\lambda\epsilon$ O (Ra.).

v. 8 עלמת : $\Gamma\epsilon\epsilon\mu\alpha\iota\theta$ c₂ ($\Gamma\epsilon\mu\mu\mu\mu$ B) : $\Gamma\epsilon\mu\epsilon\epsilon\theta$*, as in 6.45/60 G.

v. 26 לעדן : $\Lambda\alpha\delta\delta\alpha\nu$ B ($\Gamma\alpha\lambda\alpha\alpha\delta\alpha$ c₂ A, assimilated to $\Gamma\alpha\lambda\alpha\alpha\delta$ v. 14 in the previous column — 12 lines away in BM) : $\Lambda\alpha\alpha\delta\alpha\nu$ O (Ra.).

v. 32 שועא : $\Sigma\omega\lambda\alpha$ G O R : $\Sigma\omega\alpha\alpha$*.

v. 35 שלש : $Z\epsilon\mu\eta$ B ($Z\iota\mu\eta$ c₂) : $\Sigma\epsilon\lambda\lambda\eta\varsigma$ O R (Ra.) before s/ζ phonetic error and omission of final letter.

ibid. עמל : $A\mu\alpha\alpha$ G A : $A\mu\alpha\lambda$ O R (Ra.).

8.7 הגלם : $I\gamma\alpha\alpha\eta$ B (-$I\chi$ c₂) : $I\gamma\lambda\alpha\mu$*, cf. $I\gamma\lambda\alpha\alpha\mu$ O.

v. 8 שחרים : $\Sigma\alpha\alpha\rho\eta\lambda$ B, -$\eta\alpha$ c₂ : $\Sigma\alpha\alpha\rho\eta\mu$ O (Ra.).

v. 10 יעוץ : $I\delta\omega\varsigma$ G : $I\alpha\omega\varsigma$* (Wutz, p. 14, Ra.), cf. $I\omega\alpha\varsigma$ L.

v. 11f. אלפעל : $A\lambda\phi\alpha\alpha\delta$ G (-$\phi\alpha\delta$ c₂ in v. 12) : $A\lambda\phi\alpha\alpha\lambda$ O R (Ra.).

v. 29 מעכה : $M o\lambda\chi\alpha$ G : $M o\alpha\chi\alpha$*?

9.17 טלמן : $T\alpha\mu\mu\alpha\nu$ c₂ (-$\alpha\mu$ B) : $T\alpha\lambda\alpha\mu\alpha\nu$*? cf. II Esdr 17.45 $T\epsilon\lambda\alpha\mu\omega\nu$; 21.19 $T\epsilon\lambda\alpha\mu\epsilon\iota\nu$.

v. 42 עזמות : $\Gamma\alpha\zeta\alpha\omega\theta$ G : $\Gamma\alpha\zeta\mu\omega\theta$ m (Ra.).

---

[1] "List of Levitic Cities", p. 63.

11.11 יֽשׁבעם : $I\epsilon\sigma\sigma\epsilon\beta\alpha\delta\alpha$ ($I\epsilon\sigma\sigma\alpha\iota$- S) G : $I\epsilon\sigma\sigma\epsilon\beta\alpha\alpha\mu$ e₂.

v. 30 חלד : $Xoao\delta$ ($X\theta\alpha$- B) G : $Xo\lambda o\delta$* (Wutz, p. 21, Ra.).

v. 36 פלני : $\Phi\epsilon\delta\omega\nu\epsilon\iota$ B S : $\Phi\epsilon\lambda\omega\nu\iota$ m (Rothstein, Ra.). $\Phi\alpha\rho\lambda\omega\nu\epsilon\iota$ c₂ has been assimilated to $X\alpha\rho\mu\alpha\delta\alpha\iota$ v. 37, probably from an earlier $\Phi\alpha\iota\lambda\omega\nu\epsilon\iota$*.

v. 37 כרמלי : $X\alpha\rho\mu\alpha\delta\alpha\iota$ G : $X\alpha\rho\mu\alpha\lambda\iota$* (Ra.). The ending has been assimilated to $N\alpha\alpha\rho\alpha\iota$.

v. 41 אחלי : $A\chi\alpha\iota\alpha$ ($A\chi\epsilon\alpha$ S) G : $A\chi\lambda\alpha\iota$* or $A\chi\alpha\lambda\alpha\iota$*, as originally in 2.31.

12.3 יהוא : $I\eta ov\lambda$ G A N b g Arm : $I\eta ova$ c e i.

v. 6/5 בעליה : $Ba\delta a\iota a$ G : $Baa\lambda\iota a$ O (Ra.).

v. 14/13 מכבני : $M\epsilon\lambda\chi\alpha\beta\alpha\nu\nu\alpha\iota$ B (-$\alpha\iota a$ c₂, -ϵa S, assimilated to $I\epsilon\rho\mu\iota a$) : $M\alpha\chi\alpha\beta\alpha\nu\nu\alpha\iota$* (Ra.), cf. -$\beta\alpha\nu\alpha\iota$ O. After the A/Λ error E was added (Rothstein).

v. 18/17 חמס : $\dot{\alpha}\lambda\eta\theta\epsilon\dot{\iota}\alpha$ G O L R : $\dot{\alpha}\delta\iota\kappa\dot{\iota}\alpha$* (Rudolph). חמס occurs only here in Chron, but the Gk is a frequent equivalent in the LXX generally. The change was encouraged by a desire to improve the sense, marred from the beginning by reading כף for כפי by haplography, which made it apparently refer to the Benjaminites. The present Gk can hardly go back to the translator *contra* Rogers, p. 50.

v. 21/20 צלתי : $\Sigma\epsilon\mu\alpha\theta\epsilon\iota$ G : $\Sigma\epsilon\lambda\lambda\alpha\theta\epsilon\iota$* (Rothstein, Wutz, p. 17), cf. $\Sigma\epsilon\lambda\alpha\theta\epsilon\iota$ h.

v. 34/33 בלא לב ולב : $ov \chi\epsilon\rho o\kappa\alpha\dot{\iota}\nu\omega s$ B^{ab}, $ov \chi o\rho o\kappa\alpha\dot{\iota}\nu\omega s$ B*, $ov \chi\alpha\iota\rho o\kappa\alpha\dot{\iota}\nu\omega s$ S, $ov \chi\epsilon\rho o\kappa\dot{\epsilon}\nu\omega s$ c₂ O L (in doublet) R : $ov\chi \dot{\epsilon}\tau\epsilon\rho o\kappa\lambda\iota\nu\hat{\omega}s$* (Ra., following R. Smend). As well as a Λ/A error there was parablepsis from ε to ε. BH's "G ריקם?" is wrong.

25.18 עזראל : $A\zeta a\rho\iota a$ G : $A\zeta a\rho\eta\lambda$*, cf. $A\zeta a\rho a\eta\lambda$ v. 4. ι was read for η by itacism. BH unnecessarily posits עזריה.

v. 29 גדלתי : $\Gamma o\delta o\mu a\theta\epsilon\iota$ B ($\Gamma o\delta o\lambda o\mu a\theta\iota$ c₂) : $\Gamma o\delta o\lambda\lambda a\theta\iota$* (Wutz, p. 17, Ra.), cf. $\Gamma o\delta o\lambda\lambda a\theta$ L.

26.9 משלמיהו : $Mo\sigma o\mu a\mu\epsilon\iota a$ c₂, -$\epsilon\iota\delta$ B : $Mo\sigma o\lambda\lambda a\mu\iota a$ p (Ra.).

27.6 עמיזבד : $\Lambda a\iota\zeta a\beta a\theta$ c₂ (-$\beta a\zeta$ -B, -$\beta a\zeta a\epsilon$ h) : $A\mu\iota\zeta a\beta a\delta$ e₂ (δ/θ).

v. 8 שמהות : $\Sigma a\lambda a\omega\theta$ G R : $\Sigma a\mu a\omega\theta$ O L (Ra.), as in 11.27.

v. 26 כלוב : $Xo\beta ov\delta$ B (Zo- c₂) : $Xo\lambda ov\beta$* (Ra.).

v. 27 רמתי : $\dot{\epsilon}\kappa \ Pa\eta\lambda$ G : $\dot{\epsilon}\kappa \ Pa\mu a$* (Ra.). There was also a $M/N/H$ error.

v. 29 עדלי : $A\delta a\iota$ G O L R : $A\delta\lambda\iota$ Sixtine (Ra.).

II 18.7f. ימלא : $I\epsilon\mu aa$ h (-aas B c₂ by assimilation to $M\epsilon\iota\chi a\dot{\iota}as$), G : $I\epsilon\mu\lambda a$ A R Arm (Ra.).

24.26   זבד : $Z\alpha\beta\epsilon\lambda$ B h ($\Sigma\alpha\mu\epsilon\lambda$ c₂) : $Z\alpha\beta\epsilon\delta$ O R (Curtis, Ra.).

28.18   גמזו : $\Gamma\alpha\lambda\epsilon\zeta\omega$ B (-αι -c₂) : $\Gamma\alpha\mu\epsilon\zeta\omega$* cf. $\Gamma\alpha\mu\zeta\omega$ Sixtime.

Similar errors in B which are not reproduced elsewhere in the group are as follows :

I 3.20   אהל : $O\sigma\alpha$ B : $Oo\lambda$ c₂ O R (Ra., cf. Wutz, p. 20). There was also a o/c error.

8.30   עבדון : $A\beta\alpha\lambda\omega\nu$ B : $A\beta\alpha\delta\omega\nu$ c₂ (Ra.), as in v. 23.

15.18   עבד אדם : $A\beta\alpha\epsilon\delta o\mu$ B* : $A\beta\delta\epsilon\delta o\mu$ c₂ O R (Ra.), as in v. 21.

21.2   ספרו : $\delta\dot{\eta}$ $\rho\iota\theta\mu\dot{\eta}\sigma\alpha\tau\epsilon$ B* : $\dot{\alpha}\rho\iota\theta\mu\dot{\eta}\sigma\alpha\tau\epsilon$ B^(a?b) c₂ O L R (Ra.).

26.27   שלל : $\delta\alpha\phi\dot{\upsilon}\rho\omega\nu$ B : $\lambda\alpha\phi\dot{\upsilon}\rho\omega\nu$ c₂ O L R (Ra.).

27.20   פדיהו : $\Phi\alpha\lambda\alpha\delta\iota\alpha$ B (c₂ omits) : $\Phi\alpha\delta\delta\alpha\iota\alpha$ h $= \Phi\alpha\delta\alpha\iota\alpha$ Sixtine (Ra.).

II 28.20   ויצר : $\kappa\alpha\grave{\iota}$ $\check{\epsilon}\theta\alpha\psi\alpha\nu$ B* : κ. $\check{\epsilon}\theta\lambda\iota\psi\epsilon\nu$ c₂ Sixtine. Cf. v. 22   הצר : $\theta\lambda\iota\beta\hat{\eta}\nu\alpha\iota$. The plural in B* is due to the frequent phrase κ. $\check{\epsilon}\theta\alpha\psi\alpha\nu$ $\alpha\dot{\upsilon}\tau\acute{o}\nu$, e.g., in 26.23. BM wrongly restore $\check{\epsilon}\theta\lambda\iota\psi\alpha\nu$*. B^(ab) O L R read $\dot{\epsilon}\pi\acute{\alpha}\tau\alpha\xi\epsilon\nu$, a makeshift verb borrowed from v. 17.

(b)   *O-shaped letters*

ε, θ, ο, c, ϕ are another group of letters which are frequently confused. A couple of these letters can also be confused with ω, as Wutz, p. 23, and Katz[1] have observed.

I. 1.37   נחת : $N\alpha\chi\epsilon\varsigma$ B R ($A\nu\alpha\chi\epsilon\varsigma$ c₂) : $N\alpha\chi\epsilon\theta$ O L (Ra.). Ziegler, *Beiträge*, p. 65, regards this rather as a phonetic error.

v. 40   איה : $A\iota\theta$ B ($A\iota\sigma\theta$ c₂) : $A\iota\epsilon$*, as in Gen 36.24 LXX.

2.43   תפה : $\Theta\alpha\pi o\upsilon\varsigma$ G : $\Theta\alpha\pi o\upsilon\epsilon$* (Wutz, p. 20, Kahle, *Cairo Geniza*[2], p. 180).

vv. 47,49   שעף : $\Sigma\alpha\gamma\alpha\epsilon$ G : $\Sigma\alpha\gamma\alpha\phi$ O (Ra.).

v. 48   מעכה : $M\omega\chi\alpha$ G O R ($X\omega\chi\omega$ c₂) : $Moo\chi\alpha$*. Here also may be cited 3.2 $M\omega\chi\alpha$ G O R for $Moo\chi\alpha$*, cf. $Moo\chi\alpha$ m; 19.7 $M\omega\chi\alpha$ G O R for $Moo\chi\alpha$* (Wutz, p. 23), as in v. 6.

v. 52   הראה : $A\iota\omega$ G : $A\rho o\epsilon$*? (also P/I).

v. 53   ומשפחות : $E\mu o\sigma\phi\epsilon\omega\varsigma$ B (-φαι- c₂) : $O\mu o\sigma\phi\epsilon\omega\theta$*.

4.7   אתנן : $\Sigma\epsilon\nu\nu\omega\nu$ G : $E\theta\nu\omega\nu$*.

v. 8   קוץ : $K\omega\epsilon$ G O e₂ R : $K\omega\varsigma$ N b i m Arm (Ra.).

v. 24   זרח : $Z\alpha\rho\epsilon\varsigma$ G : $Z\alpha\rho\epsilon\epsilon$ *, cf. 2.43 קרח : $Ko\rho\epsilon\epsilon$.

6.64/79   קדמות : $K\alpha\delta\alpha\mu\omega\varsigma$ B (-αλα- c₂) : $K\alpha\delta\alpha\mu\omega\theta$ e.

12.12/11   עתי : $E\theta o\iota$ G : $E\theta\theta\iota$* (Ra.) $= E\theta\theta\epsilon\iota$ O R.

---

[1] *Philo's Bible*, p. 87 note 4.

15.20 יְחִיאֵל : $E\iota\theta\eta\lambda$ B (...$\epsilon\iota\theta$ $H\lambda$ S, ...$\epsilon\iota\mu$ $H\lambda$ c₂) : $I\alpha\iota\eta\lambda$*, as L in v. 18, via $I\epsilon\eta\lambda$ d p.

20.4 הַחַשְׁתִּי : $\Theta\omega\sigma\alpha\theta\epsilon\iota$ B, $\Theta o\sigma\alpha\sigma\omega\theta\epsilon\iota$ c₂ : $\acute{o}$ $\Omega\sigma\alpha\theta\epsilon\iota$*. Ziegler, *Beiträge*, p. 64f., sees here a χ/θ error.

23.7 גֵּרְשֻׁנִּי : $\Pi\alpha\rho o\sigma o\mu$ c₂ (-$\sigma\omega\mu$ B) : $\Gamma\epsilon\rho\sigma\omega\nu\iota$* via $\Gamma\iota\alpha\rho$-* ($\Gamma I/\Pi$) by metathesis for $\Gamma\alpha\iota\rho\sigma\omega\nu\iota$* (also NI/M). BH wrongly claims גֵּרְשׁוֹן as the *Vorlage*.

26.7 עָתְנִי : $\Gamma oo\nu\epsilon\iota$ G : $\Gamma o\theta\nu\iota$ O (Wutz, p. 21, Ra.).

28.9 אָבִיךָ : $\tau\hat{\omega}\nu$ $\pi\alpha\tau\acute{\epsilon}\rho\omega\nu$ σov G O L R : $\tau o\hat{v}$ $\pi\alpha\tau\rho\acute{o}s$ σov*. $\overline{\pi\rho os}$ was probably misread as $\pi\rho\omega$* and taken as $\overline{\pi\rho\omega}$ = $\pi\alpha\tau\acute{\epsilon}\rho\omega\nu$.[1] אֲבוֹתֶיךָ (BH) is less likely. Cf. II 28.2f: 34.32 below.

II 11.19 יְעוּשׁ : $I\alpha ov\theta$ G : $I\alpha ovs$* (Wutz, p. 21, Ra.).

28.2f. וְהוּא : לַבְּעָלִים : $\tau o\hat{\iota}s$ $\epsilon\hat{\iota}\delta\acute{\omega}\lambda o\iota s$ $\alpha\grave{v}\tau\hat{\omega}\nu$ G O R : ...$\alpha\grave{v}\tau\acute{o}s$*. The conjunction was omitted because of fresh division of clauses : $\tau o\hat{\iota}s$ $\epsilon\hat{\iota}\delta$. was taken with v. 3. $\alpha\grave{v}\tau\acute{o}s$* was read as $\alpha\grave{v}\tau\omega$*, then regarded as $\alpha\grave{v}\overline{\tau\omega}$, an abbreviation for $\alpha\grave{v}\tau\hat{\omega}\nu$. $\alpha\grave{v}\tau\hat{\omega}\nu$ can hardly be an explanatory addition because the only possible antecedent is singular.

34.32 אֲבוֹתֵיהֶם : $\pi\alpha\tau\rho\grave{o}s$ $\alpha\grave{v}\tau\hat{\omega}\nu$ G m : $\pi\alpha\tau\acute{\epsilon}\rho\omega\nu$ ... O L R (Ra.), as G reads in v. 33. An abbreviated $\overline{\pi\rho\omega}$ was apparently read as $\overline{\pi\rho os}$ = $\pi\alpha\tau\rho\acute{o}s$ as if it were in apposition to the preceding $\theta\epsilon o\hat{v}$.

Sometimes errors of this type in B are absent from one or more other members of the group :

I 2.46 גּוּנִי¹,² : $\Gamma\epsilon\zeta o\nu\epsilon$ B : $\Gamma\epsilon\zeta ovs$ c₂, cf. $\Gamma\alpha\zeta\alpha s$ L in the second case.

9.8 מְשֻׁלָּם : $M\alpha\sigma\epsilon\alpha\lambda\eta\mu$ B : $M\alpha\sigma\sigma\alpha\lambda\eta\mu$ c₂ (Ra.).

12.3 יוֹאָשׁ : $I\omega\alpha$ $\acute{o}$ B : $I\omega\alpha s$ S c₂ O L R (Ra.).

(c) *I-shaped letters*

I, Γ, P, T look so similar as to be mistaken by a careless copyist in reading or writing.

I. 2.22 בְּאֶרֶץ הַגִּלְעָד : $\grave{\epsilon}\nu$ $\tau\hat{\eta}$ $\Gamma\alpha\lambda\alpha\alpha\delta$ G O R : perhaps $\grave{\epsilon}\nu$ $\gamma\hat{\eta}$ Γ. n, as in 5.9.

v. 47 גִּישָׁן : $\Sigma\omega\gamma\alpha\rho$ G : $\Gamma\alpha\iota\sigma\omega[\nu]$*?, then metathesis, cf. $\Gamma\epsilon\iota\sigma\omega\nu$ L. Wellhausen,[2] Rothstein and BH ("1 frt") read גֵּרְשֹׁן according to $\Gamma\eta\rho\sigma\omega\mu$ O R, but that looks suspiciously like the substitution of a more familiar name. Does assimilation to $\Sigma\omega\beta\alpha\rho$ v. 50 lie partly behind G ?

---

[1] Cf. Gehman, *VT* iii, p. 400, for an error caused by a Gk abbreviated ending in Zech. 13.6.

[2] *De Gentibus*, p. 18f.

4.3 ישמא : $P\alpha\gamma\mu\alpha$ G : $I\alpha\sigma\mu\alpha$* (also c/г), cf. $I\epsilon\sigma\mu\alpha$ O.

5.11 בארץ הבשן : $\dot{\epsilon}\nu$ $\tau\hat{\eta}$ $B\alpha\sigma\alpha\nu$ G O : perhaps $\dot{\epsilon}\nu$ $\gamma\hat{\eta}$ B. R.

6.57/72 דברת : $\Delta\epsilon\beta\epsilon\rho\epsilon\iota$ G : $\Delta\epsilon\beta\epsilon\rho\epsilon\tau$*.

7.2 רפיה : $P\alpha\phi\alpha\rho\alpha$ G : $P\alpha\phi\alpha\iota\alpha$ O L R (Wutz, p. 18, Ra.).

8.3 אדד : $A\lambda\epsilon\iota$ B, $A\delta\iota$ c_2 : $A\delta\epsilon\rho$ e y (Wutz, p. 18, Ra.).

9.12 יחזרה : $I\epsilon\zeta\iota o\upsilon$ c_2 ($I\epsilon\delta\epsilon\iota o\upsilon$ B by a phonetic change) : $I\epsilon\zeta\rho\alpha$*. Is $E\zeta\iota\rho\alpha$ R a corruption of this? The ending was assimilated to $\upsilon\iota o\hat{\upsilon}$: it is significant that only this name in the list is Hellenized.

v. 37 גדור : $I\epsilon\delta o\upsilon\rho$ G : $\Gamma\epsilon\delta o\upsilon\rho$ O R (Wutz, p. 17, Ra.).

12.21/20 ידיעאל : $P\omega\delta\iota\eta\lambda$ G : $I\epsilon\delta\iota\eta\lambda$ O via $I\omega\delta\iota\eta\lambda$* (Ra.), assimilated to the original $I\omega\zeta\alpha\beta\alpha\delta$ earlier.

14.7 בעלידע : $B\alpha\lambda\epsilon\gamma\delta\alpha\epsilon$ G : $B\alpha\epsilon\lambda\iota\delta\alpha\epsilon$*.

26.2 ידיעאל : $I\delta\epsilon\rho\eta\lambda$ B ($I\delta\rho\epsilon\eta\lambda$ c_2) : $I\delta\epsilon\iota\eta\lambda$* (Ra.).

v. 21 בני² : $o\hat{\upsilon}\tau o\iota$ G : $\upsilon\iota o\iota$ O L R (Ra.). After the error $\tau\hat{\omega}$ (= ־הַ) O R (Ra.) probably fell out after -$\tau o\iota$.

II 6.37 בארץ שבים : $\dot{\epsilon}\nu$ $\tau\hat{\eta}$ $\alpha\dot{\iota}\chi\mu\alpha\lambda\omega\sigma\dot{\iota}\alpha$ $\alpha\dot{\upsilon}\tau\hat{\omega}\nu$ G O L R : $\dot{\epsilon}\nu$ $\gamma\hat{\eta}$ $\alpha\dot{\iota}\chi\mu\alpha\lambda\omega\sigma\dot{\iota}\alpha$s...* Cf. the rendering $\dot{\epsilon}\nu$ $\gamma\hat{\eta}$ $\alpha\dot{\iota}\chi\mu\alpha\lambda\omega\tau\epsilon\upsilon\sigma\dot{\alpha}\nu\tau\omega\nu$ later in the verse, and $\dot{\epsilon}\nu$ $\gamma\hat{\eta}$ $\mu\epsilon\tau o\iota\kappa\dot{\iota}\alpha$s $\alpha\dot{\upsilon}\tau\hat{\omega}\nu$ in the parallel III Rg 8.47.

8.11 קדש : $\dot{\alpha}\gamma\rho\dot{o}s$ G : $\ddot{\alpha}\gamma\iota os$ O L (Ra.).

18.2 ויסיתהו : $\kappa\alpha\dot{\iota}$ $\dot{\eta}\gamma\dot{\alpha}\pi\alpha$ $\alpha\dot{\upsilon}\tau\dot{o}\nu$ G O L R : κ. $\dot{\eta}\pi\dot{\alpha}\tau\alpha$ ... f j (Margolis, *AJSL* xxii, p. 110, Wutz, p. 18, Ra.). Cf. 32.11 מסית : $\dot{\alpha}\pi\alpha\tau\hat{\alpha}$. Wutz compared the variant $\dot{\eta}\gamma\dot{\alpha}\pi\eta\sigma\alpha\nu$ for $\dot{\eta}\pi\dot{\alpha}\tau\eta\sigma\alpha\nu$ Psa 78/77.36. He saw it as a Γ/Π error, but it is more probably T/Γ and metathesis. Schleusner, vol. i, p. 10, preferred to keep the error and translated "blandis verbis compellavit". The error was widely retained because of the friendly relations mentioned in v. 1.

20.17 מחר : $\alpha\dot{\upsilon}\tau\dot{o}\nu$ B* ($\alpha\dot{\upsilon}\tau o\dot{\upsilon}s$ c_2) : $\alpha\ddot{\upsilon}\rho\iota o\nu$ B^{ab} O L R (Ra.), as in v. 16.

31.1 מכל־יהודה : $\dot{\alpha}\pi\dot{o}$ $\pi\dot{\alpha}\sigma\eta s$ $\gamma\hat{\eta}s$ $'Io\upsilon\delta\alpha\dot{\iota}\alpha s$ G : ... $\tau\hat{\eta}s$ ... O L R (Ra.), cf. 17.19 בכל יהודה : $\dot{\epsilon}\nu$ $\pi\dot{\alpha}\sigma\eta$ $\tau\hat{\eta}$ $'Io\upsilon\delta\alpha\dot{\iota}\alpha$.

33.23 הוא (אמון) : $\upsilon\iota\dot{o}s$ G : $\alpha\dot{\upsilon}\tau\dot{o}s$* = *hic* La. For the corruption cf. the ms. variants $\upsilon\iota\dot{o}\nu$ for $\alpha\dot{\upsilon}\tau\dot{o}\nu$ Ruth 4.15; $\alpha\dot{\upsilon}\tau o\dot{\upsilon}s$ for $\upsilon\iota o\dot{\upsilon}s$ Judith 2.23. $\pi\alpha\tau\dot{\eta}\rho$ three words before apparently suggested $\upsilon\iota\dot{o}s$. Curtis, misled by his view of A, which with O L R adds $\alpha\dot{\upsilon}\tau o\hat{\upsilon}$ for sense, reconstructed a *Vorlage* בנו אמון and explained it and הוא א׳ as glosses which crept into different texts.

In two cases similar errors in B are not committed elsewhere in the group.

I 1.41 יתרן : $\Gamma\epsilon\theta\rho\alpha\mu$ B ($\Gamma\alpha\iota$ -c_2) : $I\epsilon\theta\rho\alpha\nu$ O L R (Ra.) by a N/M error after $I\epsilon\theta\rho\alpha\mu$ i.

II 1.1/I 29.30 וַיִּתְחַזֵּק : κατενίσχυσεν B : καὶ ἐνίσχυσεν c₂ (Ra., so G O L R in II 1.1).

(d) *Other uncial letters*

Γ and C are sometimes confused : cf. Wutz, pp. 24, 95 for this type of error. A number of examples are cited in other sections, but the following may be cited here.

I 8.36 עַלְמֶת : Σαλαιμαθ G : Γαλαιμαθ h = Γαλεμαθ A N (Ra.), cf. 9.42 Γαμελεθ G.

II 28.7 עַזְרִיקָם : Εγδρεικαν G : Εσδρικαμ* (Ra.). The ending has been assimilated to Μαασαίαν.

32.30 גִּיחוֹן : Σειων G f h y : Γιων O L (Wutz, p. 24, Ra.), cf. 33.14 Γιον G.

Ζ and Χ are substituted at times.[1]

II 22.1 לְמַחֲנֶה : οἱ ʾΑλιμαζονεῖς G O : Λαμαχανα* or the like?[2] Evidently the translator transliterated because he failed to understand his *Vorlage*. He may himself have Hellenized the word as descriptive of the Arabians.

25.18 חוּת[1,2] : χοζ (cf. οχοζ by dittography A h Arm), αχοζ c₂ : χοχ*, αχοχ*. In the first case B reads χοζει, in the second αχουχ = O. χοζει clearly once stood at the end of the verse too : -ει comes from εἶπας at the beginning of v. 19. The error of dittography spread to the first instance. Then the second form was replaced by the O reading.

Η and Ν are sometimes interchanged.

I 8.2 נוֹתָה : Ιωα G : Νωα O R (Ra.) via Ηωα*, cf. Ηωλ h.

II 36.8 (גְּ-עֻזֹּה) : Γανοζαη G : Γανοζα R (Ra.) via Γανοζαν O by internal assimilation.

Λ and Χ are twice confused (cf. Wutz, p. 15).

I 6.10/25 אֲחִימוֹת : Αλειμωθ G : Αχιμωθ O R (Wutz, Ra.).

26.21 לְעָדָן[1] : Χαδαν G : Λαδαν R (Wutz, Ra.), as twice in this verse.

---

[1] Cf. Fischer, *Das Alphabet*, p. 12; Wutz, p. 27; Ziegler, *Beiträge*, p. 76.

[2] Cf. the analogous case at 14.14/15, discussed in Part I, p. 167.

M and Π can be interchanged : see Wutz, p. 16.

I 4.17 מרד : $\Pi\omega\rho\alpha\delta$ B ($-\alpha\beta$ c₂) : $M\omega\rho\alpha\delta$ O R (Wutz, Ra.).

P and Φ can be confused :

I 4.20 רנה : $\Phi\alpha\nu\alpha$ G (transposed) : $P\alpha\nu\alpha$*.

(e) *Minuscule errors*

F. Nau wrote a significant little article entitled "Permutations des lettres M N B dans le codex Vaticanus".[1] He claimed that these interchanges could not be explained in terms of transcription of uncials, since the forms were too dissimilar. But in the cursive script they are close enough to create confusion. He found in these errors "traces de la plébéienne origine" of B : at some stage in its history it had a minuscule exemplar.

All Nau's examples are taken from II Par. His single instance of β and ν confusion from II 17.8 must be ruled out as due rather to internal assimilation.[2] His β and μ examples, from 21.10; 36.2a, are doubtful : they are probably to be explained as ב/מ errors. Of his μ and ν errors, the case in 17.8 comes rather into the category of substitution of a familiar name; the case at 31.13 is only apparent, for two names have been transposed.

But although some of his examples were chosen superficially, they can be replaced for β and μ, and μ and ν. There are two β and μ errors within the G group.

I 15.24 שבניהו : $\Sigma o\mu\nu\iota\alpha$ B m : $\Sigma o\beta\nu\epsilon\iota\alpha$ S (Ra. $\Sigma\omega\beta\eta\iota\alpha$ c₂ by N/H error).

19.7 מידבא : $B\alpha\iota\delta\alpha\beta\alpha$ S : $M\alpha\iota\delta\alpha\beta\alpha$ B c₂ (Ra.). Gilbert saw here a מ/ב error,[3] but it is more likely to be an inner-group Gk error : cf. $B\alpha\delta\alpha\beta\alpha$ y for $M\alpha\delta\alpha\beta\alpha$ i n. This case suggests that S too had a minuscule ancestry.

There are quite a few cases of μ and ν error. A number are mentioned in other sections, but the following may be cited here.

I 1.43 המלכים אשר מלכו בארץ אדום : $oi\ \beta\alpha\sigma\iota\lambda\epsilon\hat{\iota}s\ \alpha\dot{\upsilon}\tau\hat{\omega}\nu$ G : ... $A\iota\delta\omega\mu$*. $\alpha\dot{\upsilon}\tau\hat{\omega}\nu$ is odd because this verse has no link with what goes

---

[1] *Revue d'Oreint Chrétien*, xvi, p. 428f.

[2] See p. 2.

[3] *AJSL* xiii, p. 292.

before : the Edomite kings are a new subject. It is most probably a misreading of $E\delta\omega\mu$* spelt as $Ai\delta\omega\mu$*, as e₂ sporadically mis-spells in this very verse and in II 8.17 ; 21.9,10. The error was basically a μ/ν one. The translator omitted part of the Heb phrase as superfluous.[1] Benzinger, Kittel, *SBOT*, Curtis, Rothstein and BH posit מלכיהם, but it is exceedingly difficult to see how this reading could have arisen.

2.6,8 איתן : $Ai\theta a\mu$ B ($E\theta a\mu$ h c₂), G : $Ai\theta a\nu$ Oᵐˢˢ R (Ra.).

v. 54 נטופתי : $M\epsilon\tau\omega\phi a\theta\epsilon\iota$ G : $N\epsilon\tau\omega\phi a\theta\iota$ O (Ra.).

ibid. מנחתי : $Ma\lambda a\theta\epsilon\iota$ G : $Ma\nu a\theta\iota$ L (Ra.), probably via $N/M/\Lambda$.

4. 18 מרד : $N\omega\rho\omega\eta\lambda$ B (Δ/Λ influenced by $X\epsilon\tau\iota\eta\lambda$), $\Omega\rho\eta\delta$ c₂ from $N\omega\rho\eta\delta$* by haplography : $M\omega\rho\eta\delta$ O R (Ra.).

v. 32 עיטם : $Ai\tau a\nu$ G A N ($Ai\tau a$ c₂) : $Ai\tau a\mu$ O L (Ra.).

5.26 תגלת פלנסר : $\Theta a\gamma\nu a\phi a\mu a\sigma a\rho$ G : $\Theta a\gamma\lambda a\phi a\lambda\nu a\sigma a\rho$ O (Ra.), cf. v. 6. Was N originally a correction of M, which displaced Λ?

6.27/42, 29/44 איתן : $Ai\theta a\mu$ c₂, G L : $Ai\theta a\nu$ B,[2] $Ai\theta a\nu$ O R (Ra.).

v. 55/70 ענר : $A\mu a\rho$ G : $A\nu a\rho$* (Albright, "List of Levitic Cities", p. 63, Ra.).

7.12 שפם : $\Sigma a\pi\phi\epsilon\iota\nu$ G : $\Sigma a\pi\phi\epsilon\iota\mu$*.

ibid., v. 15 חפס : $A\pi\phi\epsilon\iota\nu$ B ($A\mu\phi\iota$ c₂), $A\mu\phi\epsilon\iota\nu$ G (Π/M) : $A\pi\phi\epsilon\iota\mu$*, $A\pi\phi\epsilon\iota\mu$ f.

v. 27 נון : $No\upsilon\mu$ G A b : $No\upsilon\nu$ O e₂ R.

v. 32 חותם : $X\omega\theta a\nu$ G : $X\omega\theta a\mu$ O (Ra.). חותן (BH) is less likely.

9.14 עזריקם : $E\sigma\rho\epsilon\iota\kappa a\nu$ G : $E\sigma\rho\iota\kappa a\mu$ R (Ra.).

15.18 מקניהו : $Ma\kappa\epsilon\lambda\lambda\epsilon\iota a$ (-$\lambda\lambda a$ S) G : $Ma\kappa\epsilon\nu\iota a$ O (Ra.) as in v. 21, by $N/M/\Lambda\Lambda$ errors.

27.27 שפמי : $\Sigma\epsilon\phi\nu\iota$ G O : $\Sigma\epsilon\phi\mu\iota$*. שפני, which BH tentatively suggests as the basis of Par, is much less likely.

II 5.12 ידתון : $I\delta\epsilon\iota\theta o\upsilon\mu$ G Oᵐˢˢ b R : $I\delta\iota\theta o\upsilon\nu$ Oᵐˢˢ e₂ (Ra.).

31.12 כונניהו : $X\omega\mu\epsilon\nu\iota as$ G : $X\omega\nu\epsilon\nu\iota as$ O L R (Nau, Ra.), cf. $X\omega\nu\epsilon\nu\iota o\upsilon$ v. 13.

v. 15 עדן : $O\delta o\mu$ G O : $O\delta o\nu$*, cf. $\Omega\delta\omega\nu$ f.

35.15 ידתון : $I\delta\epsilon\iota\theta\omega\mu$ G : $I\delta\iota\theta\omega\nu$* (Ra.).

There are some cases where B has unique errors of this kind among the G group.

I 5.29/6.3 עמרם : $A\mu\beta\rho a\nu$ B* ($A\beta\rho a\mu$ b c₂) : $A\mu\beta\rho a\mu$ Bᵇ e₂ R (Ra.).

29.8 גרשני : $\Gamma\eta\rho\sigma o\mu\nu\epsilon\iota$ B : $\Gamma\eta\rho\sigma o\nu\nu\iota$ R, cf. $\Gamma\eta\rho\sigma o\nu\iota$ p c₂.

---

[1] Cf. Part I, pp. 51, 111f., 114.

[2] See Part I, p. 155.

II 8.5 בית חורון : Βαιθωρωμ B : Βαιθωρων c₂ O L R (Ra.).

16.7 חני : Αναμει B : Αvανι c₂ O (Nau, Ra.).

17.8 יהורם : Ιωραν B : Ιωραμ c₂ O L R (Nau, Ra.).

Here too should be mentioned a similar error in S. In the G errors above S has not been extant.

I 15.17 איתן : Αιθαμ S L : Αιθαν B (Ναιθαν c₂) O R (Ra.).

(f) Phonetic errors

Itacism is a frequent source of error, of which a selection will be given here.

I 2.45 בית־צור : Βεσουρ c₂ (Γεδσουρ B, assimilated to Γαιφαηλ v. 46) : Βεθσουρ f i = Βαιθσουρ R (Ra.).

5.7 אחיו : ἀδελφὴ αὐτοῦ G : ἀδελφοὶ αὐτ. O L R (Ra.).

6.45/60 גבע : Γαβαι G : Γαβεε O R (Ra.).

II 18.29 התחפש : κατακάλυψόν με G O R : κατακαλύψομαι L f j (Schleusner, ii, p. 176, Ra.). The later imperative ἔνδυσαι caused the change.

33.14 גיחון : Γιον G : Γιων* (Ra.) = Γειων L (in doublet).

B, which so frequently writes ει for ι, has a number of such errors, which are not found throughout the group.

I 6.26/41 זרח : Ζααραι B : Ζαρε R, cf. Αζααρε c₂, Ζαρε 1.37.

11.40 יתרי : Ηθηρει B : Ιθηρει S c₂.

13.2 אחינו : πους ἀδελφοὺς ὑμῶν B c₂ ... ἡμῶν S O L R (Ra.).

29.11 לך : συ B d e h m p : σοι c₂ O L R (Thackeray, Grammar, p. 94, Ra.)

II 15.2 בהיותכס : ἐν τῷ εἶναι ἡμᾶς B g : ...ὑμᾶς c₂ O L R Cyprian[1] (Ra.).

28.10 אלהיכם : θεῷ ἡμῶν B p : ...ὑμῶν c₂ O L R (Ra.).

Similar-sounding consonants are also confused.

I 4.2 להד : Λααθ G b' : Λααδ L (Ra.).

v. 8 צבבה : Σαβαθα G : Σαβαβα*.

v. 22 כזבא : Σωχηθα B (Σωχηθ Λ c₂) : Χωσηβα*.

7.10 אהוד : Αωθ G L (Ιωαθ c₂) : Αωδ O.

v. 33 פסך : Βαισηχι G : Φαισηχ m (dittography of iota).

---

[1] Cf. Weber, pp. xix, 30f.

11.44 חותם : $K\omega\theta\alpha\nu$ G : $X\omega\theta\alpha\nu$ O L R (Ra.). The ending has been assimilated to $B\epsilon\theta\alpha\nu\epsilon\iota$ v. 43.

12.21/20 יוזבד : $I\omega\sigma\alpha\beta\epsilon\theta$ S c_2 (-$\alpha\iota\theta$ B) : $I\omega\sigma\alpha\beta\epsilon\delta$*.

26.4 יהוזבר : $I\omega\zeta\alpha\beta\alpha\theta$ G : $I\omega\zeta\alpha\beta\alpha\delta$ O L R (Ra.).

II 11.8 זיף : $Z\epsilon\iota\beta$ G : $Z\epsilon\iota\phi$ O L R (Ra.).

30.1ff. פסח : $\phi\alpha\sigma\epsilon\kappa$ G R : $\phi\alpha\sigma\epsilon\chi$ O L, as in 35.1ff.

Errors in B when it is not representative of the group are as follows :

I 4.12 פסח : $B\epsilon\sigma\sigma\eta\epsilon$ B, $B\epsilon\sigma\sigma\eta$ i : $\Phi\epsilon\sigma\sigma\eta\epsilon$ c_2 (Ra.).

5.8 בלע : $B\alpha\lambda\epsilon\kappa$ B : $B\alpha\lambda\epsilon\chi$ h c_2.

6.26/41 עדיה : $A\zeta\epsilon\iota\alpha$ B : $A\delta\epsilon\iota\alpha$ c_2 L (Ra.).

(g) *Combined letters*

In certain cases a couple of letters and another letter can be confused.

ιϲ and κ interchange as follows :

I 4.21 הביץ : $\alpha\beta\alpha\kappa$ G : $\alpha\beta\epsilon_{S}$* via $\alpha\beta\alpha\iota_{S}$*.

24.21/22 ישיה : $\kappa\alpha\iota$ G O (in doublet) R (ditto) : $I\sigma\alpha\iota\alpha$*, as in v. 25.

27.18; II 21.2 מיכאל : $M\epsilon\iota\sigma\alpha\eta\lambda$ G, G O : $M\epsilon\iota\kappa\alpha\eta\lambda$* (haplography of *iota*).

II 13.19 ישנה : $K\alpha\nu\alpha$ B (-$\nu\alpha\nu$ c_2) : $I\sigma\alpha\nu\alpha$* (Wutz, p. 22, Ra.), cf. $I\sigma\acute{\alpha}\nu\alpha\nu$ Jos., *Ant.* viii, 285.

N and AI (and the like) can be mistaken for each other.

I 7.30 ימנה : $I\nu\iota\nu\alpha$ B ($K\omega\iota\nu\alpha$ c_2 : ιϲω assimilated to ιϲονα) : $I\mu\nu\alpha$* (Wutz, p. 17).

8.25 פניאל : $\Phi\epsilon\lambda\iota\eta\lambda$ B ($A\phi$-c_2) : $\Phi\epsilon\nu\iota\eta\lambda$* (haplography of *iota*).

9.11 מריות : $M\alpha\rho\mu\omega\theta$ G : $M\alpha\rho\alpha\iota\omega\theta$ R (Wutz, p. 17, Ra.) by $AI/N/M$ errors.

11.47 מצביה : $M\epsilon\iota\nu\alpha\beta\epsilon\iota\alpha$ G : $M\iota\sigma\alpha\beta\iota\alpha$* (Ra.) by $E/AI/N$ errors. A צ/י confusion (Rothstein) is unlikely.

14.7 אליפלט : $E\nu\phi\alpha\lambda\epsilon\tau$ S ($E\mu\phi$- B, $N\epsilon\phi$- c_2) : $E\lambda\iota\phi\alpha\lambda\epsilon\tau$ O R (Ra.)

15.9,11 אליאל : $E\nu\eta\lambda$ S c_2 ($E\nu\eta\rho$ B, assimilated to $\Gamma\eta\rho\sigma\alpha\mu$ v. 7), $E\nu\eta\lambda$ B c_2 (...$\epsilon\lambda\eta\mu$ S) : $E\lambda\iota\eta\lambda$ O L R (Ra.).

v. 18 אליפלהו : $E\lambda\iota\phi\alpha\nu\alpha$ c_2 (-$\epsilon\nu\alpha$ B S) : $E\lambda\iota\phi\alpha\lambda\alpha$ O. This became -$\phi\alpha\lambda\iota\alpha$* through the influence of $M\alpha\tau\tau\alpha\theta\iota\alpha$.

v. 21 אליפלהו : $E\nu\phi\alpha\nu\alpha\iota\alpha_{S}$ B c_2 (-$\nu\iota\alpha_{S}$ S) : $E\lambda\iota\phi\alpha\lambda\alpha$*, assimilated to $B\alpha\nu\alpha\iota\alpha_{S}$ v.20.

25.2 נתניה : $N\alpha\theta\alpha\lambda\iota\alpha_{S}$ G : $N\alpha\theta\alpha\nu\iota\alpha_{S}$ O L R (Ra.) by haplography of *iota*.

v. 27 אליתה : $A\iota\mu a\theta a$ B ($K\epsilon\mu$- c₂) : $E\lambda\iota a\theta a$ Sixtine (Ra.), cf. $E\lambda\iota a\theta$ O, by $\varLambda I/N/M$ errors.

26.7 אליהו : $E\nu\nu o\upsilon$ G : $E\lambda\iota o\upsilon$ O L R (Ra.).

II 11.18 אביהיל : $A\beta a\iota a\nu$ B^ab vid c₂ ($B a\iota a\nu$ B*) : $A\beta a\iota a\iota\lambda$* by $AI\varLambda/NA$ errors and metathesis.

B has unique errors of this kind in two places.

I 6.37/52 אמריה : $A\lambda\iota a\rho\epsilon\iota a$ B : $A\mu a\rho\iota a$ c₂ O L R (Ra.) by $M/N/AI$ errors.

II 15.2 ואסא : $a\dot{\upsilon}\tau\hat{\omega}\nu$ $\dot{\epsilon}\nu$ B : $A\sigma a$ $\kappa a\acute{\iota}$ c₂ O L R (Ra.). ⲁⲥⲁⲕⲁⲓ was read as ⲗⲟⲛⲉⲛ*, and the meaningless ⲗⲟⲛ was "corrected" to $a\dot{\upsilon}\tau\hat{\omega}\nu$.

There is at least one apparent M/NI error.

I 2.46 מוצא : $I\omega\sigma a\nu$ B ($'I\omega\sigma\epsilon\acute{\iota}a\nu$ c₂) : $M\omega\sigma a$ O (Ra.). NM was read as NNI, and N was dropped by haplography. The ending was assimilated to $A\rho\rho a\nu$.

There may be one case of a M/NA error.

I 4.3 עיטם יורעאל : $A\iota\tau a\nu$ B ($E\tau\rho a\nu$ c₂) $A\zeta\rho a\eta\lambda$ B ($A\zeta a\eta\lambda$ c₂) : $A\iota\tau a\mu$ R (Ra.) $I\zeta\rho a\eta\lambda$*.

M and $\varGamma I$ are once confused in G.

I 6.15/30 חגיה : $A\mu a$ G : $A\gamma\iota a$* (Wutz, p. 16) $= A\gamma\gamma\iota a$ O R (Ra.).

$\varPi$ and TI or IT are twice confused.

I 14.14f. בכאים : $a\grave{\iota}\tau\acute{\iota}\omega\nu$ B* S ($\dot{a}\gamma\gamma\acute{\iota}\omega\nu$ h, $\dot{\epsilon}\tau\acute{\iota}\omega\nu$ c₂) : $\dot{a}\pi\acute{\iota}\omega\nu$ O R (Ra.). In v. 14 c₂ reads $a\pi$ before $\dot{\epsilon}\tau\acute{\iota}\omega\nu$ by way of correction.

II 11.6 עיטם : $A\pi a\nu$ G : $A\iota\tau a\mu$ b R (Ra., cf. Wutz, p. 16) via $A\iota\tau a\nu$ B^ab e₂ (μ/ν).

(iii) Wrong division of words

The customary close writing of words in Gk mss. easily led to misunderstanding and to words being wrongly joined together or divided.[1] The second Gk form is the corrected one.

I 1.32 וישבק (transposed) מדן : $M a\delta a\mu$ ($M a\lambda a\kappa$ c₂ vid) $\varSigma o\beta a\kappa$ G : $M a\delta a N$ $I\sigma o\beta a\kappa$*. Gilbert wrongly thought in terms of a N/M error.[2]

---

[1] See, e.g., Würthwein, Text of the OT, p. 73.

[2] Loc. cit., p. 291.

4.19 אשתמע המעכתי : Εσθαιμωνη (-θεμ -c₂) Νωχαθει G : Εσθαμω*[1] Ημοοχαθει*.

v. 28f. ובבלהה : חצר שועל : Εσηρεουλαβ · Αβελλα B* (-βαλ · Αβελδα c₂) : Εσηρσουαλ* (Ra., cf. Εσερσουαλ O) Βαβελαα* (cf. Αβελαα h).

6.11/26 ונחת : Καιναθ G Aᵃ? N i : καὶ Νααθ R (Ra.). Gilbert, p. 296, note 2, suggested καὶ Ναθ*.

7.34 וארם (Qere; Kethib וחבה (יחבה : καὶ Ωβαβ (+ καὶ c₂) Ακαραν G : καὶ Ωβα* (cf. Οβα O) καὶ Αραμ O L R (Ra.).

9.15 בקבקר חרש : Βακαρ Καραραιηλ (...καὶ P. B) G : Βακαβκαρ* or Βακβακαρ O L R (Ra.) Αραις* (= Αρες O R). The second name suffered assimilation to Γαληλ* following.

11.26 דודו מבית לחם : Δωδωε Καθλαεμ S, ...Βαιθ - B, ...καὶ Καιεθ Λασιμ c₂ : Δωδω* (Ra.) ἐκ O Βαιθλαεμ.

v. 34 השם הגזוני : ὁ Σομογεννουνιν (ὁ Σομολογ. B, influenced by the familiar word ὁμολογεῖν) G : Οσομ* (Pa.) ὁ Γεννουνι* (Ra.). νν may represent Heb or Gk internal assimilation : Rehm, pp. 54, 115, thinks of a ז/נ error. There is doubt concerning the adjective : see Rudolph.

12.5f./4f. גדרתי : אלעוזי : Γαδαραθειειμ (Γαδαρα S) Αζαι (Αζε c₂, Αζει S) : Γαδαραθι m (Ra.) Ελλαζαι * (cf. Ελαζι R).[2]

26.4 נתנאל : Νααs Ιειηλ G : Ναθαναηλ O L R (Ra.) before errors of Θ/C, N/ΑΙ and assimilation to Αμειηλ v. 5.

There is one error of this kind in B only :

I 2.46 עיפה : Γαιφαηλ B* : Γαιφα (Γεφα c₂) ἡ Bᵇ c₂ O R (Ra.).

(iv) *Metathesis*

I 1.33 אלדעה : Ελλαδα G : Ελδαα O (Ra.).

2.44 רחם : Ραμε c₂ (Ραμεε B) : Ραεμ O R (Ra.).

3.3 יתרעם : Ιθαραμ G : Ιθρααμ*.

4.1 חצרון : Αρσων G : Ασρων*.

v. 28 מולדה : Μωαλδα B (-αλα c₂) : Μωλαδα O R (Ra.).

5.13 יעכן : Χιμα G : Ιαχαν O (Ra.) via Ιαχαμ m, assimilated to Μοσολαμ.

v. 14f. אחי : בוז : Ζαβουκαμ G : Βουζ L R. Αχαμ* (Katz, *TLZ* lxi, coll. 272, 276). Noth[3] and BH wrongly state that Par omits אחי.

---

[1] See p. 4 on v. 17.

[2] See p. 77.

[3] *Personennamen*, p. 235.

The ending -αμ, doubtless originally -αι*, has been assimilated to Μοσολαμ v. 13.

6.38/53 אחימעץ : Αχεισαμα G : Αχιμαας O L R (Ra.).

7.2 יחמי : Ειικαν B (Ισι c₂) : Ιχαμει* (χ/κ, μ/ν).

v. 25 רשף : Σαραφ B (c₂ omits) : Ρασαφ*. BH wrongly records "G^B Σαφαρ".

v. 26 אלישמע : Ελεισαμαι G : Ελισεμα*? (usually -σαμα).

v. 35 צופח : Σωχαθ G : Σωφαχ* (φ/θ phonetic error), cf. v.36.

v. 36 וחרנפר : צופה סוח : Σωφας B R Χουχι B Αναρφαρ B (Σωφα Σχουχια καὶ Αρφαρ c₂) : Σωφαχ* Σουχ* Ιαρναφαρ* (ו/י).

ibid. שועל : Σουλα G : Σουαλ O (Ra.).

8.26 שחריה : Σαραια G L : Σααρια O (Ra.).

v. 38 שעריה : Σαραια G O : Σααρια L (in doublet).

9.7 הסנאה : (υἱὸς) Αανα B (Αναα c₂) : Ασανα*, as in the corresponding II Esdr. 21.9, via Σαανα L.

v. 42 עלמת : Γαμελεθ G m : Γαλεμεθ O R (Ra.).

11.46 אליאל : Λειηλ B S (Δ-c₂) : Ελιηλ R (Ra.).

12.7/6 יועזר : Ιωζαρα G : Ιωαζαρ* (Ra.).

16.5 שמירמות : Σαμαρειμωθ B S (Σαμαριμωβ... c₂) : Σαμιραμωθ O L R (Ra.).

23.21 מחלי : Μοηλ G : Μοολι O R (Ra.), as just before, via Μολη* which was assimilated to Οζιηλ v. 20.

24.12 אלישיב : Ελιαβει c₂ (-βιει B) : Ελιασειβ O (Ra.). c was lost before o.

v. 14/13 בלגה : Γελβα B : Βελγα*=O L v. 14. Βεαγα c₂ has probably been corrected according to this form.[1]

v. 31 ויפילו : καὶ ἔλαβον G L R : κ. ἔβαλον O (Margolis, AJSL xxii, p. 113; Wutz, p. 30; Katz, TLZ lxi, col. 269; Ziegler, Beiträge, p. 45), as in 25.8 (ἔλαβον R); 26.13,14 (ἔλαβον q).[2]

25.4 ישבקשה : Ιειβασακα G : Ιεσβακασα* (Ra., c lost after ε internal assimilation).

27.11 זרחי : Ζαρια G : Ζαραι O L R (Ra.), cf. Ζαρει G v. 13.

28.10 עתה כי : τοίνυν G : νῦν ὅτι O.

II 8.3 חמת צובה : Μαισωβα c₂ (Βαι- B, assimilated to Βαιθωρων v. 5) : Ημαθ* Σωβα (H. as in v. 5 : H/I, Θ lost before c).

31.6 קדשים : αἰγῶν G O R; ἁγίων L (Schleusner, vol. i, p. 71, BH,

---

[1] See p. 52.

[2] For other examples of this common error see Margolis, Ziegler and Montgomery, Kings, p. 328.

Rudolph, Gehman, *VT*, iii, p. 398). Gehman rightly explains the error as due to the two types of animal mentioned earlier in the verse. Compare the opposite error in 35.7 (listed in section i, b) and Exod. 35.26 αἰγείας : ἁγίας A. Wutz, pp. 30, 197, 338, strangely insisted upon an underlying תישים.

v. 13 ו (transposed) נחת : Θαναι G : Νααθ* (= L earlier) καί A a g z L Arm.

Similar errors occur in B when it is not representative of the group.

I 1.51 הדד : Αδδα B : Αδαδ c₂ O L R (Ra.), as in v. 50.

2.5 חצרון : Αρσων B* : Ασρων* cf. Ασρωμ i, as in Gen 46.12. Εσδρωμ c₂ has probably been corrected on the lines of Εσρωμ O L R.

5.3 חצרון : Αρσων B : Ασρων a b c h m c₂.

7.31 בריעה חבר : Βεριχα Γαβερ B : Βεριγα Χαβερ c₂ O R (Ra.), cf. Βεριγα v. 30, Χαβερ v. 32.

9.16 נטופתי : Νωτεφατει B c₂ : Νετωφατ(ε)ι h L (Ra.).

II 1.13 במה : Μαβα B : Βαμα c₂ O (Ra.).

(v) *Substitution of a familiar name*

"Manchmal kommt es vor, dass ein häufiger E(igen)N(ame) den Abschreiber beeinflusst, besonders dann, wenn er graphisch oder phonetisch in der Nähe liegt".[1]

I 1.42 בלהן : Βαλααμ G O L R : Βαλααν O (Ra.). The other name was suggested by Βαλακ v. 43 (Rothstein).

2.21f. שגוב : Σερουχ G : Σεγουβ O L (Ra.), probably via Σεβουγ*.

v. 38 יהוא¹,² : 'Ιησοῦν, 'Ιησοῦς G : Ιηου O L R (Ra.).

3.1 היזרעאלית : τῇ 'Ισραηλίτιδι G O (L) R : τῇ 'Ιζραηλίτιδι, N, cf. II 22.6 below.

4.8 אחרחל : ἀδελφοῦ Ρηχαβ G O R : ἀ. Ρηχαλ*?

v. 14 יואב : Ιωβαβ G L : Ιωαβ O (Ra.).

v. 18 חבר : Αβεισα B, Αβισσα c₂ : Αβερ O L R (Ra.), probably via Αβει* (P/I).

6.56/71 עשתרות : Ασηρωθ B (-ων c₂) : Ασταρωθ L, cf. Ασταρωθει G in 11.44. "An obvious scribal confusion with the Hazeroth of the wilderness wanderings".[2]

7.13 שלום : Σαλωμων B (-ομ -c₂) : Σαλωμ* (Ra.), as in 5.13f. G.

---

[1] Ziegler, *op. cit.*, p. 62.

[2] Albright, "List of Levitic Cities", p. 69.

8.18 יובב : $I\omega\alpha\beta$ G : $I\omega\beta\alpha\beta$ O L R (Ra.).

9.10 ידעיה : $I\omega\delta\alpha\epsilon$ G R : $I\alpha\delta\alpha\iota\alpha$*? assimilated to $I\omega\alpha\rho\epsilon\iota\mu$. The other name is the standard one for יְ֫דַ֫עְיָה: יהוידע (BH) is not pre-supposed.

v. 15f. גלל : $\Gamma\alpha\lambda\alpha\alpha\delta$ G, G L : $\Gamma\alpha\lambda\eta\lambda$*, cf. $\Gamma\alpha\lambda\epsilon\lambda$ R. in v. 16. The initial $\Gamma\alpha\lambda$- and the form ...$\alpha\rho\alpha\iota\eta\lambda$ just before in v. 15 for $A\rho\alpha\iota\varsigma$* together suggest $\Gamma\alpha\lambda\eta\lambda$*.

11.46 יושויה : $I\omega\sigma\epsilon\iota\alpha$ G A : $I\omega\sigma\omega\iota\alpha$*, cf. $\Omega\sigma\omega\iota\alpha$ O^{mss} b with haplo-graphy of *iota*.

12.7/6 ישיהו : $I\eta\sigma\upsilon\nu\epsilon\iota$ G : $I\eta\sigma\iota\upsilon$*.

15.8 אליצפן : $E\lambda\epsilon\iota\sigma\alpha\phi\alpha\tau$ G : $E\lambda\iota\sigma\alpha\phi\alpha\nu$ O b R (Ra.).

23.10f. יעוש : $I\omega\alpha\varsigma$ G O L : $I\alpha\omega\varsigma$*. cf. $I\alpha\upsilon\varsigma$ 7.10.

25.15 ישעיהו : $I\omega\sigma\epsilon\iota\alpha$ G R : $I\sigma\alpha\iota\alpha$ b, as originally in v. 3 = $H\sigma\alpha\iota\alpha$ e$_2$.

26.3 יהוחנן : $I\omega\nu\hat{\alpha}\varsigma$ G : $I\omega\alpha\nu\alpha\nu$ O (Ra.).

v. 25 ישעיהו : $'\Omega\sigma\alpha\iota\acute{\alpha}\varsigma$ G O for $'I\omega\sigma$. R (haplography) : $'I\sigma\alpha\acute{\iota}\alpha\varsigma$*.

27.17 קמואל : $\Sigma\alpha\mu\upsilon\eta\lambda$ G : $K\alpha\mu\upsilon\eta\lambda$ O L R (Ra.). This is more likely to be a Gk error than to imply שמואל (BH) in the *Vorlage*.

v. 22 ירחם : $I\omega\rho\alpha\mu$ G O : $I\rho\alpha\alpha\mu$*, as in 8.27; 9.8,12.

II 8.17 אילות : $A\iota\lambda\alpha\mu$ B O R ($E\lambda$ -h c$_2$) : $A\iota\lambda\alpha\theta$ b i y (Ra.).

9.29 יעדי : $I\omega\eta\lambda$ G O L R : $I\omega\delta\iota$*? via $I\omega\eta\delta$* (Rudolph). A *Vorlage* יועל (BH) or יועד (Kittel, *SBOT*) is unlikely.

11.7 שׂוכו : $\Sigma\omega\kappa\chi\omega\theta$ G R : $\Sigma\omega\kappa\chi\omega$ O L.

17.7 עבדיה : $A\beta\epsilon\iota\alpha$ c$_2$ ($'A\beta\acute{\iota}\alpha\nu$ B assimilated to -$\acute{\iota}\alpha\nu$ following) : $A\beta\delta\epsilon\iota\alpha$*. Ra. restores $'A\beta\delta\acute{\iota}\alpha\nu$ with O L R, but the original form was probably originally indeclinable, as in I 3.21 (cf. 7.3): 8.38; 9.16,44; 12.10/9; II 34. 12.

v. 16 עמסיה : $M\alpha\sigma\alpha\acute{\iota}\alpha\varsigma$ G O : $'A\mu\alpha\sigma\acute{\iota}\alpha\varsigma$ L R (Ra.).

18.10,23 כנענה : $X\alpha\nu\alpha\alpha\nu$ G O e$_2$ R : $X\alpha\nu\alpha\nu\alpha$* (Ra.), cf. $X\alpha\nu\alpha\alpha\nu\alpha$ A; $X\alpha\nu\alpha\nu\alpha$ A f j m n (Ra.).

20.34 יהוא : $'I\eta\sigma\upsilon\hat{\upsilon}$ G b : $I\eta\upsilon$ O e$_2$ R or $I\upsilon$* (Ra.), cf. $H\upsilon\upsilon$ g and $I\upsilon\upsilon$ 19.2.

v. 37 אליעזר : $E\lambda\epsilon\iota\alpha\delta\alpha$ G : $E\lambda\iota\alpha\zeta\alpha\rho$* by a ζ/δ error.

22.6 יזראאל[1,2] : $I\sigma\rho\alpha\eta\lambda$ B, $I\overline{\eta}\lambda$ h ($I\lambda\overline{\eta}\mu$ c$_2$) : $I\zeta\rho\alpha\eta\lambda$* as originally in I 4.3,[1] cf. $I\zeta\rho\alpha\epsilon\lambda$ A. See I 3.1 above.

24.1 צביה : $A\beta\iota\alpha$ G O : $\Sigma\alpha\beta\iota\alpha$ L R (Ra.). A צ/ﬡ error (Rehm, p. 40) is unlikely.

---

[1] See p. 26.

25.1 יהועדן : *Ιωνα* c₂ (*Ιωναα* B by dittography : *ἀπό* follows) : *Ιωαδαν** via *Ιωαν**.

26.6 יבנה : *Αβεννηρ* G : *Ιαβνη* O L R (Ra.). through loss of *iota* after *eta*.

28.12 עמשא : *'Αμασίας* G O L R; *Αμασα** assimilated to two *-ίας* endings earlier.

29.13 שמרי : *Ζαμβρι* G a g n : *Σαμβρι* O L (Ra.).

ibid. זכריהו : *'Αζαρίας* G : *Ζαχαρίας* O L R (Ra.). These two names are frequently confused in the LXX, probably partly because an Azariah and a Zechariah ruled as contemporaries on the thrones of Israel and Judah.[1] עזריהו (BH) is less likely.

31.14 ימנה : *Αιμαν* G : *Ιαμνα** by metathesis.

34.20 עבדון : *Αβδοδομ* G : *Αβδων* O L (Ra.), probably via *Αβδωμ**.

Similar errors in B by degeneration of the group reading are as follows.

I 9.19 שלום : *Σαλωμων* B : *Σαλωμ* c₂ O (Ra.).

19.6 צובה : *Σωβαλ* B c₂ : *Σωβα* S m (Ra.).

II 17.8 נתניהו : *Μανθανίας* B : *Ναθανίας* O L (Ra.), cf. *Ναθανούας* c₂ assimilated to *Σαμούας*.

24.20 זכריה : *'Αζαρίαν* B O R : *Ζαχαρίαν* c₂ L. This son of the chief priest was confused with the chief priest of 26.17,20. עזריה (Curtis, BH) is hardly likely.

26.1 עזיהו : *'Οχοζείαν* B : *'Οζίαν* c₂ O L R (Ra.), cf. *'Οζίας* vv. 3ff.

(vi) *Misunderstanding*

At times the text has clearly suffered change because copyists misunderstood the context and adapted a word slightly here and there by an error of judgment.

I 5.9 מקניהם : *κτήνη αὐτῷ* G a : ...*αὐτῶν* O L R (Ra.). An abbreviated *-ῶ* was misunderstood because of the singular subject earlier.

23.11 הרבו ... ויהיו : *ἐπλήθυνεν* G ...*καὶ ἐγένετο* G R : *ἐπλήθυναν* O L R (Ra.) ...*καὶ ἐγένοντο* O (Ra.). *καὶ Ιωας* was taken with the preceding list (cf. *Σιως ὁ γ'* c₂) and *Βερια* was taken as the sole subject.

II 6.36 ואנפת בם : *καὶ πατάξεις αὐτούς* G O R : *καὶ ἐπάξεις αὐτοῖς** (Margolis, *AJSL* xxvi, p. 50, n. 205; C. F. Burney, *Kings*, ad I 8.46; Katz, "Septuagintal Studies", p. 203, note 2). Margolis noted similar

---

[1] Cf. Rahlfs, *LXX-Studien*, iii, p. 129.

confusion between the verbs in Lev 26.25; IV Rg 6.19, etc. He saw here an instance of ἐπάγειν with the subject to be understood. Burney, discussing the parallel text, which reads the same as Par, made the same suggestion and supposed an ellipse of ὀργήν. He compared Psa 7.12; Isa 26.21 where ἐπάγειν ὀργήν occurs. However, Katz gave Gk parallels for an intransitive sense "fall upon somebody as an enemy". He took the Gk as an appropriate loose rendering, and this view seems best. Three other opinions should be mentioned. Rogers, p. 24, finds here the translator's removal of an anthropopathism. Wutz, p. 225, found double corruption : καὶ παρατάξεις* for ואגפת, comparing Ezek 17.21 אגפיו : παρατάξει. Rehm, p. 40, and Rudolph also think in terms of a different *Vorlage* : ונגפת, comparing the Heb of v. 24. Probably the present Gk is an attempt to make sense of a phrase which was not understood.

10.17 רחבעם : Ιεροβοαμ G R : Ροβοαμ O L (Ra.). This is a consequence of earlier misunderstanding. G R take the Israelites mentioned earlier as members of the Northern Kingdom and differentiate, by adding καί, from the southerners "who live in Judah", as Rahlfs observed.[1] So the name of the southern king easily came to mind.

15.11f. ויבאו ... הביאו ... ויזבחו : καὶ ἔθυσεν G O R ... ἤνεγκεν B (ἀνήνεγκεν c₂²) ... διῆλθεν G O : κ. ἔθυσαν A ... ἤνεγκαν O L R (Ra.) ... διῆλθον L R. αὐτῶν at the end of v. 12 suggests that the last verb was originally plural. This in turn suggests plurals earlier. The mention of Asa at the end of v. 10 prompted the substitution of singular verbs as in v. 8f. This phenomenon undoubtedly explains καὶ ὤμοσαν ἐν (τῷ) κυρίῳ G Oᵐˢˢ for וישבעו ליהוה in v. 14. ὤμοσεν A g was intended, but the correct final syllable was treated as a separate word.

32.18 לבהלם : κατασπάσαι G O L R : κατασπεῦσαι* (Wutz, p. 31). For the error compare κατέσπασαν c e g Syh for κατέσπευσαν in 26.20. בהל is also rendered κατασπεύδειν in 35.21. The error came about to make more obvious sense in the context.

35.3 Qere המבינים : τοῖς δυνατοῖς G O L R : τ. συνετοῖς*. Compare מבין : συνετός I 15.22; 27.32; συνίων I 25.7; II 26.5; 34.12. The following infinitive led to the change. Cf. Dan Theod. 2.20, where Q rightly reads δύναμις for σύνεσις, as Montgomery has noted.[3]

v. 26 חסדיו : ἡ ἔλπις αὐτοῦ G O L (in doublet) R : τὸ ἔλεος a.*

---

[1] *Op. cit.*, iii, p. 241.

[2] See Part. I, p. 101.

[3] *Daniel*, p. 159.

(Rudolph), as in 32.32. Rehm, p. 61, posits a different, unknown *Vorlage*.

36.4 **וימלך** : καὶ κατέστησεν … βασιλέως G : … βασιλέα O L R (Ra.). The preceding genitive caused the slip. In the parallel IV Rg 23.34 many mss. have been contaminated with this corrupted reading. BH misunderstands Par and posits **מלך** for **על**.

Errors in B when apparently it does not represent the group are as follows :

I 5.3 **בני** : υἱοῦ B d e m : υἱοί c₂ O L R (Ra.). The phrase was wrongly taken with v. 2 and related to Joseph.

29.25 **ויתן** : καὶ ἔδωκαν B : κ. ἔδωκεν c₂ O L R (Ra.). Israel just before was taken as subject instead of Yahweh.

II 4.3 **הבקר** : τοὺς μόχλους B : τ. μόσχους c₂ O L R (Ra.). Presumably "bolts" entered a copyist's mind as better suiting constructional work.

8.8 **אחריהם** : μετ᾽ αὐτοῦ B e m e₂ : μετ᾽ αὐτούς c₂ O b R (Ra.). Israel at the end of v. 7 was wrongly taken as the antecedent.

28.6 **ויהרג** : καὶ ἀπέστειλεν B : κ. ἀπέκτεινεν c₂ O L R (Wutz, p. 31, Ra.). The great defeat of v. 5 apparently caused a copyist to think that the reason must be a great force sent into battle.

v. 23 **ויאמר** : καὶ εἶπαν B : κ. εἶπεν c₂ O L R (Ra.). The following θεοί was wrongly taken as the subject.

29.17 **באחד** : τῇ ἡμέρᾳ τῇ τρίτῃ B* : … πρώτῃ Bᵃᵇ c₂ O R (Ra.). The change represents a mathematical correction to make the rest of the dates tally with the reading "13th" for "16th" later.[1] The first part of the work took five days and the next eight so that the total number of days was thirteen, as required. So Rudolph has rightly explained, but he mistakenly considers πρώτῃ not to be original.[2]

2. Addition

(i) *Assimilation*

(a) *Internal assimilation*

I 25.4 **אליאתה** : Ηλιαθαθ G : Ηλιαθα g e₂ (Ra.).

---

[1] See p. 85.

[2] See Part I, p. 172.

(b)　*Local assimilation*

Letters are often added to names by the influence of names or other words nearby, which are given as the second Gk form in each case.

I 1.5　מדי : *Μαδαιμ* B (*Μαλ*-c₂) : *Μεστραιμ* v. 8 : *Μαδαι* O L R (Ra.).

v. 9　סבא : *Σαβατ* G : *Σαβατα* : *Σαβα* O L R (Ra.).

ibid.　חוילה : *Ευειλατ* G L : *Σαβατα* : *Ευιλα* O R.

ibid.　שבא : *Σαβαν* G c e i n (*Σεβ*-c₂) : *Ιουδαδαν* : *Σαβα* O L R (Ra.).

v. 32　שבא : *Σαβαι* G : *καί* : *Σαβα* O L (Ra.).

2.6　הימן : *Αιμουαν* G : *Ιεμουηλ* v. 5 : *Αιμαν* O L (Ra.).

v. 17　עמשא¹,² : *Αμεσσαβ* G : *Ιωαβ* v. 16 : *Αμεσσα* O L R (Ra.).

v. 27　רם : *Αραμ* G R : *Αραν* O v. 25 : *Ραμ* O L (Ra.).

3.1　דניאל : *Δαμνιηλ* G : *Αμνων* : *Δανιηλ* g (Ra.).

v. 18　פדיה : *Φαλδαίας* G : *Ηφαλ* 4.6 in the next column (12 lines away in BM) : *Φαδαίας* O R (Ra.).

v. 20　ברכיה : *Βαραχιαι* G : *καί* : *Βαραχια* O L R (Ra.).

4.12　רכה : *Ρηχαβ* G L : *Ρηχαβ* v. 8 : *Ρηχα**.

v. 17　יתר : *Ιεθερει* G : *Εσρει* : *Ιεθερ* O L R (Ra.), as later.

v. 18　שוכו : *Σωχων* G A N h i : *Μαιων* v. 17 : *Σωχω* b R.

ibid.　זנוח : *Ζαμων* G A : *Σωχων* : *Ζανω* O R (Ra., *ν/μ*).

v. 21　לעדה : *Μαδαθ* G : *Ζωαθ* v. 20 : *Λααδα* O (Ra., *ΛΑ/Μ*).

v. 23　גדרה : *Γαβαηρα* G, formerly *Γαβδηρα** : *Μωαβ*, *αβεδηρειν* v. 22 : *Γαδηρα* O e₂ (Ra.).

v. 34　יושה : *Ιωσια* G O : *Αμασεια* : *Ιωσα**.

6.6/21　זרח : *Ιααρα* G : *Ζαραια* 5.32/6.6 in the preceding column (12 lines away in BM) : *Ζαρα* O L R (Ra.). The intended addition *ΙΑ* displaced *Ζ*.

7.8　עמרי : *Αμαρεια* G O L R : *Ζαμαρια* : *Αμαρει**.

v. 28　נערן : *Νααρναν* G : *ΓΑΙΑΝ* : *Νααραν* O (Ra.).

v. 38　פספה : *Φασφαι* G : *καί* : *Φασφα* O L R)Ra.).

8.11　חשים : *Ωσιμεν* G : *ἐγέννησεν* : *Ωσιμ* O L R (Ra.).

v. 16　יוחא : *Ιωαχαν* G : *Ιωναθαν* v. 33 (12 lines away in BM) : *Ιωχα* O (Ra.).

v. 20　אליאל : *Ελιηλει* G O : *Σαλθει* : *Ελιηλ* L R.

v. 21　שמעי : *Σαμαειθ* G : *Σαμαραθ* : *Σαμαι* O R (Ra.).

v. 37　אלעשה : *Σαλασαθ* B, *Ελλασαδ* c₂ : *Σαλαισαθ* v. 36 : *Ελλασα**, cf. *Ελασα* R (Ra.).

9.7　סלוא : *Σαλωμ* G L : *Σ*. v. 17 in the next column (12 lines away in BM) : *Σαλω* O R (Ra.).

v. 43 אצל : *Eσαηλ* G R (*Aσ-* b c₂) : original *Eλeασa*[1] : *Eσηλ* O (Ra.), as in v. 44.

14.6 נגה : *Nαγeθ* B, -*eτ* S (c₂ omits) : *Eλιφαλeθ* or -*eτ* : *Nαγe* b′ (Ra.), cf. *Nαγαι* 3.7.

15.18 אליאב : *Eλιαβα* G (-*ιβα* S) : *Bαναια* : *Eλιαβ* O L R (Ra.).

20.5 לחמי : *Eλeμee* G : *Eλλαν* : *Λeeμαι** (*αι/e*).

25.4 הותיר : *Ωθηρeι* G : *Mανθeι* : *Ωθηρ* z.

II 16.4 דך : *Δανω* G : *Iω* : *Δαν* O L R (Ra.).

28.7 זכרי : *Eζeκρeι* B a h (-*κeι* c₂) : ʿ*Eζeκίας* v. 12 in the next column (11 lines away in BM) : *Zeκρι**.

29.12 זמה : *Zeμμαθ* G O : *Mααθ* : *Zeμμα* L R.

34.22 משׁנה : *Mαασαναι* G : *καί* : *Mασανα* R (Ra.).

B sometimes commits this type of error while the correct form is preserved elsewhere in the group.

I 2.18 ישׁר : *Iωασαρ* B : *Eλιωθ* : *Iασαρ* c₂ L R. יועזר (BH) is hardly presupposed.

6.20/35 עמשׁי : ʾ*Aμαθeίου* B : *υἱοῦ* : *Aμαθeι* c₂ from *Aμασeι** (c/Θ).

v. 27/42 זמה : *Zαμμαμ* B : *Aιθαμ* c₂[2] : *Zαμμα* c₂ O (Ra.).

7.19 לקחי : *Λακeeιμ* B c₂ : *Iααιμ* : *Λακeeι* h.

Words and phrases are frequently added from the context.

I 7.30 ושׁרח : +*καί* G, due to the sequence of name + conjunction.

9.4 עותי בך : *καὶ Γωθeι καὶ υἱός* G (R), mechanically following the pattern of *καὶ Mανασση*.

11.20 חלל : *ἐν καιρῷ ἐνί* G O L R, from v. 11 in the preceding column (13 lines away in BM) where the phrase, itself not original,[3] occurs after the same three Gk words. BH wrongly posits an addition in the *Vorlage*.

15.27 הארון : + *διαθήκης κυρίου* G O L R, added from v. 28.

19.7 להם : + *ἄρματα καὶ ἱππeῖς* G, repeated from the end of v. 6 (Ra.). A Gk copyist's eye strayed back three whole lines (36 letters) and he copied out three words before realising his error.[4] An addition in the *Vorlage* (BH) would be less easy to explain.

27.15 הנטופתי : *ὁ ἐκ Neτωφατeι* G O R. *ἐκ* was added by analogy with v. 13 *ὁ ἐκ Neτουφατ* (Ra.).

---

[1] p. 51.

[2] See Part I, p. 155.

[3] See Part I, p. 145.

[4] See p. 50.

II 2.6/7 חכם : + καὶ εἰδότα G O L R, from v. 12/13 in the next column (12 lines away in BM). BH wrongly suggests a Heb addition.

4.12 והגלות : καὶ ἐπ᾿ αὐτῶν γωλαθ G O R. The prepositional phrase has been imported from v. 19 in the next column (10 lines away in BM).

6.2 בית : + τῷ ὀνόματί μου G O L R, added from v. 9 οἶκον τῷ ὀν. μου in the next column (11 lines away in BM).

v. 15 לו : + λέγων G O R, from the same phrase in v. 16, but here no direct speech follows. The error was probably Gk.

7.2 יהוה¹ : + ἐν τῷ καιρῷ ἐκείνῳ G O L R, from v. 8 in the next column (about 12 lines away in BM).

v. 14 ויכנעו : καὶ ἐὰν ἐντράπῃ G O R, due to the sequence καὶ ἐάν twice in v. 13.

9.14 לשלמה : τῷ βασιλεῖ Σ. G O L R, assimilated to the same phrase in v. 12 (Heb אל־המלך).

11.20 לקח : + ἑαυτῷ G O (L R), added from v. 18 (ויקח־לו).

13.11 אלהינו : τοῦ θεοῦ τῶν πατέρων ἡμῶν G O L R. τῶν πατ. has come from the similar phrase in v. 12.

v. 23/14.1 הארץ : ἡ γῆ Ιουδα G O L R, assimilated to 14.5/6 ἐν γῆ Ιουδα (ביהודה). BH annotates "G^BAL + יהורה".

15.19 היתה : + μετ᾿ αὐτοῦ G O (L) R, copied from v. 9 in the preceding column (11 and 13 lines away in BM).

16.9 עם־לבבם : ἐν πάσῃ καρδίᾳ G O (L) R, influenced by ἐν πάσῃ τῇ γῇ (בכל־הארץ) earlier.

17.4 ובמצותיו : καὶ ἐν ταῖς ἐντολαῖς τοῦ πατρὸς αὐτοῦ G O R. τοῦ πατ. has been added from seven words before.

v. 17 חיל : + καί G, a mechanical reproduction of the sequence δυνάμεως. καί in v. 16f.

18.25 יואש : + ἄρχοντα G O L R, because it follows the first name.

20.12 נעשה : + αὐτοῖς G O (L) R. The copyist's eye strayed back to ἐν αὐτοῖς earlier, and he repeated αὐτοῖς after -εν.

22.7 ובבאו : καὶ ἐν τῷ ἐξελθεῖν G A c, an error for ... ἐλθεῖν O L R (Ra.) due to ἐξῆλθεν following.

v. 11 מפני : + τοῦ βασιλέως Ιωας G, repeated from earlier in the verse; a copyist was misled by the repetition of καὶ ἔκρυψεν αὐτόν.

23.13 וההצצרות : + ἄρχοντες G O (L R), copied from two lines above.

24.17 ואחרי : καὶ ἐγένετο μετὰ τήν G O L R, assimilated to v. 23 καὶ ἐγ. μετὰ τήν in the next column (10 lines away in BM).

25.1 בן : καὶ ἐβασίλευσαν ὧν G. The first two words are copied from 24.27b.

v. 14 ולפניהם ישתחוה : καὶ ἔστησεν B ἐναντίον αὐτῶν προσκυνεῖν G. ἔστ. is repeated from καὶ ἔστ. in the preceding clause. The infinitive is a necessary adaptation of the original προσεκύνει O L R (Ra.). In c₂ a reviser cut out ἔστ., but left the infinitive.

ibid. ולהם : καὶ αὐτὸς αὐτῷ B* (c₂ omits the clause). αὐτός was wrongly written at first, probably due to αὐτός v. 21 in the next column (12 lines away in BM). αὐτῷ was originally αὐτοῖς Bᵃᵇ (O L), miswritten under the influence of αὐτοὺς αὐτῷ earlier in the verse.

30.22 את־המועד : + τῶν ἀζύμων G O L R, added from the phrase in v. 21 (את־חג המצות).

31.7 הערמות : οἱ θεμέλιοι σωροί G. A copyist's eye slipped to -οι θεμελιοῦσθαι, and he doubtless wrote θεμελιου* before realising his error; the ending was adapted.

32.19 ירושלם : + καί G, mechanically assimilated to Ιερουσαλημ. καί v. 25f. in the next column (12 lines away in BM).

34.3 שנה : + τῆς βασιλείας αὐτοῦ G O L R, from the dating earlier in the verse. The error is probably Gk since the phrases are less similar in the Heb.

35.8 לפסחים : εἰς τὸ φασεκ πρόβατα καὶ ἀμνοὺς καὶ ἐρίφους G O L R. προβ. is an explanatory addition used to cover the plural Heb in the sense of "passover offerings" : cf. v. 9 (G) O L R. צאן is hardly presupposed : cf. Rudolph. The last four words are copied from v. 7, where צאן does occur for πρόβ.

B has a number of individual errors of a similar kind.

I 6.45/60 בנימן : + καί B a, due to the sequence καὶ τήν in the context.

11.2 יהוה : Ισραηλ κύριος B. The first word came in by vertical dittography from the preceding line.

21.12 חרב : + ἐξ B, an anticipation of ἐξολεθρεῦσαι four words later. Rehm, p. 58, posits a different *Vorlage*.

23.8 ויואל : + καί B*, due to the sequence of name + conjunction.

v. 9 וחזיאל : καὶ Ειειηλ καὶ τρεῖς B*. A copyist's eye went back to Ιωηλ καὶ τρεῖς in v. 8.

II 16.9 שלם : + ἐπὶ τοῦ B, anticipating ἐπὶ τούτῳ four words later (Ra.).

20.26 וביום : καὶ ἐγένετο τῇ ἡμέρᾳ B. The verb has come in by attraction to the similar καὶ ἐγένοντο ἡμέραι v. 25.

26.9 וְעַל־שַׁעַר : + γωνίας B*, repeated from earlier in the verse where it occurs after the same Gk words. γωνίαν B^{ab} R is an adaptation of B*.

28.13 חֲרוֹן אַף : (ὀργὴ κυρίου[1]) + θεοῦ B g, under the influence of ὀργὴ κυ. θεοῦ v. 9 (9 lines away in BM).

v. 18 אֶת־בֵּית־שֶׁמֶשׁ : + ἐν οἴκῳ κῡ ... τῷ βασιλεῖ B (R), added from v. 21 (Ra.). A copyist's eye slipped from the context of ἔλαβον in v. 18 to that of ἔλαβεν in v. 21.

(c) *The influence of a similar passage elsewhere in Par*

II 25.14 וַיָּבֹא : +πρὸς αὐτούς G O (L R), a misplaced gloss on αὐτῷ (אֵלָיו) in v. 15, assimilating to πρὸς αὐτούς (בָּהֶם) in 24.19. The addition continues the trend towards assimilation already noted.[2] It is significant that R reads πρὸς αὐτούς for αὐτῷ in v. 15.

(ii) *Dittography*

(a) Letters belonging to the next word are at times repeated at the beginning or end of words.

I 4.35 שְׂרָיָה : Σαρααυ (υἱός) B (-αου c2) : Σαραια O L R (Ra.). *Iota* was omitted between vowels.

7.2 שְׁמוּאֵל : (καὶ) Ισαμουηλ G : Σαμ. O L R (Ra.).

ibid. תּוֹלָע : Θωλαει (ἰσχ.) G : Θωλαε*, cf. v. 1 in B below.

8.26 שִׁמְשְׁרַי : (καὶ) Ισμασαρια G : Σαμσαρι R via Σαμσαρια O assimilated to Σααρια.

9.36 עַבְדּוֹן : (-τόκος) Σαβαδων G : Αβαδων* (Ra.), as in 8.23.

11.35 אוּר : (υἱός) Σουρ G L (Σθυρ B) : Ουρ R (Wutz, p. 29, Ra.).

v. 47 עוֹבֵד : (καὶ) Ιωβηδ c2 A L (-ηλ S, -ηθ B) : Ωβηδ O (Ra.), unless ι = ע.

26.10f., 16 חֹסָה : (καὶ) Ιοσσα G : Οσσα 74, Οσσα*, Οσσα* cf. καὶ Οσσα 16.38.

Sometimes B has an individual error of this kind.

I 2.23 יָאִיר : (κώμας) Σαειρ B* : Ιαειρ B^{ab} c2 O L R (Ra.), as in v. 22.

3.3 אֲבִיטָל : (τῆς) Σαβειταλ B : Αβιταλ c2 O R (Ra.).

7.1 תּוֹלָע : Θολαεκ (καί) B : Θωλαε*, cf. Θολοε c2.

---

[1] See p. 101.

[2] p. 15.

9.4 עמיהוד : (υἱὸς) Σαμμιου B : Αμμιουδ* (Ra.), cf. Αμιουδ O and Αμμια c₂ assimilated to Ασαια v. 5.

11.31 ריבי : Ρεβιε (ἐκ) B : Ραιβι*, cf. Ρεβι c₂, Ραβειαι S.

15.18 מתתיהו : (καὶ) Ιματταθια B : Ματ. S c₂ (Ra.).

II 18.25 יואש : Ιωασα (ἄρχ) B : Ιωας c₂ O L R (Ra.).

20.2 תמר : Θαμαρα (αὔτη) B : Θαμαρ c₂ O L R (Ra.).

25.24 עבד אדום : (τῷ) Ιαβδεδομ B* : Αβδεδομ c₂ R (Ra.). According to Wutz, p. 74, ι stands for ע.

(b) Words or parts of words are occasionally repeated.

I 10.3 ויחל : καὶ πόνοις καὶ ἐπόνεσεν/αν G O (L) R. Probably a copyist wrote ΚΑΙ ΠΟΝΕϹ*, then he abandoned his error, which was subsequently adapted to suit the context (Benzinger, following Klostermann, *Samuel*). Rehm, p. 27 sees here a Heb doublet ויחלי ויחל.

12.7/6 וישבעם : Καινα καὶ Σοβοαμ S (... Σωβ- c₂, ... Σοβοκαμ B) : originally καὶ Ιασοβοαμ*. A copyist wrote ΚΑΙΑ omitting ι, then started again. ΚΑΙΑΙΑ was subsequently taken as a name (Α/ΙΝ), and καί was inserted.

21.18/17f. ו : κύριε. καί G O R. The first word is an adapted dittography of the second via κε̄.[1]

II 6.23 מן־השמים : ἐκ τοῦ οὐρανοῦ τοῦ οὐρανοῦ G O e₂.

18.23 עבר רוח־יהוה מאתי : πνεῦμα παρ᾽ ἐμοῦ πνεῦμα πρός σε πνεῦμα κυρίου παρ᾽ ἐμοῦ G. A copyist made several attempts to write correctly. πρός σε comes from the end of the verse. The muddle caused the omission of παρῆλθεν O L R (Ra.).

26.19 בזעפו : ἐν τῷ ναῷ ἐν τῷ θυμωθῆναι αὐτόν G O (L R). A dittograph of ἐν τῷ was filled out with the aid of ναόν in v. 16.

29.14 ומן־בני : καὶ τῶν υἱῶν ὧν G.

There are a couple of similar errors in B.

II 20.6 בשמים : ἐν οὐρανῷ ἄνω B L R. c₂ O (Ra.) omit ἄνω. The error is found frequently in the LXX. J. S. Sibinga explains it as partly due to liturgical phraseology.[2]

23.7 כלין : σκεῦος σκεῦος B. c₂ O (Ra.) omit the repetition.

(iii) *Letters added*

Occasionally the original reading has clearly been adapted by the

---

[1] For confusion of the two words see Ziegler, *op. cit.*, p. 57, and Part I, p. 152.

[2] *The OT Text of Justin Martyr*, i, p. 90f.

addition of one or more letters. Mainly the cause is pseudo-dittography, as follows.

I 5.8 בעל מעון : Βεελμασσων B (-με -c₂) : Βεελμαων O R (Ra.).

7.10 אחישחר : ΑχεισαΔΑρ B (-ακ c₂) : Αχισααρ O R (Ra.).

11.47 אליאל : ΔΑλειηλ B S (Δανιηλ c₂) : Αλιηλ O R (Ra.).

II 19.10 כל־ריב : πᾶς ἀνHP KPίσιν G O L R : πᾶσαν* κ. (Rudolph). כל becomes πᾶς ἀνήρ only here in Par. (πλ)ήρ(ει) in v. 9 may have contributed to the error.

B has one of these errors when another member of the group preserves an uncorrupted reading.

I 4.4 בית לחם : ΒαιθλΑΔεν B (-δαιν c₂) : Βαιθλαεμ A c n (Ra.) via Βαιθλαεν h.

There are examples of other letters, unrelated to existing ones, being added.

I 26.7 אחיו : Αχιουδ G N : Αχιου O R (Ra.), on the analogy of the standard form Αβιουδ for אביהוא.

II 31.16 מלבד : ἕκαστος G m : ἐκτός O L R (Ra., Rudolph). "According to great and small" just before encouraged the error; notice too the frequent combination κα in v. 15. Benzinger wrongly suggested a *Vorlage* איש on the basis of the mistake.

There is one individual error of this kind in B.

II 28.3 כתעבות : καὶ τὰ βδελύγματα B* e m : κατὰ βδ. h*.

(iv) *Amplifying glosses*

Par sometimes exhibits additional phrases which appear to be later than the translator and to have been added by way of explanation or amplification.

I 9.2 ישראל : + υἱοί G, a gloss intended to make it clear that Ισραηλ does not qualify πόλεσιν but is part of the predicate.

10.13 לדרוש : + καὶ ἀπεκρίνατο αὐτῷ Σαμουηλ ὁ προφήτης G O L R. Thackeray suggested that the clause is a later Gk gloss since the passive of ἀποκριν. is used throughout the LXX.[1] In fact, in Par elsewhere only the passive is used, seven times.

16.40 ישראל : + ἐν χειρὶ Μωυσῆ τοῦ θεράποντος τοῦ θεοῦ G O (L) R. Thackeray again suggested a Gk gloss on the grounds that θεράπων occurs only here in Par, being characteristic mainly of the Pentateuch.[2]

---

[1] *Grammar*, p. 239.

[2] *Op. cit.*, p. 7f.

Par generally uses παῖς and occasionally δοῦλος. BH unwisely puts the gloss into Heb dress.

21.26 העלה : + καὶ κατανάλωσεν τὴν ὁλοκαύτωσιν G O R. Rothstein, BH and Rudolph "restore" the clause to Chron, claiming homoeoteleuton. But it is significant that in II 7.1 the verb in this sense is rendered κατέφαγεν, the regular verb in the LXX when אכל occurs with אש (e. g., Lev 9.24; Num 11.1). This fact probably implies that the extra clause does not go back to the *Vorlage* but is a later Gk amplification.

II 5.6 הנועדים עליו : καὶ οἱ φοβούμενοι καὶ οἱ ἐπισυνηγμένοι αὐτῶν G O (L) R. οἱ φοβ. is an interpretative gloss on the next phrase, which was taken to be a group distinct from Israel and interpreted as non-Jewish adherents to the Jewish faith or "God-fearers". Sc. τὸν θεόν and cf. Acts 10.2,22; 13.16,26 for the technical term. La significantly has *qui timebant deum*. It lacks the second Gk phrase : evidently the gloss displaced the original.

23.6 הכהנים והמשרתים ללוים : οἱ ἱερεῖς καὶ οἱ Λευῖται καὶ οἱ λειτουργοῦντες τῶν Λευιτῶν G O (L R). The last Gk phrase obviously means "those of the Levites on duty". It cannot be an objective genitive : the dative would have been used as, e.g., in 17.19; 22.8. It was evidently misunderstood later as "the servants of the Levites". Since the Levites figure in the ensuing narrative they were re-introduced here. BH's assumption that הלוים (why not והלוים?) stood in the *Vorlage* is unlikely. La has *et qui ministrant levitae* for והמ' לל' = καὶ οἱ λειτ. οἱ Λευῖται* : the gloss displaced τῶν Λευιτῶν.

3. OMISSION

(i) *Local assimilation*

Names at times show signs of shortening through the influence of other words in the context. The second Gk form is the cause of the error.

I 2.6 כלכל : Χαλκα G : Δαρα : Χαλκαλ R.

v. 52 המנחות : ... α Μωναιω G : Αιω : Αμωναωθ* ?

v. 55 רכב : Ρηχα G : Μεσημα : Ρηχαβ O L R.

4.20 חנן : Ανα G (transposed) : Φανα : Αναν*, as O L R later.

v. 22 שרף : Σαια B (Σωα c₂ from Σαρα*) : Ιωαδα : Σαραφ O L R (Ra.).

6.28/43 יחת : Ηχα G : Ζαμμα : Ιχαθ*.

v. 30/45 חשביה : $A\sigma\epsilon\beta\epsilon\iota$ G O : $A\beta\delta\epsilon\iota$ v. 44 : $A\sigma\epsilon\beta\iota\alpha$*.

7.8 זמירה : ᾿$A\mu\alpha\rho\iota\alpha s$ G : $A\mu\alpha\rho\epsilon\iota\alpha$: $Z\alpha\mu\alpha\rho\iota\alpha s$ a g (Ra.) = זמריה. It is hardly necessary to posit with Rothstein an underlying אמריה by a ז/א error.

8.4,7 נעמן : $Nοο\mu\alpha$ G, G O : $A\chi\iota\alpha$: $Noo\mu\alpha\nu$*, $Noo\mu\alpha\nu$ p.

9.16 ברכיה : $B\alpha\rho\alpha\chi\epsilon\iota$ G : $Z\epsilon\chi\rho\epsilon\iota$ v. 15 : $B\alpha\rho\alpha\chi\iota\alpha$ e₂ R (Ra.).

12.10/9 עזר : $A\zeta\alpha$ G : $A\beta\delta\epsilon\iota\alpha$: $A\zeta\alpha\rho$*.

24.18 מעזיהו : $M\alpha\alpha\sigma\alpha\iota$ B ($M\alpha\sigma$- c₂) $A\delta\alpha\lambda\lambda\alpha\iota$: $M\alpha\alpha\sigma\alpha\iota\alpha$*.

27.2 ישבעם : $\Sigma o\beta\alpha\alpha$ c₂ (-$\beta\alpha\lambda$ B) : $\Sigma o\beta o\chi\alpha\iota$ v. 11 in the next column (12 lines away in BM) : $I\sigma o\beta\alpha\alpha\mu$*. M was lost after AA. Many read ישבעל on the basis of B, comparing 11.11.

II 28.18 גדרות ... אילון : $A\iota\lambda\omega$ ... $\Gamma\alpha\lambda\eta\rho\omega$ G : $\Sigma\omega\chi\omega$: $A\iota\lambda\omega\nu$ O R (Ra.) ... $\Gamma\alpha\delta\eta\rho\omega\theta$ O L (Ra., Δ/Λ).

29.12 עמשי : $M\alpha\sigma\iota$ G : $M\alpha\alpha\theta$: $A\mu\alpha\sigma\iota$ O R (Ra.).

B occasionally has such errors when elsewhere in the group the text is preserved.

I 3.8 אליפלט : $E\lambda\epsilon\iota\phi\alpha\lambda\alpha$ B h : $E\lambda\epsilon\iota\delta\alpha$: $E\lambda\iota\phi\alpha\lambda\alpha\theta$ c₂.

15.24 בניהו : $B\alpha\nu\alpha\iota$ B c₂ O L R : $A\mu\alpha\sigma\alpha\iota$: $B\alpha\nu\alpha\iota\alpha$ h, as in v. 18.

II 25.12 ראש : $\kappa\rho o\nu$ B* : $\kappa\rho\eta\mu\nu o\hat{\nu}$: $\check{\alpha}\kappa\rho o\nu$ Bᵃᵇ c₂ O L R (Ra.).

Once a couple of words are omitted by assimilation to a nearby phrase.

I 23.17 היו לאליעזר בנים : $\hat{\eta}\sigma\alpha\nu$ $\upsilon\iota o\iota$ G, assimilated to $\hat{\eta}\sigma$. $\upsilon\iota o\iota$ earlier in the verse. $\tau\hat{\omega}$ $E\lambda\iota\epsilon\zeta\epsilon\rho$ O L R (Ra.) originally stood in the text. The earlier phrase $\upsilon\iota o\iota$ $\tau\hat{\omega}$ $E\lambda$. G O L R for בני אלי was probably originally $\upsilon\iota o\iota$ $E\lambda$. : $\tau\hat{\omega}$ came in by assimilation to the later phrase which was subsequently omitted.

In I 21.3 B* e* read $\check{\iota}\nu\alpha$ for ולמה¹. $\tau\iota$ Bᵃᵇ c₂ O L R (Ra.) was omitted by analogy with the final conjunction $\check{\iota}\nu\alpha$ later.

(ii) Haplography

(a) Letters belonging to the beginning or end of one word are at times omitted if they recur at the end or beginning of an adjacent word.

I 2.33 ירחמאל : ($\upsilon\iota o\iota$) $P\alpha\mu\epsilon\eta\lambda$ G : $I\rho\alpha\mu\epsilon\eta\lambda$*.

3.6; 14.5 יבחר : ($\kappa\alpha\iota$) $B\alpha\alpha\rho$ G : $I\beta\alpha\alpha\rho$* (Ra.).

4.7 צרת ($\Lambda o\alpha\delta\alpha s$) $A\rho\epsilon\theta$ G : $\Sigma\alpha\rho\epsilon\theta$ O (Ra.).

v. 17 ילון : ($\kappa\alpha\iota$) $A\mu\omega\nu$ G : $I\alpha\lambda\omega\nu$ O L (Ra.).

4.20; 5.24 יִשְׁעִי : (υἱοὶ) Σεει G : Ισει* (Ra.).

v. 23 נְטָעִים : (ἐν) Αζαειμ B (Εζ- c₂) : Ναταιμ* (Ra.).

5.11 סלכה : (ἕως) Ελχα G L : Cελχα O R (Ra.).

v. 19 יְטוּר : (καὶ) Τουραίαν c₂ (-αία B) : Ιτουραίων O (Ra.).

7.2 יְרִיאֵל : (καὶ) Ρειηλ G : Ιρειηλ* (Wutz, p. 29).

v. 6 יְדִיעֲאֵל : (καὶ) Αδειηλ G g : Ιαδιηλ O (Ra.).

v. 7 יְרִימוֹת : (καὶ) Αρειμωθ G : Ιαριμωθ*.

v. 8 יְרֵמוֹת : (καὶ) Αυρημωθ G : Ιαριμωθ*.

v. 12 עִיר חֻשִׁם : (υἱοὶ) Ραωμ G : Ιρασομ* (ωc/ο). Wutz, p. 23, suggested Ιρασεμ. Rothstein wrongly posited רח(ו)ם.

v. 19 אַחִין : (Σεμειρα) Ιααιμ B (-Ιαλ c₂) : Αιμ R before pseudo-ditto-graphy of IM, ultimately from Αειν O (ν/μ).

v. 29 תַּעֲנָךְ : Θαανη (καί) c₂ (Θαλμη B : Α/Λ, ν/μ) : Θαανακ*. The ending was assimilated to Μανασση after haplography.

v. 37 יִתְרָן : (καὶ) Θερα G : Ιθεραν*. The ending was assimilated to Σαλεισα.

8.16 יִשְׁפָּה : (καὶ) Σαφαν G : Ισαφα*, assimilated to Ιωαχαν..

v. 18 יִזְלִיאָה ... יִשְׁמְרַי : (καὶ) Σαμαρει (καὶ) Ζαρεια G : Ισμαρι g (Ra.) ... Ιζαλια*, assimilated to Σαμαρει.

9.8 יִבְנְיָה : (καὶ) Γανααμ G : Ιβαναια*, assimilated to Ιρααμ. At the end of the verse Βαναια G marks an intermediate stage of the corruption.

11.35 שָׂכָר : (υἱὸς) Αχαρ B S h i y Arm (-αμ c₂) : Σαχαρ O (Ra.).

v. 46 יִתְמָה : (καὶ) Εθεμα B S (Θεμα c₂) : Ιεθεμα O (Ra.).

v. 47 יַעֲשִׂיאֵל : (καὶ) Εσειηλ S c₂ (Εσσ- B A L) : Ιεσιηλ O R (Ra.).

12.4 יִשְׁמַעְיָה : (καὶ) Σαμαιας B c₂ O L R (-με -S) : Ἰσαμαίας*.

v. 6/5 יְרִימוֹת : (καὶ) Αρειμουθ B d c₂ (ἀριθμούς S) : Ιαριμουθ O R (Ra.).

v. 8/7 יְרֹחָם : (υἱοὶ) Ρααμ G : Ιρααμ* (Ra.), as in 8.27; 9.8,12.

15.18 יַעֲזִיאֵל : (καὶ) Οζιηλ G : Ιοζιηλ*? Rothstein and Rudolph posit עֻזִּיאֵל and BH so reads according to v. 20, but the *Vorlage* may well have agreed with MT.

16.6 יַחֲזִיאֵל : (καὶ) Οζειηλ G O R (S omits) : Ιοζιηλ m (cf. Rudolph). It is less likely that עֻזִּיאֵל (Rothstein, BH, Goettsberger) was read. Cf. II 20.14 below.

23.23 יְרֵמוֹת : (καὶ) Αρειμωθ G : Ιαριμωθ O (Ra.).

24.16 יְחֶזְקֵאל : (τῷ) Εζεκηλ G g : Ιεζεκηλ*.

v. 30 יְרִימוֹת : (καὶ) Αρειμωθ G : Ιαριμωθ* (Ra.).

25.3 יְשַׁעְיָהוּ : (καὶ) Σαια G : Ισαια* (Ra.. following Lagarde) = Ησαια e₂.

26.30 בני חיל : (αὐτοῦ) οἱ δυνατοί G : υἱοὶ δυν. O R (Ra.). The article reads awkwardly in the context.

27.19 ירימות : (Νεφθαλει) Ερειμωθ G : Ιεριμωθ R (Ra.).

II 20.14 יחזיאל : (τῷ) Οζιηλ G O R : Ιοζιηλ*.

31.13 יחיאל : (καὶ) Ειηλ G : Ιειηλ O L R (Ra.).

Individual errors in B are as follows :

I 2.3 שוע : (θυγατρὸς) Αΰας B* : Σαυας Bᵃᵇ c₂ O R (Rothstein, Ra.).

7.2 יבשם : (καί c₂ O L R, omitted in B¹) Βασαν B : Ιβασαμ*, cf. Ιβασα c₂. After the haplography the form was changed to a familiar name. יבשן (BH) is less likely.

25.17 שמעי : (δέκατος) Εμεει B : Σεμει c₂ (Ra.), as in v. 3.

(b) *Syllables within words are occasionally omitted by haplography.*

I 12.13/12 יוחנן : Ιωαν G : Ιωαναν O L R (Ra.).

20.5 אלחנן : Ελλαν G : Ελλαναν *(Ra.), as in II Rg. 21.19 L.

B has one such individual error.

II 20.9 הזה : τοῦ B* : τούτου Bᵃᵇ c₂ O L R (Ra.).

(c) *Words are at times omitted by this fault.*

I 4.23 היוצרים : (οὗτοι) κεραμεῖς G O R : οἱ κ. L. This could theoretically be a case of Heb haplography, but the Gk has an unnatural ring, compared with, e.g., v. 38 οὗτοι οἱ ...

II 6.15 אשר¹ : ἅ O L R (Ra.), omitted in G m after καρδία v. 14.

B has this type of error by itself within the group as follows :

I 22.2 אשר : τούς c₂ R. B O L omit after -τους.

II 8.4 אשר : ἅς c₂ Oᵐˢˢ R (Ra.). B Oᵐˢˢ L omit after ὀχυράς. As Rudolph notes, BH's proposal "dl c GV" is ill-founded.

9.14 מביאים : ὧν ἔφερον c₂ O R (Ra.), as required in the context. B omits ὧν after -ων.

(iii) *Parablepsis*

This section is concerned with cases apart from haplography, where the eye of a copyist has apparently jumped from syllable to syllable, from word to word or from line to line. In most cases homoeoteleuton or homoeoarcton are involved, but in some instances a whole line, or

---

¹ See p. 47.

even lines, appear to have been skipped over without either of these
factors.[1]

(a) *Syllables within words*

I 2.18 שׁוּבָב : *Ιασουβ* B (-σσ-c₂) : *Σουβαβ**. The beginning was assimilated to the original *Ιασαρ* earlier.

v. 31 אַחְלִי : *Αχαι* G : *Αχαλαι**. The omitted *αλ* was added in the
wrong place : cf. v. 30 סְלֵד[1],[2] : *Αλσαλαδ, Σαλαδ*.

3.24 פְּלִיָּה : *Φαρα* G from *Φαια** (*I/P*) : *Φαλαια* O (Ra.).

7.34 אֲחִי וְרֹהֲגָה : *Αχιουια* G : *Αχιουραογα* O (Ra., *P/I*).

8.31 וְגָדוֹר : *καὶ Δουρ* G : *κ. Γαιδουρ** = *Γεδ*. O (Ra.).

11.29 הַחֻשָׁתִי : *ὁ Αθει* B c₂ (*Ιαθει* S) : *ὁ Ισαθει**, as in 27.11. ιc fell
out after *O*.

v. 36 הַמְּכֵרָתִי :*Μοχορ* G : *ὁ Μοχοραθι** (Ra. : "*αθι* excidit ante *αχι*").
The article was dropped because it was apparently no longer linked
with an adjective.

16.28 מִשְׁפָּחוֹת : *πατρί* BS, cf. *τῷ π.* Justin : *πατριαί** (Ra.). cf.
αἱ π. c₂ O L R. *τῷ κυρίῳ* just before encouraged the error.

23.3 וַיִּסְפְּרוּ : *καὶ ἠρίθμησαν* G O b R : *-μήθησαν* a n z e₂ Arm
(Ra.). וַיִּסְפְּרוּ (BH) is unlikely.

v. 4 מֵאֵלֶּה לְנֶצַח : *ἀπὸ τῶν ἐργοδιωκτῶν* G m : *ἀπὸ τούτων* O L R
(Ra.) *-ῶκται* O R (Ra.). After the omission the noun-ending was
adapted.

25.1 וַיַּבְדֵּל : *καὶ ἔστησεν* G O L R : *κ. διέστησεν** (Rudolph) ? He
is countering Rothstein's suggestion to read וַיַּעֲמֵד with Par. But the
equivalent is only found in Isa. 59.2. *διέστειλεν** is expected : this
verb is used for the Niphal in 23.13. It may well be that after *ΔΙ* was
lost after *ΑΙ* the verb was adapted for sense. For the initial error cf.
II 23.3 *καὶ διέθεντο* : *κ. ἔθεντο* R.

v. 24 יִשְׁבְקָשָׁה :(-os) *Βακατα* G : *Ισβακασα**. -*ατ*-has been assimilated
to -*δέκατος*. In v. 27 c₂ reads *Κεμαθα* for *Αιμαθα* : *K* may well
stand for ιc, a misplaced correction.

v. 16 יְעֵץ : *ἐβούλετο* G O R : *ἐβουλεύετο**.

28.6 הוּא־יִבְנֶה : *κληρονομήσει* B : *αὐτός** *οἰκοδομήσει* c₂ = L R
(Ra.). An abbreviated ΑΥΤΟΛΟΜΗCΕΙ* was read under the influence of *κληρονομήσητε* v. 8.

---

[1] The omission of *υἱοῦ*[2] c₂ O L (Ra.) in B at I 6.32/47 and of *ἐπί*[2] O R (Ra.) in G L
(in doublet) at II 5.8 appears to be pure carelessness on the part of Gk copyists.

v. 11 גוכיו : τῶν ζακχω αὐτοῦ G O R. γαν*- (Wutz, p. 43) was lost after τῶν.

II 4.17 בין צרדחה : ἀναμεσιρδαθαι G : ἀνὰ μέσον O L R Σιρδαθα* (Ra.). -αι has been assimilated to καί.

6.30 וסלחת : καὶ ἱλάσῃ c₂ R (κ. ἰάσῃ B O L). Thackeray, *Grammar*, p. 270, and Ra. so read. But ἵλεως ἔσῃ* is more likely according to the consistent rendering in vv. 21, 25, 27, 39; 7.14 and also to the parallel III Rg 8.39. La so reads : *et propitius eris*. Probably this became ιλεϲη* by parablepsis and was then adapted. B's form has suffered pseudo-haplography, perhaps under the influence of 7.14 where the context is similar.

13.11 עלות : ὁλοκάντωμα G d : -ώματα O R (Ra.). Elsewhere in Par the plural is always rendered -ωσ(ε)ις or -ώματα.

28.12 חדלי : Χοαδ G : Χοδλει* (Ra.). ει was lost before ἐπί.

29.34 להתקדש : ἥγνισαν G : ἡγνίσθησαν O R (Ra.).[1]

34.8 מעשיהו : Μααaσα G : Μαασαια* (Kittel, *SBOT*).

Individual errors of the same kind appear in B as follows :

I 1.54 מגדיאל : Μεδιηλ B : Μεγεδιηλ c₂ Oᵐˢˢ (Ra.), as in Gen. 36.43 LXX.

3.11 אחזיהו : Οζεια B : Οχοζια a h m n, cf. -ίας c₂ L R.

v. 24 אלישב : καὶ Ασειβ B : κ. Ελιασειβ O L (Ra.), cf. Λιασειβ c₂.

17.5 משכן : καλύμματι B : καταλύματι S c₂ O L R (Wutz, p. 34, Rehm, pp. 69, 83, Ra.). After the loss of τα the word was adapted.

II 3.1 לבנות : οἰκοδομή B* : -μῆσαι Bᵃ c₂ O L R (Ra.). ϲαι was lost before εν.

10.6,9 נועצים : βούλεσθε B A a b' c f h m z Arm, B A c g h i : βουλεύεσθε c₂ O L R (Ra.).

13.12 תצליחו : εὐοδώσεται ὑμῖν B n : -ωθήσεται ὑ. c₂ O (Ra.) before a jump from Θ to ϲ.

17.16 זכרי : Ζαρει B : Ζαχαρει m c₂.

25.25 יהואחז : Ιωας B c₂ : Ιωαχας h, encouraged by Ιωας just before.

v. 26 ספר : βλιου B* : βυβλίου Bᵃ, βιβλίου c₂.

30.15 (ו)יתקדשו : ἥγνισαν B* : ἡγνίσθησαν Bᵃᵇ c₂ O L R (Ra.).

v. 18 הִטֶּהָרוּ : ἥγνισαν B : ἡγνίσθησαν c₂ O L R (Ra.).

(b) *Single words*

καί is frequently overlooked.

---

[1] Cf. Part I, p. 105.

I 1.35 G : καί O L R (Ra.) before Κορε; the conjunction is necessary.

5.16 וישבו : κατοίκων G for καὶ L κατῴκουν O R (Ra.). -ων has been assimilated to ἄρχων, πατρῖων v. 15.

15.27 G : καί O L R (Ra.) before 'IEχονίας.

16.22 G : KAI O L R (Ra.) before EN.

21.17 G O R : καί L before κακ-.

29.2 G O R : καί *before κατά. Cf. Boh et; καὶ ἐγὼ κατά L.

v. 27 G : καί O L R (Ra.) before ἐν.

II 2.6/7 G e₂ : καί O b R (Ra.) before ἐν.

8.13 G d, G : καί O L R (Ra.) before ἐν.

18.21 G : καί O L R (Ra.) after ιc and before Δ.

26.19 G O : καί L R (Ra.) before ἐν.

32.10 G O : καί L R (Ra.) before καθ-.

34.10 G O : καί L R between -σαι and κατ-.

36.13 G O L R : καί* before ἐν.

v. 22 G O L R : καί* before ἐν.

B omits καί as follows :

I 7.2 B : καί c₂ O L R (Ra.) after καν-.

15.4 B Omss R : KAI S c₂ Omss L (Ra., comparing vv. 11,14) after -N.

16.30 B c₂ O L R : καί S* Justin before κατ-.

v. 32 ועץ (read for יעלץ) : ξύλον B : καὶ ξ. S c₂ O R (Ra.) after -ατι.

II 30.18 B : καί c₂ O L R (Ra.) after -χαρ.

Other words are overlooked.

I 4.32 עץ omitted in G : Aιν* (Katz, TLZ lxi, col. 276) was lost after καί; cf. Ev L and II 20.2 Ev = Aιν.

11.28 עקש התקועי : Εκτης ὁ Θεκω(ε) G : Εκκης O L R (Ra.) ἐκ τῆς Θ. After the name fell out the next two words were taken as a name and ὁ B S (c₂ omits) was inserted according to the pattern of name + ὁ + name in the context.

v. 39 יואב omitted in G. In the sequence σκεύη Ιωαβ vi. O L R (Ra.) probably the eye jumped from υηι to υι, and only two letters were restored.

13.9 כידן omitted in G O : Καιδων* before καί.

16.14 הוא omitted in G : αὐτός O L R (Ra.) after αὐτοῦ.

17.10 ובית יבכה-לך : καὶ οἰκοδομήσει σε G : originally κ. οἶκον οἰκ. σοι f (Ra.). After the omission the pronoun was adapted for sense. But Rogers, p. 11f., sees here the avoidance of an anthropomorphic notion of God as house-builder.

18.4 אִישׁ רַגְלִי : ἀνδρῶν G. Rehm, p. 17, claims this as a short rendering, but rather πεζῶν O L R (Ra.) dropped out : cf. 19.18 א'ר' : πεζῶν.

v. 10 וּנְחֹשֶׁת omitted in G O : καὶ χαλκᾶ L R omitted between καὶ χρυσᾶ and καί

20.8 אֵל נוֹלְדוּ לְהָרָפָא : οὗτος ἐγένετο Ραφα G. τῷ L R fell out after -το. οὗτοι O L R (Ra.) ἐγένοντο O R (Ra.) is original. After the omission of the article the name was taken as subject or predicate, and the earlier elements were made singular.

21.7 וַיֵּרַע בְּעֵינֵי : καὶ πονηρὸν ἐναντίον G : ἐφάνη O L R (Ra.) was lost before ἐναντίον. Cf. Gen 38.10 וַיֵּרַע : κ. πονηρὸν ἐφάνη.

v. 12 אֶת-שֹׁלְחִי : τῷ ἀποστείλαντι G. ΜΕ O L R (Ra.) fell out before ΛΟ. Rehm, p. 58, posits לְשֹׁלֵחַ.

v. 17 בָּעָם : τῷ λαῷ B g : ἐΝ O L R (Ra.) was lost after ΑΙ. c₂ adapts to τὸν λαόν.

ibid. נָא omitted in G O L R : δή* before ἡ ?

22.7 אֱלֹהַי : θεοῦ G O : μου L R fell out, unless Heb abbreviation is the cause.

24.24 בְּנִי omitted in G R : probably originally υἱός* (= בֵּן) lost after -τος.

26.24 נָגִיד omitted in G : ἐπιστάτης*, the equivalent in II 31.12, was lost before ἐπί.

27.5 לַחֹדֶשׁ : τὸν μῆνα G O R : probably εἰς* was lost after -ος. The Gk construction is either εἰς τ. μ. vv. 7, 15 or τῷ μηνί vv. 8,9, etc.

28.9 בְּנִי omitted in B a f g h : probably τέκνον*, as rendered in 22.7, has been lost after -ων. υἱέ c₂ O L R is probably the result of revision.

II 2.1/2 סַבָּל omitted in G : νωτοφόρων O L R, the equivalent in v. 17/18, fell out after -ων.

6.16 מִלְּפָנֵי : ἀπὸ προσώσου G : μου Bᵃ O L R (Ra.) was lost.

v. 22 מִזְבַּחֶךָ : τοῦ θυσιαστηρίου G O L R : σου*, as in the parallel III Rg. 8.31 was lost.

v. 32 עַמְּךָ : τοῦ λαοῦ G Oᵐˢˢ· : σου Oᵐˢˢ· L R (Ra.), as found continually in the context, was lost.

15.8 אָסָא omitted in G O R : ΑϹΑ* was overlooked after -ϹΑΙ, cf. τὸν Α. L.

17.6 עוֹד omitted in G d m : ἔτι O L R (Ra.) fell out before -ἐ.

v. 13 לוֹ omitted in G : αὐτῷ O L R (Ra.) was lost after -το.

22.7 יֵהוּא omitted in G : Ιου b (Ra.) as in v. 8f., fell out before υἱόν.

25.26 מַלְכֵי omitted in G : probably βιβλίου βασιλέων Ιουδα O R (Ra.) was reduced to βιβλιουδα* and adapted.

26.11 לעזיהו : 'Οζεία G : τῷ O L R (Ra.) fell out after -το.

29.12 יואח omitted in G : Ιωαχ* fell out between ωνι and ἀπό. Ιωαχα at the end of the verse has been assimilated to the form which earlier stood here by dittography of α.

31.16 ביומו לעבודתם : εἰς ἡμέρας λειτουργίαν G g : εἰς O L R (Ra.) was omitted after -ας. O⁻ᵍ Arm R correct to ἡμέραν, but the plural is original after ἡμερῶν G O L R for יום.

32.12 הלא omitted in G : οὐχί* as in v. 11, or οὐχ O L R (Ra.) was dropped between -ουρ and οὗτος.

v. 26 הוא omitted in G O : αὐτός L R was lost after αὐτοῦ.

33.15 וישלך חוצה : καὶ ἔξωθεν G (O R) : ἐξέβαλεν L fell out. Cf. 24.10 ἐνέβαλλον for the rendering.

34.12 עשים omitted in G O R : probably ποιοῦντες* fell out after -ες.[1]

v. 13 מנצחים omitted in G O R : ἐπιστάται L (Rudolph), as rendered in 2.1/2, or ἐπίσκοποι*, as for מפקדים v. 12 (cf. ἐπισκοπεῖν for לנצח in that verse), fell out before ἐπί. Benzinger is unjustified in striking out מנ' on the basis of Par's omission.

v. 16 לאמר omitted in G O : λέγων L R fell out after λόγον. Cf. for the opposite process λέγων y, λέγον g. for λ. λ.

35.9 לפסחים : εἰς τὸ φασεχ G : πρόβατα O L R (Ra.) is essential before the neuter plural numeral. It dropped out before π.

II Ki.23.27/35.19d פני : προσώπου G : μου O L R (Ra.) must be restored.

ibid. הזאת omitted in G O L R and in IV Rg L K R : ταύτην* was lost between -ιν and ἥν.

v. 26 יתר omitted in G O L R : λοιποί y (Rudolph) before λόγοι. Cf. 28.26 for the rendering. Rehm, p. 61, wrongly posits ויהי for ויתר.

II Ki.23.35/36.4a יהויקים omitted in G O L R : ΙΩΑΚΕΙΜ* was lost after ΕΛΩΚΕΝ The name is necessary since the subject changes.

v. 14 מעל כעל תעבות : ἀθετήματα βδελυγμάτων G L : originally ἀθέτημα κατὰ τὰ βδελύγματα R La via the contracted ἀθετήματα βδελύγματα O. The text was adapted for sense after the omission.

ibid. הקדיש omitted in G O L R : ἁγιαζόμενον*, as in the parallel I Esdr 1.47, was probably lost after τόν. According to Rogers, p. 43, the translator omitted to tone down the flagrancy of the profanation.

v. 22 כורש omitted in G : Κύρου O L R (Walde, *Esdrasbücher*, p. 30, Ra.) was overlooked after πρώτου.

---

[1] For the Gk participle cf. Part I, p. 42.

Another type of omission is encountered in I 11.15 : חנה omitted in
G : παρεμβεβλήκει O L R (Ra). Thirteen letters are involved, probably
representing a line. A line of the exemplar has probably been omitted.
If this is so, Rothstein's view on the basis of Par that (מ)חנה is a
dittograph of מחנה is erroneous. Compare the omission in II 2.17/18 :
מנצחים omitted in B* b' : ἐργοδιώκτας Bᵃᵇ c₂ O L R (Ra.). This has a
ring of originality : a reviser would have chosen ἐπιστάτας, the equivalent in v. 2. The rendering is authenticated by its presence in I 23.4
for לנצח. Eleven letters are involved.

H. L. Allrik has drawn from a study of I Esdr. 5.8ff. the inference
that the prototype exemplar of B had from twelve to fifteen letters
in a line.[1] Similarly, Westcott and Hort observed that longer portions
of the text omitted in B consist usually either of twelve to fourteen
letters or of multiples of the same and that its exemplar was doubtless
written in lines of this length.[2] These two independent deductions are
reinforced by the present writer's own observation that in Par R
often uniquely omits portions of the text consisting of about twelve
letters, e.g., II 7.1 ἐκ τοῦ οὐρανοῦ, 13.2 ἐν Ιερουσαλημ, 15.8 ἐν ὄρει
Εφραιμ, 19.11 καὶ οἱ Λευῖται. In the light of this cumulative evidence
it is clear that line omission involving twelve letters or so is a factor
to be reckoned with in the textform of G. In fact S has lines of this
average length. More examples will be given in the next section, but
first remaining individual omission of words in B are to be listed.

I 17.9   בראשונה : ἀρχῆς B S : originally ἀπ' ἀ. c₂ O L R (Ra.), as in
the parallel II Rg 7.10 and in II 23.8 G O R.

v. 22   היית omitted in B : ἐγενήθης S c₂ O R. The eye jumped from
K̄C̄ (B only κύριος for κύριε) to Η̄C̄.

II 2.17/18 has been considered above.

5.2 ; 29.27 ישראל omitted in B : Ισραηλ is present in c₂ O L R (Ra.).
The abbreviation ιC̄Λ̄, as found in A, has been overlooked before ΚΑ.

v. 13   וכהרים : καὶ ὕψωσαν B* N e Arm : ὡς Bᵃᵇ c₂ O L R (Ra.)
was lost before -ωσ-.

6.21   עמך : λαοῦ B : σου c₂ O L R (Ra.) dropped out.

14.8/9   אלף omitted in B m : χιλίαις c₂ O L R (Ra.) fell out before
χιλιάσιν.

16.13   ἐνάτῳ dropped out before ἐν τῷ in B*.[3]

---

[1] ZAW lxvi, p. 274.

[2] The NT in the Original Greek, ii, p. 233f.

[3] See p. 12f.

26.3 במלנו omitted in B : ἐβασίλευσεν c₂ O R (Ra.), as in 22.2 G O.
-ωN and -cεN were confused.

(c) *Phrases*

Two or more words are frequently absent from G in circumstances
which suggest oversight on a copyist's part.

I 2.16 ואביגיל omitted in G : καὶ Αβιγαια O L R (Ra.), as in v. 17;
3.1, after -ια. ἀδελφὴ αὐτῶν G O R for אחיתיהם was doubtless
ἀδελφαὶ αὐτῶν n before the omission.
7.20 שותלח וברד בנו ותחת : Σωθαλαθ B (Σωλαθ c₂). The copyist's
eye went from Σωθαλα O R (Ra.) to Θααθ O L R (Ra.). The first name
may have been assimilated to B's form before the parablepsis. BH
marks the omission inaccurately.
8.12 ואת־לד omitted in G : καὶ ... before καί.
9.5 ובניו omitted in G a g : καὶ υἱοὶ αὐτοῦ O R (Ra.) after αὐτοῦ, as
Ra. notes.
v. 34 ללוים omitted in G : τῶν Λευιτῶν O L R after -ων. Rudolph
rightly condemns Rothstein's deletion from the Heb on the Gk evidence.
v. 43 אלעשה בנו omitted in G R : ... υἱὸς αὐτοῦ O L (Ra.) after v. a.
The following Εσαηλ B (Ασ- c₂) for אצל shows the influence of -σα
originally preceding.
11.4f ויאמרו ישבי יבוס : ישבי הארץ : οἱ κατοικοῦντες τὴν Ιεβους εἶπαν
G : γῆν O L R καὶ οἱ κατ* has been lost after the similar οἱ κατ. τήν;
so the unusual article in G suggests. The verb was evidently transposed to a Gk order. BH (cf. Rothstein) assumes a divergent *Vorlage* :
"G^B יבוס" (for הארץ), "1 c G^B ויאמרו" (for יבום ... ויא'.).
v. 9 וגדול omitted in G : καὶ μεγαλυνόμενος O L R (Ra.) as in the
parallel II Rg 5.10, was lost after -όμενος, as Ra. notes. Rehm, p. 17,
considers this a case of shorter rendering, but the clause reads badly
without the addition.
v. 33 אליחבא השעלבני : Σαμαβα ὁ Ομει B, Ελμαβα (-βαμα c₂)
ὁ Σωμει S c₂ : originally Ελιαβα O R (Ra.) ὁ Σααλαβωνι* (cf. Σαλαβωνι
O L). In B's text the eye has slipped from εΛ to cΛ. The final word
must at some stage have taken the form Σααλαβαωμει* : -βα- was
assimilated to Ελιαβα, and ν became μ. This was then divided up
according to the pattern ὁ + gentilic adjective in the context, taking
ω as οο and confusing ΛΛ with Μ. In the text of S c₂ similar changes
took place, but εΛ was left instead of cΛ. ο cω represents pseudo-
dittography of ω.

17.6 אֲשֶׁר צִוִּיתִי omitted in G : ᾧ* ἐνετειλάμην O L R, as in II Rg. 7.7 (the context is very similar to Rg). The eye slipped from λΗλ to ΜΗΝ in a line omission of twelve letters.

19.13 בְעֵינָיו omitted in G : ἐναντίον αὐτοῦ*, as in 21.23, a line omission of thirteen letters and the eye slipped from ЄΝ to ΚΑΙ.

21.9 דָּוִיד לֵאמֹר omitted in G : Δαυιδ λέγων O (Ra.) was overlooked after ὦντα. BH's omission marks are misplaced.

24.13 לְיֶשְׁבְאָב : τῷ Γελβα B, τ. Βεαγα c₂ = לְבִלְגָה v. 14. Ιεσβααμ* (ב/מ;¹ cf. Ισβααλ O b R, Ιεσβαλ e₂) was confused with the next name (ΤШΙ ΙЄϹΒΑΑΜ, ΤШΙ ΓЄΛΒΑ) and omitted. In the list all the subsequent names were moved one place backwards to fill up the gap. This phenomenon is easily explained if it be assumed that each name and number (in alphabetic form?) occupied a single line, and names and numbers were copied separately. The last number, in v. 18, was left without a name, and so was omitted.

v. 26 בָּנוּ : τοῦ G : υἱοῦ αὐ(τοῦ)* was lost in the sequence λ.ΥΙΟΥ.ΑΥΤΟΥ.

26.29 בָּנָיו לַמְּלָאכָה : υἱοὶ τῆς ἐργασίας G R. O L (in doublet) add αὐτοῦ, but this is inadequate. Probably ἐπί* too dropped out : cf. ἐπί frequently for עַל in the context. This would suit the genitive. The eye slipped from οι to ЄΠΙ.

27.32 וְסוֹפֵר הוּא omitted in G : καὶ γραμματεὺς αὐτός O L R (Ra.) fell out between -τός and καί. The omission thus has no significance for the Heb text *contra* Curtis and Rothstein.

29.30 וְהָעִתִּים omitted in G : καὶ οἱ καιροί O L (Ra.) once stood in G as a necessary antecedent to οἵ. The nominative has an original ring : had the text been supplemented in O L, they would have read the genitive like R. οἱ κ. fell out before οἵ, then καί was dropped.

II 2.6/7 וְתַכְלֶת omitted in G : καὶ ἐν τῷ ὑακίνθῳ O L R (Ra.; = וּבַת) before καὶ ἐ-. This equivalent appears in v. 13/14; 3.14.

v. 17/18 בָּהָר omitted in G O : ἐν τῷ ὄρει L R omitted before καί.² Rehm, p. 17, claims a shorter rendering on the translator's part.

9.12 הִיא וַעֲבָדֶיהָ omitted in G O L R; probably αὐτὴ καὶ οἱ παῖδες αὐτῆς* was lost after αὐτῆς. *Ipsa et pueri eius* La probably attests this original fuller text.

v. 20 מַשְׁקֵה omitted in G O R : τοῦ οἴνου* lost before τοῦ, cf. the corrupted τοῦ οἴκου L, assimilated to οἴκου after σκέυη later in the

---

¹ See p. 110.

² Cf. the cases of omission of καί before ἐν on p. 47.

verse. A specification of the type of vessels is needed in the context. Cf. v.4 משקין : οἰνοχόων αὐτοῦ for the rendering.

12.7 ביד שישק omitted in G O R : ἐν χειρὶ ϹΟΥϹΑΚΕΙΜ L, as in v. 5, after ΙΕΡΟΥϹΑΛΗΜ. According to Rogers, p. 27, the translator omitted to remove pagan collaboration in God's wrath.

14.4f./5f. ויבן ערי : ותשקט הממלכה לפניו : καὶ εἰρήνευσεν. πόλεις G O (R) : ... ᾠκοδόμησεν* (cf. -ησε a L) after -σεν.

15.4 בצר omitted in G O R : ἐν θλίψει L La after -ψει. Cf. θλίψει for צרה v. 6.

16.10 כי־בזעף עמו omitted in B*. Bᵃᵇ c₂ O L R (Ra.) supply ὅτι ὠργίσθη which has an original ring with its avoidance of the preposition.[1] ὅτι ... was lost before ἐπί. The original phrase may well have included αὐτῷ*. There is no occasion for a personal dative with ὀργίζεσθαι in Par but it is frequent in the Gk Old Testament. Then a line of fourteen letters was overlooked.

19.10 בעריהם omitted in G : ἐν πόλεσιν αὐτῶν after -των (cf. ἐν ταῖς π. α. O L R). A line of fourteen letters was overlooked.

ibid. לדם omitted in G f j : καὶ αἵματος p Arm Lucifer after αἵματος, as the rendering of the next, parallel phrase suggests.

v. 11 בן ישמעאל : ὁ τοῦ Ισμαηλ* before ὁ. cf. v. 2 בן : ὁ τοῦ.

20.7 עמך omitted in G : τοῦ λαοῦ σου O L R (Ra.) after -ου.

21.2 ועזריהו omitted in G : καὶ Ἀζαρίας O L R (Ra.) after Ζαχαρίας.

22.7 להכרית omitted in G O R : τοῦ ἐξολεθρεῦσαι L, as rendered in I 17.8, before τόν. A line of fifteen letters was omitted. The following accusative demands a verb.

25.23 בן־יהואחז omitted in G O : τοῦ Ιωαχας* after τοῦ Ιωας. Cf. the confusion of the two names later in this very verse. It is more likely that parablepsis occurred in the Gk than that Par used an older Heb text lacking the phrase, as Rudolph claims.

29.8 לשמה omitted in G : καὶ εἰς ἀφανισμόν O L R (Ra.) before καὶ εἰς, as Ra. notes. The use of ἀφ. (for השחית) in 36.19 authenticates the wording here.

29.15 ויבאו omitted in G O L R : καὶ εἰσῆλθαν*, as in B v. 18, after -ίσθησαν.

30.8 כאבותיכם omitted in G O : ὡς οἱ πατέρες ὑμῶν L R after ὑμῶν. The presence of the phrase must have been a partial cause of the

---

[1] Cf. Part I, p. 44.

Gk assimilation to Psa 95/94.8 earlier[1] : cf. οἱ π. ὑμῶν in v. 9 of the psalm.

31.10 עַד־לָרוֹב omitted in G : ἔτι (= עַד) εἰς πλῆθος* (cf. ἕως εἰς π. O L R) before ὅτι. ἔτι was wrongly restored between κατελίπομεν[2] and τὸ πλῆθος in O L R (Ra.), and subsequently corrupted to ἐπί G N.

v. 20 וְהָאֱמֶת omitted in G O R : καὶ τὸ ἀληθές L after -θές. A reviser would have used ἀλήθεια, as found in 32.1.

34.8 שָׁלַח omitted in G : ἀπέστειλεν τόν O L R (Ra.) after -ον. QA line of thirteen letters was overlooked. BM restores only the verb.

v. 19 אֶת־דִּבְרֵי omitted in G : τοὺς λόγους O L R (Ra.) before τοῦ. ἀκούειν often takes a genitive of the thing heard but an accusative occurs in v. 27. Rehm, p. 17, sees here a shorter rendering.

v. 24 וְעַל־יוֹשְׁבָיו omitted in G O L R : καὶ ἐπὶ τοὺς κατοικοῦντας αὐτόν*, as in v. 27, after τοῦτον. Twenty seven letters, or two lines, were involved.

v. 31 לַעֲשׂוֹת omitted in G O : τοῦ ποιεῖν* before τούς, cf. τοῦ φυλάσσειν for לִשְׁמוֹר just before.

II Ki.24.1/36.5a וַיָּשָׁב omitted in G O L R : καὶ ἀπέστρεψεν*, as rendered in 32.21 ; 34.7, before καὶ ἀπέστη.

v. 20 מִן־הַחֶרֶב omitted in G O L R : ΕΚ τῆς μαχαίρας* before ΕΙΣ. A line of thirteen letters was overlooked.

v. 21 כָּל־יְמֵי הֻשַּׁמָּה שָׁבָתָה : σαββατίσαι G. O L R (Ra.) add what was doubtless the original text : πάσας τὰς ἡμέρας (τῆς) ἐρημώσεως αὐτῆς ἐσαββάτισεν. G has suffered omission by homoeoteleuton of αὐτῆς, then the verb was conformed to the preceding infinitives. Presumably the fragment in G was obelized in the LXX column of the Hexapla.

In a number of these cases it has been observed that line omission has played a part together with other factors. At times it is the sole or major cause of omission.

I 29.1f. הַבִּירָה omitted in B and ו in G O R : ἡ οἰκοδομὴ καί*, a line of twelve letters. O R put ἡ οἰκ. earlier according to the order in MT. c₂ reads οἰκ. in the same place by revision.

II 1.6 מוֹעֵד omitted in G O : τοῦ μαρτυρίου L R, as in v. 3, overlooked as a line of twelve letters. Rehm, p. 16, claims a shorter rendering, but elsewhere in Par אֹהֶל מוֹעֵד is always rendered in full.

9.30 ; 19.4 ; 35.1 בִּירוּשָׁלַם omitted in G O R, G (before καί), G O L R :

---

[1] See p. 15.

ἐν Ἰερουσαλημ K, O L R (Ra.),* overlooked in each case as a line omission of twelve letters. Rogers, p. 41f., finds the translator's broader theology in the last omission.

12.9 על־ירושלם omitted in G O : ἐπὶ Ἰερουσαλημ L R, as in v. 2, lost as a line of thirteen letters. Rogers, p. 108, again claims a deliberate omission by the translator, out of veneration for Jerusalem.

15.11 מן־השלל omitted in G : ἀπὸ τῶν σκύλων O L R (Ra.), an omission of a twelve letter line.

20.25 לאין משא omitted in G O L R. Yet משא is rendered ἆραι in 35.3. Has καὶ οὐκ ἦν ἆραι* fallen out before καί and by a twelve letter line omission? Cf. I 22.4 לאין : οὐκ ἦν; II 36.16 עד־לאין : ἕως οὐκ ἦν.

33.18f./19 מלכי ישראל omitted in G O L R : βασιλέων Ἰηλ καί* fell out as a line of fourteen letters.

A few phrases have fallen out of B individually.

I 4.12 ואשתון omitted in B : καὶ Ασσαθων c₂ O (Ra.) after Ασ.

6.50/65 בשמות omitted in B* : ἐπ’ ὀνόματος B^ab c₂ O R (Ra.) after αὐτάς.

7.16 פרש ושם אחיו omitted in B : Φαρας (-ες O L R) καὶ ὄνομα ἀδελφοῦ (c₂ omits) αὐτοῦ c₂ O L R fell out after αὐτοῦ (Ra.). Rothstein claims a Vorlage omission, but this is less likely.

I 1.18 ויבאו omitted in B* : καὶ ἦλθον S B^a c₂ O L R (Ra.) over-looked after καὶ ἐλαβον.

II 6.42 משיחך[1] : σου B O^mss : τοῦ χριστοῦ O L R (Ra.; cf. χ̄ῡ = χριστοῦ c₂) dropped out before σου. פניך (BH) is hardly implied.

18.24 אשר omitted in B : ἐν ᾗ c₂ O L R (Ra.) lost after ἐκείνῃ.

20.3 על־כל־יהודה omitted in B* : ἐν παντὶ Ιουδα B^ab c₂ O L R (Ra.) fell out before καί and as a twelve letter line.

v. 10 ומואב omitted in B* : καὶ Μωαβ B^ab c₂ O L R (Ra.) fell out before καί (Ra.).

28.24 בירושלם omitted in B*; ἐν Ἰερουσαλημ B^ab c₂ O L R (Ra.) was overlooked as a twelve letter line and before καί.

(d) Clauses

I 16.24 G O omit the whole verse by homoeoteleuton of αὐτοῦ.

17.23f. עד־עולם ... ועשה (עד־עולם) is omitted in G O. The words were once represented in Par since λεγόντων (= "when men say") for לאמר following would otherwise be λέγοντος agreeing with αὐτοῦ.

---

[1] BH prints משיחיך with "L" but rightly counsels that חך־ be read "c mlt MSS".

Rogers, p. 13, thinks that the translator omitted the final words of v. 23 because they suggest giving a command to God.

19.13 חזק ... אלהינו is omitted in B S h. O L R (Ra.) have ἀνδρίζου καὶ ἐνισχύσωμεν ... ἡμῶν. This has an original ring : cf. ἐνισχύειν for חזק in II 1.1 and ἀνδρίζου I 22.13 ; 28.20. c₂ patches the omission with ἀνδ. καὶ ἴσχυε, apparently derived from 22.13. Sixty two letters or five lines were overlooked.

21.4 has been considered earlier.[1]

B has the following cases of omission :

II 5.5 ויעלו את־הארון omitted in B : καὶ ἀνήνεγκαν τὴν κιβωτόν c₂ O L R (Ra.) after τὴν κ. (Ra.).

6.6 שם ... ואבחר omitted in B a g. The words in c₂ O L R (Ra.) fell out by homoeoarcton of καὶ ἐξελεξάμην (Ra.).

20.8 ויבנו לך בה omitted in B* a. c₂ O R (Ra.) add καὶ ᾠκοδόμησαν ἐν αὐτῇ which fell out after ἐν α. (Ra.)[2]

(iv) *Letters omitted*

Sometimes the original reading has been marred by the loss of letters. Pseudo-haplography is often the cause.

I 2.55 ספרים : γραμμάτων G : γραμματέων O R (Ra.) which is expected in the context.

4.38 הבאים : οἱ διελόντες G : οἱ διελθ. O R (Ra.)

5.26 חלח : Χααχ G : Χαλαχ* (Ra.).

11.13 פס דמים : Φασοδομη G : Φασοδομιν O (Ra.) via -ΗΝ*.

12.5/4 יחזיאל : Ιεζηλ B S (Ιερμηλ c₂, assimilated to 'Ιερμίας) : Ιεζιηλ O L R (Ra.).

17.26 ; II 33.13 האלהים : θεός G e₂ R, G b : ὁ θ. O b (Ra.), O L R (Ra.).

23.8 ; II 21.2 יחיאל : Ιηλ B a m (Ισλ̄ c₂), G : Ιειηλ O L R (Ra.).

24.15 הפצץ : Αφεση (ὁ) : Αφεσης*.

v. 23 יקמעם : Ιακομ c₂ (Ιοκ- B) : Ιακμοαμ 144.

26.1f. משלמיהו : Μοσολαηλ G, Μοσολαηα R (-ηλ c₂) : Μοσολλαμια* (Ra.).

27.12 הענתתי : ἐξ Αναθωθ G : ὁ ἐξ A. O L R (Ra.).

II 24.26 שמעת : Σαμα B f h j (Ζα- c₂) : Σαμαθ Omss (Ra.).

---

[1] p. 11.

[2] For לך see p. 145.

26.21 הַמֶּלֶךְ : βασιλεύς G : ὁ β. O L R (Ra.), omitted after -ς.

31.15 אַמַרְיָהוּ : Μαρίας G O : 'Αμαρίας L R (Ra.).

34.8 אֲצַלְיָהוּ : Σελια G O : Εσελια R (Ra.).

v. 12 יַחַת : Ιε G : Ιεθ O R (Ra.).

B has individual errors of this kind as follows :

I 9.7 מְשֻׁלָּם : Μοολλαμ B : Μοσολλαμ O (Ra.), cf. Βοσ- c₂.

17.26; 25.5 הָאֱלֹהִים : θεός B n y, B : ὁ θ. S c₂ O L R (Ra.), c₂ O L R (Ra.).

II 30.18 הַטּוֹב : ἀγαθός B : ὁ ἀ. c₂ O L R (Ra.), omitted after -ς.

Iota falls out occasionally between vowels.

I 3.21 רְפָיָה : Ραφαλ G from Ραφαα* (cf. Ραφα R) : Ραφαια O L (Ra.).

4.2 רְאָיָה : Ραδα G from Ραα* : Ραια* (Ra.)., cf. Ραιαλ L.

II 11.10 אַיָּלוֹן : Ααλων c₂ (-Αλδ B) : Αιαλων O L (Ra.).

B has two such cases :

I 3.22 שְׁמַעְיָה¹ : Σαμαα B* : Σαμαια Bᵃᵇ c₂ O (Ra.). as later.

24.18/17 דְּלָיָהוּ : Αδαλλα B : Αδελαια c₂ from Δαλαια O L R (Ra.) in v. 18.

Other omissions of letters are as follows :

I 2.8 עֲזַרְיָה : Ζαρεια G : Αζαρια O R (Ra.).

v. 29 מוֹלִיד : Μωηλ G : Μωληδ* = Μωλιδ O (Ra.).

3.3 עֶגְלָה : Αλα G : Αγλα O R (Ra.).

4.16 זִיפָה : Ζαφα G : Ζαιφα A i.

v. 19 הַגַּרְמִי : Αταμει B (Ασταμι c₂) : Αγαρμι* (Ra.), cf. ὁ Ταρμι O, ὁ Γαρμι L.

5.5 מִיכָה : Ηχα G : Μηχα g = Μιχα O L R (Ra.).

7.20 אֶלְעָדָה : Λααδα G : Ελααδα m.

8.35f. אָחָז : Ζαχ c₂ (-κ B) : Αχαζ R (Ra.), as in 9.42.

11.39 צֶלֶק : Σελη G : Σεληκ e g (Ra.).

24.1 מַחְלְקוֹתָם : διαιρέσει G : -σεις O L R (Ra.).

v. 23 יַחֲזִיאֵל : Ιαση G : Ιασιηλ*.

27.7 זְבַדְיָה : 'Αβδείας G : Ζαβδίας O e₂ R (Ra.).

v. 13 מַהְרַי : Μεηρα G : Μεηραι*.

II 11.9 אֲדוֹרַיִם : Αδουραι G : -αιμ O (Ra.).

29.1 אֲבִיָּה : Αββα G from Αβα* : Αβια L R.

v. 12 יְהַלֶּלְאֵל : Ελλη G : Ιαλεληλ*, cf. Ιλαεληλ R, Ιαλλεληλ O.

v. 13 אָסָף : Ασα G : Ασαφ O L R (Ra.).

The following individual errors occur in B :

I 3.21 פלטיה : Φαλεττι B : Φαλλετια O (Ra.). cf. Φελλετια N c₂.

4.2 צרעתי : Αραθει B R : Σαραθι O (Ra.), cf. Σαραιθι c₂.

v. 32 תכן : Θοκκα B c₂ : Θοκκαν h.

5.31/6.5 בקי¹,² : Βωε B = Βωαι* : Βωκαι O (Ra.), cf. Βω h c₂ with haplography of καί.

11.30 נטופתי : Ετωφατει B*vid : Νετωφατει Bᵃ, cf. Νετωφαθι S c₂ O L (Ra.).

25.22 ירמות : Ερειμωθ B : Ιεριμωθ O (Ra.), cf. Ιεριμω c₂.

27.8 יזרח : Εσραε B (... ερσααι c₂) : Ιεσραε h (Ra.).

II 1.8 אתה : ὅ B : συ c₂ O L R (Ra.). After υ was dropped σ became ο.

16.4 עיון : Ιω B : Ιων* (Ra.), cf. Ινω c₂.

28.5 בו : ἑαυτῷ B : ἐν αὐτῷ c₂ O R (Ra.).

(v) *Omission of* κύριος

There are nineteen places in Par where no equivalent appears for יהוה. They are as follows : I 6.17/32 G; 9.19 G; 15.12 G O, 13 G O, 14 G Oᵐˢˢ, 25 G; 16.8* G (ליהוה), 11* G; 17.27 G; 21.28* G; 22.19 G; 23.4* G; II 7.2 G O; 8.12 G R; 20.21 G O R (ליהוה); 29.11 G; 30.6 G O; 33.16 G, 18 G. An asterisk indicates places where the omission leaves an awkward gap in the sense of the context. To this list may be added three places where no equivalent appears for האלהים : I 14.11 G (L R add k̄s̄); 17.20 G O; II 31.14 G O L R (Pesh יהוה). It will be noted later that κύριος frequently stands for (ה)אלהים.[1] I 17.25 should also be taken into account, where O R read κύριε for אלהי.[2]

How may these omissions be explained ? In II 8.12 Rehm, p. 86, suggested that the omission was deliberate on the part of the translator because τῷ κυρίῳ precedes. In I 23.4 it is conceivable that κ̄ῡ has dropped out after -κου. But what of the rest of the cases ? What is needed is an explanation which will do justice to all the twenty three cases.

It is significant that the phenomenon is not unknown elsewhere. A.S. Hunt has observed that Papyrus iv. 656, a third century A.D. papyrus of Genesis, has a "decided tendency to omit the word κύριος".[3] In three passages a second hand filled in the blank with

---

[1] p. 146f.

[2] See Part I, p. 194.

[3] *The Oxyrhynchus Papyri*, vii, p. 2 (cited by Waddell, *JTS* xliv, p. 158 note 5).

κύριε. A blank space, sufficient for four letters, was left by the original scribe. Why four letters? Papyrus Fouad 266 provides the answer. The remains of this papyrus of the LXX of Deuteronomy, which Waddell assigned to the second or first century B.C., shows no example of κύριος, but everywhere the Tetragrammaton written in the square script. In at least one case "the scribe of the Gk text left a space in which another hand inserted the Heb letters so small as not to fill the space".[1] This practice of writing the Heb is not only attested by Origen and Jerome as characteristic of LXX mss.,[2] but is also found in a papyrus containing fragments of Lev 2-4, which was discovered at Qumran in Cave Four.[3] "Thus the indications are that the Tetragrammaton in the LXX was at first written in Heb letters and not in Gk".[4]

It may be suggested that here lies the answer to the missing cases of κύριος in Par. At some stage in the history of the text a Gk copyist left gaps for somebody else to write in יהוה. The second copyist was careless in his task and overlooked twenty three of the gaps.

---

[1] Würthwein, *op. cit.*, p. 132.

[2] Waddell, *loc. cit.*, p. 158, gives the references.

[3] Kahle, *Cairo Geniza*,[2] p. 224.

[4] Roberts, *OT Text and Versions*, p. 174. P.W. Skehan, *Supplements to VT* iv, p. 151, considers the transcription ΙΑΩ (for which see Part I, p. 146) even earlier.

CHAPTER TWO

GREEK OR HEBREW TEXTUAL CHANGES

There are a number of variants which it is impossible to put into one clear-cut category. At some point along the textual line changes of various kinds have evidently taken place in the text, but whether within the course of Heb or Gk transmission it is now hard to determine.

1. Assimilation

The context or a similar passage elsewhere sometimes moulds the text to a different shape.

(a) *Substitution*

I 2.42 מֵישָׁע : $Mαρεισα$ B O, assimilated to M.[2] = מרשה (Rudolph). Benzinger, Kittel, Rothstein and Goettsberger change with Par, striking out אבי as a gloss.

12.3 פלט : $Iωφαλητ$ (not -$ετ$, as BH prints) G, assimilated to the beginning of יואל just before in the *Vorlage* or to $Iωηλ$. Rothstein suggested that יו has been lost in MT after ו, comparing the form אליפלט, but this is less likely.

24.15/14 חזיר : $Xηζειν$ B, corresponding to a *Vorlage* חזין according to BH. The form has been influenced either by יכין in v. 17 or by $Iαχειν$* in v. 16. For the Heb name see Rudolph's comment.

25.25 לחנוי : $'Aνανίας$ G R. Cf. v. 23 לחנניהו : $'Aνανίας$ G O L.

29.14 עמי : ὁ λαός σου G O. Either this stands for עמך, influenced by v. 17f., or else μου LR is original and σου has been influenced by σου at the end of v. 13.

v. 20 אלהיכם (יהוה) : (κύριον) τὸν θεὸν ἡμῶν G O. Either אלהינו (BH) is presupposed under the influence of v. 16 יהוה אלהינו; or ὑμῶν L R is original and has been assimilated to κύριε ὁ θεὸς ἡμῶν.

II 1.9 דברך (יאמן) : τὸ ὄνομά σου G O R. Cf. I 17.24 שמך ... ויאמן. G O omit, but the clause once stood in Par.[1]

---

[1] See p. 55.

7.9 ויעשׂו ... עשׂו : καὶ ἐποίησεν ... ἐποίησεν G O L R. Cf. v. 7 עשׂה :
ἐποίησεν twice, and v. 8 ויעשׂ : καὶ ἐποίησεν.

18.8 מלך ישׂראל : ὁ βασιλεύς G R, influenced by המלך : ὁ βασ. at
the end of v. 7.

20.37 אניות : τὰ πλοῖά σου G O (L) R = perhaps אניותיך (BH),
assimilated to מעשׂיך. Or else τὸ ἔργον σου G O was the magnet.

31.4 ויאמר : καὶ εἶπαν G R = ויאמרו ? The number has been mechanically assimilated to the next verb יחזקו : κατισχύουσιν/ωσιν.

34.33 (כל־הנמצא) בישׂראל : ἐν Ιερουσαλημ καὶ ἐν Ισραηλ G O L (R).
Cf. v. 32 כל־הנמ׳ בירושׁלם. Four Heb mss. so read here. On the other
hand the two names are notorious variants in Gk mss because of the
similarity of their abbreviated forms ΙΛΗΜ and ΙΗΛ. At some stage
the correction has slipped into the text alongside the error.

ibid. סרו ... אבותיהם : ἐξέκλινεν ... αὐτοῦ G O L R. Cf. v. 2 לא־סר :
οὐκ ἐξ. After the verb was adapted either the suffix or the pronoun
was made singular.

36.19 וישׂרפו ... וינתצו ... שׂרפו : καὶ ἐνέπρησεν G O L R ... κ. κατέσ-
καψεν G O L ... ἐνέπρησεν G O L R. In the first two cases h has
plurals. The verbs have been conformed to the singulars before and
after.

(b) Addition

I 6.33/48 לכל־עבודת : εἰς πᾶσαν ἐργασίαν λειτουργίας G O R. Either
לכל־מלאכת ע׳ (Rothstein) is presupposed, in which case מל׳ has
come in from v. 34/49, or else the original Gk was εἰς π. λειτουργίαν*
and ἐργ. came in from εἰς π. ἐργασίαν in the next verse, and λ. was
made genitive.[1]

15.24 לארון : + τοῦ θεοῦ G O L R. The fuller phrase occurs earlier
in the verse.

16.4 ארון יהוה : τῆς κιβωτοῦ διαθήκης κυρίου G O L R. Rothstein
takes the fuller phrase back to the Vorlage. Cf. 15.28f.

v. 9 נפלאתיו : + ἃ ἐποίησεν κύριος G O L R. Cf. v. 12 נ׳ אשׁר עשׂה
(BH). κύριος is doubtless a Gk amplification (contra BH) linked with
the Gk omission of ליהוה v. 8.

17.4 לשׁבת : +ἐν αὐτῷ G O L R. Cf. II 2.2/3 לשׁבת בו : κατοικῆσαι
ἐν αὐτῷ.

23.5 להלל : + τῷ κυρίῳ G O (L) R. Cf. the phrase מהללים לי׳ :

---

[1] S. Daniel, Le Vocabulaire du culte, p. 90 note 114, suggests a longer Gk rendering
for clarity's sake.

αἰνοῦντες τῷ κ. earlier in the verse. Rudolph rightly calls the insertion
an unnecessary textual change. He criticises BH's note "ins c 10 MSS
post להלל" : in fact the mss. put it before the verb. Rothstein adopts
the addition.

25.1 ויהי מספרם : + κατὰ κεφαλὴν αὐτῶν G O L R, influenced by
23.3 וי׳ מס׳ לגלגלתם. The Gk is the same.

v. 8 ויפילו : + καὶ αὐτοί G O L. Cf. 24.31 ויפ׳ גם-הם. BH wrongly
reconstructs as המה גם. Rothstein remarks that גם-הם could have been
overlooked in MT, but surely attraction is the more likely explanation
of the variant.

28.10 לבנות : + αὐτῷ G O L R .Cf. the frequent phrase לב׳ לו בית,
e.g., 14.1, 17.25; II 2.2/3.

II 6.20 אל-המקום : + τοῦτον G O L R (R omits the earlier τοῦτον,
doubtless by error for this one), corresponding to the phrase at the
end of the verse.

v. 28 כי-יהיה : + ἐπὶ τῆς γῆς G on the pattern of כי-יה׳ בארץ just
before.

7.6 מחצצרים : + ταῖς σάλπιγξιν G O L R, corresponding to the phrase in 5.12.

9.27 את-הכסף : τὸ χρύσιον καὶ τὸ ἀργύριον G O L R, as in 1.15
for את-הכ׳ ואת-הזהב. If the transposition there was pre-Gk the
assimilation could have taken place already in the *Vorlage*. It is
significant that III Rg 10.31 reads the same. Rehm, p. 96, claims
that Par has taken over Rg, but it is more likely to be the other way
around in view of Rg's assimilation to Par elsewhere in the context.[1]

17.4 (דרש ...) לאלהי: τὸν κύριον θεόν G O L R. Cf. 16.12 דרש את- יהוה.

v. 6 מיהודה : ἀπὸ τῆς γῆς Ιουδα G O L R. Cf. 19.3 מן-הארץ :
ἀπὸ τ. γ. Ιουδα G O L (R). The phrases stand in similar contexts. At
some stage has double assimilation occurred, resulting in conflated
texts at both points ?

19.6 לאדם : + ὑμεῖς G O L R. Cf. אתם : ὑμεῖς earlier in the verse.

20.11 והנה : καὶ νῦν ἰδού G O, influenced by v.10 ועתה הנה : κ.
ν. ἰδού.

29.9 בשבי : + ἐν γῇ οὐκ αὐτῶν G O L R = בארץ לא להם according
to Curtis. This is a reminiscence of Jer. 5.19 בא׳ לא לכם : ἐν γῇ οὐχ
ὑμῶν. It is significant that "sword", "sons" and "daughters" in this
verse are also mentioned in Jer 5.17[2].

---

[1] See Part I, p. 202.

[2] Gen. 15.13 בארץ לא להם : ἐν γῇ οὐκ ἰδίᾳ is a less likely source.

v. 31 ותודות : + εἰς οἶκον κυρίου G O L R, assimilated to the phrase earlier in the verse.

34.9 כל שארית ישראל : παντὸς καταλοίπου ἐν Ισραηλ G O. Cf. v. 21 הנשאר ביש׳ : παντὸς τοῦ καταλειφθέντος ἐν I. G O R. Double conflation has occurred.

36.4 נכו : Φαραω Νεχαω G O L R, assimilated to פרעה נכו earlier in the verse in the *Vorlage* or in the Gk.

(c) *Omission*

I 22.18 (עמכם) אלהיכם (יהוה) is omitted in G O L R under the influence of יהוה עמך : κύριος μετὰ σοῦ in v. 16.

2. PARABLEPSIS

(a) *Haplography*

I 5.14 ישישי : Ισαι G.
23.30 בבקר² : G O L R omit.
26.17 שנים² : G R omit.
II 31.6 ערמות² : G N omit.

(b) *Homoeoteleuton or -arcton*

I 1.27 אברם הוא אברהם : Αβρααμ G Omss. Rothstein observes that the omission could be parablepsis in Par or the *Vorlage*. Benzinger, ever partial to Par, omits with the LXX as an addition in MT assimilating to Gen. Curtis thinks of a Gk error, but only because he undervalues B.

v. 38 ודישן ואצר ודישן : Δησων Ωναν G. The second name probably developed in Par from a dittograph of (Δησ)ων, which was adapted by assimilation to the name in v. 40.

16.36 (העולם) ועד־העלם : G omits.
17.18 (ואתה את־ע׳) את־עבדך : G O R omit. Many delete with II Sam 7.20. Curtis and Rehm, p. 69, explain as an anticipation of the later phrase. But Rudolph plausibly finds here parablepsis, either Heb or Gk (from σε τὸν παῖδά σου* to καί συ τ. π. σου).

24.20 (שובאל) לבני שובאל : G O omit.
25.4 (חניה) חנני : G omits. Αιμανει earlier for הימן probably attests a Gk attempt to restore the omission. Ανι*, a corruption of Αανι O was wrongly taken as a correction of the end of the earlier name. Αιμανει at the end of v. 6 has been influenced by the resultant form here.

28.4 (אבי) ובבני אבי : G R omit.

3. TRANSPOSITION

There are many cases where it is impossible to determine at what stage the order of words was changed, whether already in the *Vorlage* or in the process of translation or in the course of Gk transmission. In the following list the earlier word or words in MT is put on the right of the oblique stroke.

I 1.32   מדן/מדין G.

ibid.   שבא/דדן G.

v. 34   (read as יעקב) עשׂו/ישׂראל G. Benzinger and Kittel so read, but Rudolph wisely keeps as the *lectio difficilior* : the Gk order corresponds to v. 28.

4.5   חלאה/נערה G.[1]

v. 20   רנה/חנן G.[2]

v. 40   ושקטת/ושלוה G O R. Cf. the renderings in 22.9.

5.14   ירוח/יחדו G.

6.42f./57f.   יתר/חילז G O. BK wrongly claims a plus in Par in v. 42.

9.2; II 11.13   הכהנים/הלוים G.

11.11   חלל/בפעם אחת ... על .[3]

v. 23   את־ההנית/מיד המצרי G O.

12.18/17   עליכם/לבב ליחד G O R.

v. 19/18   דויד/ועמך G.

v. 41/40   בחמורים/בגמלים G O.

13.12   אלי/את ארון האלהים G.

14.14   עוד/דויד G O R.

15.13   למבראשונה/לא G O L R. Rothstein wrongly claims that Par read לא instead of ל.

18.10   זהב/כסף G, in the order of v. 11.

21.3   זאת/אדני G O.

v. 10   אני/נטה B Omss.

v. 24   ליהוה/והעלות ... חנם .[4]

v. 26   שם/דויד G O.

26.8   ובניהם/ואחיהם G O.

v. 31   בהם/גבורי חיל G O L R.

27.1   לכל דבר/המחלקות .[5]

---

[1] See p. 112.

[2] See pp. 22, 41.

[3] See Part I, p. 145.

[4] See Part I, p. 145.

[5] See Part I, p. 145.

28.3 לי/לא־תבנה G O L R.

29.1 הבירה/כי ליהוה אלהים.[1]

v. 11 כל בשמים ובארץ/לך G O L (in doublet) R.

v. 12 העשר והכבוד/מלפניך G O L (in doublet) R.

ibid. מושל/בכל G O L R (44 = MT).

v. 18 לעולם/ליצר מחשבות לבב עמך G O L R.

v. 24 המלך/דויד G.

v. 29 דויד/המלך G O R.

II 1.10 הזה/הגדול G O L.

v. 15; 16.2f. כסף/זהב G O, G O, G O L.

2.2/3; 21.12 דויד/אבי(ך) G O, G.

v. 7/8 עבדי/עבדיך G O R.

v. 11/12 שׂכל/בינה G R.

v. 13/14 אדני/דויד G O.

3.1 אשר הכין/במקום G O L R. Kautzsch, Benzinger, Curtis and BH
so read. But there may well be a gloss here (Ehrlich, Rudolph).

4.3 הבקר/יצוקים G O.

v. 11 הסירות/היעים G O L R.[2]

v. 21 והנרות/והמלקחים G O R.

5.6 צאן/בקר G O L R (c e = MT).

6.33 שמך/נקרא G O.

v. 35 תפלתם/תחנתם G O. So III Rg 8.45 with the same Gk (Rehm,
p. 38).

8.14 להלל/לשרת G.

9.2 דבר/משלמה.[3]

v. 10 חורם/שלמה G O R.

12.16 עם־אבתיו/ויקבר.[4]

13.8 אתם/אמרים G O.

15.5 ליוצא/לבא G O.

17.12 ביהודה/בירניות G O.

18.34 נכה ארם/עד־הערב G O.

19.8; 30.21 הלוים/הכהנים G O, G O R.

v. 10 קצף/עליכם G O.

20.17 תיראו/תחתו B.

21.9 לימם/מימים G O L R.

27.7 ישראל/יהודה G O.

---

[1] See p. 54.

[2] See p. 170.

[3] See Part I, p. 147.

[4] See Part I, p. 147.

28.6   מאה ... אלף/ביום אחד G O L R.

29.19   המלך/אחז G.

30.25   קהל יהודה/הקהל G O.

31.10   התרומה/לביא G.

v. 13   נחת/מחת G. Nau overlooks the transposition.[1]

ibid.   יחזקיהו/המלך G O.

v. 17   מבן ... ולמעלה/במשמרותיהם G O L R. BH (cf. Curtis) notes "trsp frt c G huc במח/*".

32.12   במותיו/מזבחתיו G O R.

v. 28   ותירוש/ויצהר G O.

33.17   עוד/העם G O.

34.6   מנשה/אפרים G O L, in the order of v. 9.

v. 7   המזבחות/האשרים G O L.

35.11   מידם / (הדם).[2]

v. 14   העולה/החלבים G O.

36.15   מלאכיו/השכם ושלוח G (so O L R in doublet).

---

[1] *Revue d'Orient Chretien*, xvi, p. 429. See p. 22.

[2] See p. 138.

CHAPTER THREE

VARIANTS IN PAR DUE TO DIFFERENT VOCALISATION : POINTING AND VOWEL LETTERS

1. POINTING

In many cases the translator of Par clearly had the consonantal text of MT before him, but interpreted it in a different way from the pointed text. In most of these instances the MT tradition of pointing clearly interprets aright, and the translator has misunderstood the text. But occasionally his rendering represents an improved vocalisation of the consonantal text.

Below are set out the variant forms presupposed in Par. Once again the textform of G is taken as basic. Name-variants such as כְּנַנְיָהוּ/כְּנַנְיָהוּ I 15.22 are not listed; variants involving the definite article of the type בָּאֵשׁ : ἐν πυρί = בָּאֵשׁ have also been ignored as of little significance.

(i) Names in MT taken as common nouns

Erroneous pointing in MT :

I 8.38; 9.44 בֹּכְרוּ : πρωτότοκος αὐτοῦ G O L R = בְּכֹרוֹ "c Ec 1 pl MSS" (BH). MT "has clearly arisen from the falling of one of the six sons from the text and this supplies the deficiency. The absence of the connective before בכרו shows also that the word originally was first born" (Curtis, cf. Rudolph). MT's *paseq* before בְּ in both cases seems to indicate an awareness of the anomaly.

24.23 בְּנֵי : υἱοί G O (L) = בְּנֵי (BH). The pointing in MT is again due to an early omission in the Heb : see Curtis and BH.

Erroneous or less likely pointing presupposed in Par :

I 8.14,31 אַחְיוֹ : ἀδελφὸς αὐτοῦ G = אָחִיו (BH *ad* v. 31). Bertheau and BDB, p. 26b, adopt G's pointing in v. 14, but Rothstein rightly rejects the change.

9.8 אֵלָה : οὗτοι G L (in doublet) R (in doublet) = אֵלֶּה (BH : so "nonn MSS").

v. 37 וְאָחִיו : καὶ ἀδελφὸς αὐτοῦ c₂ (B S lack αὐτοῦ by oversight :
וְאָח is hardly to be presupposed *contra* BH) = וְאָחִיו.

13.7 אֶחָיו : οἱ ἀδελφοὶ αὐτοῦ G O L R = אָחִיו (BH). The parallel
II Rg.6.4 is identical.[1]

26.10 שֹׁמְרִי : φυλάσσοντες G O L (in doublet) R = שֹׁמְרֵי.

II 3.17 בְּעֹז : ἰσχύς G O R = בְּעֹז (BDB, p. 127a; R.B.Y. Scott,
JBL lviii, p. 148).

31.13 בָּנֵיהוּ : οἱ υἱοὶ αὐτοῦ G O L R in doublet[2] = בָּנָיהוּ.

(ii) *Common nouns taken as names*

Erroneous pointing in MT :

I 20.2 מַלְכָּם : Μολχολ G (O) R in doublet = מִלְכֹּם (BH).[3]

Erroneous pointing in Par :

I 26.7 אָחִיו : Αχιουδ G (O R) = אֶחָיו.

(iii) *Different forms of common noun, including participial*

Erroneous pointing in Par :

I 9.18,24 הַשְּׁעָרִים : αἱ πύλαι G (O) R, G O R = הַשְּׁעָרִים. Rudolph so
reads in v. 24, but Rothstein rightly calls the change unnecessary.

v. 22 לִשְׁעָרִים : ταῖς πύλαις G O (R) = לַשְּׁעָרִים.

v. 26 ; 26.12 הַשְּׁעָרִים : τῶν πυλῶν G O R, G O L R = הַשְּׁעָרִים (BH
ad v. 26).

12.9/8 לְמִצַּד מִדְבָּרָה : ἀπὸ τῆς ἐρήμου G L = (Aramaic) לְמִצַּד מִדְבְּרָה.
BH counsels "dl לְמִצַּד c G" !

24.4 הַגְּבָרִים : τῶν δυνατῶν G O L (R) = הַגִּבֹּרִים (BH : so "pl MSS").
Rothstein comments that Par's pointing is unsuitable.

II 3.7 הַקְּרֹות : τοὺς τοίχους G O L R = הַקִּרֹות. BH without citing
Par notes that "Ec l" so reads.

22.5 הָרֹמִים : οἱ τοξόται G O L R = הָרֹמִים : "l c G ... vel c pc
MSS ... 2 R 8, 28 M הָאַרַמִּים" (BH). Rehm, p. 118, prefers the latter.

---

[1] Cf. Driver, *Samuel, ad loc.*

[2] See Part I, p. 164.

[3] See Part I, p. 162.

MT is probably merely a case of syncopation from הָאֵר׳, like הַסוּרִים for הָאֲסוּרִים in Eccles. 4.14.[1]

23.4 לְשַׁעֲרֵי : εἰς τὰς πύλας G O (L) (in doublet) R = לִשְׁעָרַי (Rehm, p. 21).

24.7 הַמִּרְשַׁעַת : ἡ ἄνομος G O L R = הַמִּרְשַׁעַת.

35.12 לַבֹּקֶר : εἰς τὸ πρωί G O L (R) = לַבֹּקֶר. BH does not cite Par but notes that "pl MSS" read thus and also I Esdr. 1.11 τὸ πρωινόν. It is false, as Rudolph says; it was clearly prompted by עַד־לַיְלָה in v. 14.

(iv) *Nouns taken as verbs*

MT is preferable in all cases.

I 16.11 וְעֻזּוּ : καὶ ἰσχύσατε G O L R = וְעֻזּוּ (BH). The same tradition underlies the LXX of Psa. 105/104.4 καὶ κραταιώθητε.

17.6 הַדָּבָר = II Sam. 7.7 : εἰ λαλῶν G O L R = Rg = הֲדִבֶּר. Rothstein, BH and Rehm, pp. 40, 111, prefer Par, but MT is satisfactory.

II 6.38 שָׁבִים אֲשֶׁר־שָׁבוּ אֹתָם : αἰχμαλωτευσάντων αὐτούς G O L (in doublet) R (ditto) = ... שָׁבִים. According to BH and Rehm, p. 70, שֹׁבֵיהֶם was read, and BH considers that the last three words are omitted in Par. In fact אֲשֶׁר־שָׁבוּ, taken as synonymous with שָׁבִים, was doubtless omitted by the translator.[2]

23.13 קֶשֶׁר : ἐπιτιθέμενοι G O R = קָשָׁר.

24.5 לְדַבֵּר : λαλῆσαι G O (L) R = לְדַבֵּר.

v. 6 וְהַקְהֵל : ὅτε (O Lmss for ὅτι which remaining mss. read) ἐξεκ-(κ)λησίασεν G O L R = וְהַקְהֵל (Curtis).

II Ki.24.1/36.5a עֶבֶד : δουλεύων G O L R = עָבַד (Rehm, p. 48).

(v) *Verbs taken as nouns or adjectives*

MT is preferable in all cases.[3]

I 4.31 מֶלֶךְ : βασιλέως G O (L) R = מֶלֶךְ (BH : so "pl MSS"; Soisalon-Soininen, *Die Infinitive*, p. 114).

---

[1] Cf. *Gesenius' Hebrew Grammar*, section 35d.

[2] In accord with the principle enunciated in Part I, p. 112.

[3] For I 5.41/6.15 see Part I, p. 117.

5.2 גִּבֹּר : δυνατός G O L R = גֻּבַּר.

13.4 יָשֵׁר : εὐθής G O L R = יָשַׁר.

23.1 וְשָׂבֵעַ : καὶ πλήρης G O L R = וְשָׂבַע.

II 15.9 הַגֵּרִים : τοὺς προσηλύτους G O L R in doublet[1] = הַגָּרִים.
Geiger saw in MT a deliberate repointing : for the Chronicler moving
from Israel to Judah would imply foreign travel.[2] But the following
עמהם suggests a participle.

24.14 הָעֹלוֹת : ὁλοκαυτωμάτων G O (L) R = הָעֹלוֹת.

31.1 לְכַלֵּה : εἰς τέλος G O (L) R = לְכָלָה.

(vi) *Singular nouns for plural in MT*

MT is preferable in all cases.

I 6.29/44) אֲחֵיהֶם : ἀδελφοῦ αὐτῶν G O R = אֲחֵיהֶם (Rudolph,
"möglich").

10.12 גּוּפֹת : τὸ σῶμα G L R = גּוּפַת.

II 26.6 חוֹמֹת[1,2,3] : τὰ τείχη [1,2,3] G O L R = חוֹמֹת.

35.9 אֶחָיו : ἀδελφὸς αὐτοῦ G O L R = I Esdr. 1.9 ἀδελφός = אָחִיו.

(vii) *Plural nouns for singular*

Erroneous pointing in MT :

I 4.27 מִשְׁפְּחֹתָם : αἱ πατριαὶ αὐτῶν G O (L) R = מִשְׁפַּחְתָּם. The
contrast with Judah shows that the reference is to the tribe of Simeon
(Rothstein, BH, Rudolph).

6.46/61, 56/71 מִמִּשְׁפְּחֹת : ἐκ τῶν πατριῶν G O R, ἀπὸ πατριῶν
G O R = מִמִּשְׁפַּחַת, as in the parallel Jos. 21.5,27. In both cases the
genitives require plurals before.

Erroneous or less likely pointing in Par :

I 9.2 בַּאֲחֻזָּתָם : ἐν ταῖς κατασχέσεσιν αὐτῶν G O L R = בַּאֲחֻזָתָם ?

16.13 עֲבָדוֹ : παῖδες αὐτοῦ G O (L) R = עֲבָדָיו (BH).

24.27 בְּנוֹ : υἱὸς αὐτοῦ G O R = בָּנוּ.

---

[1] See Part I, p. 164.
[2] *Urschrift,*[1] p. 359.

26.22 אָחִיו : οἱ ἀδελφοί G (L) R = אָחִיו (Rothstein). He considers that αὐτοῦ has fallen out, but more probably the suffix was not rendered as ill-fitting. Rudolph's suggestion is worthy of mention : that Par is perhaps right and the word was originally a gloss on בני since the persons mentioned are brothers in 23.8.

II 6.23 דַּרְכּוֹ : ὁδοὺς αὐτῶν G O L R = דַּרְכוּ (Rehm, p. 59).

v. 39 : מִשְׁפָּטָם : κρίματα G O R = מִשְׁפָּטָם (Rehm, p. 59).

22.5 בַּעֲצָתָם : ἐν ταῖς βουλαῖς αὐτῶν G O L R = בַּעֲצָתָם.

30.12 מִצְוַת : κατὰ τὰ προστάγματα G = מִצְוֹת.

(viii) *Absolute and construct confused*

MT is erroneous in one case :

I 19.8 צָבָא : τὴν στρατ(ε)ιάν (τῶν) G O Ł R = צְבָא to be read with Rothstein, BH, Rehm, Rudolph. Rehm, p. 110, notes that this is one of many cases where Chron MT has been influenced by the pointing in Sam (II 10.7 הַצָּבָא).

MT is preferable in the other cases :

I 4.38 בְּשֵׁמוֹת : ἐν ὀνόμασιν (ἀρχόντων) G O L R = בְּשֵׁמוֹת.

II 36.15 בְּיַד : ἐν χειρί, G = בְּיָד, as in 25.20.

(ix) *Confusion over prepositions*

MT is preferable in all cases :

I 12.19/18 לְךָ : πορεύου G O L (in doublet) R = לְךָ (Curtis, Rothstein).

ibid. עַמְּךָ : ὁ λαός σου G O L R = עַמְּךָ (Curtis, Rothstein, BH).

19.6 עָם : λαός G O L R = עַם (Ackroyd, *JTS* ii, p. 32).

II 1.14 עָם : ὁ λαός G O L R in doublet[1] = עָם.

31.10 עַד : ἔτι O L R (G ἐπί[2]) = עֹד.

(x) *Confusion over pronouns*

II 29.3 הוּא : καὶ ἐγένετο G O L R = וְהוּא. The conjunction has

---

[1] Cf. Part I, p. 197.

[2] See p. 54.

come about as the result of dittography of the preceding (אבי)ו. A copyist or the translator expected something like ויהי in the context and thought of the Aramaic equivalent.

35.21 אַתָּה : ἥκω G O L R = אָתָה. Benzinger invoked בָּאתִי to explain the Gk. BH would read אֲנִי אָתָה "c G V S." Curtis, without citing Par, suggested אָתָה. Surely this is the basis of the Gk. The verb suits the rest of the clause as it stands in MT, but it occurs in the rest of the Old Testament only in poetry. Probably the present pointing should be kept as an emphatic pronoun.[1]

(xi) *Verbs : different roots*

Par is correct in one case only :

II 6.26 תַעֲנֵם "answer" : ταπεινώσεις αὐτούς G O L R = תַעֲנֵם "humble". Par is generally followed. The parallel I Ki.8.35 reads the same as Chron : Rehm, p. 111, notes this as a case of the influence of parallel texts.

Par is less likely in these cases :

I 4.43 וַיֵּשְׁבוּ : τοὺς καταλειφθέντας G O (in doublet) R (ditto), by error for -ληφθ-*[2] = וַיִּשְׁבּוּ. Cf. λαμβάνειν for שבה in II 14.14/15. The Heb verb is rendered with a Gk participle, a liberty of a type illustrated in Part I.[3] According to BH וַיֵּשְׁבוּ שָׁם is omitted, but in fact only שָׁם is not represented. The translator rendered שְׁאֵרִית הַפְּלֵטָה by the one term τοὺς καταλοίπους, omitting a synonym as so often.[4] It may well be that the adaptation of the verb represents an attempt to obtain an equivalent for the supposedly missing term and that the order in G τοὺς καταλειφθ. τοὺς καταλοίπ. τοῦ Ἀμαληκ is a further expedient towards this end. The order τοὺς καταλοίπ. τοὺς καταλειφθ. in O R, taken over in Rahlfs, *LXX*, is hardly likely : ἐκ or ἀπό would surely be required before τοῦ Ἀμ. The original order was doubtless τοὺς καταλοίπ. τοῦ Ἀμ. τοὺς καταληφθ., corresponding to the order in MT.

II 21.17 וַיֵּשְׁבוּ : καὶ ἀπέστρεψαν G O R = וַיָּשֻׁבוּ.

---

[1] Cf. Rudolph, *ad loc.*

[2] For confusion of the two Gk words cf. Jer 3.8 LXX κατελήφθη/κατελείφθη and Ziegler, *Beiträge*, pp. 38, 93. This is another case to add to Ziegler's list.

[3] p. 42.

[4] Cf. Part I, pp. 112ff.

(xii) *Verbs : change of conjugation or voice*

Par's interpretation is preferable in these instances :

I 23.6; 24.3 וַיְחַלְּקֵם : καὶ διεῖλεν αὐτούς G O L R = וַיֵּחָלְקֵם,
cf. 24.4f., or וַיְחַלְּקֵם. The pointing is generally changed.[1]

II 3.13 פְּרֻשִׂים : διαπεπετασμέναι G O L R = פְּרֻשִׂים, generally
adopted, e.g., by Benzinger, BH and Rudolph.

32.31 הַמְשֻׁלָּחִים : τοῖς ἀποσταλεῖσιν G O L R = הַמְשֻׁלָּחִים, to be
read with Kautzsch, BH ("c G V T"), Curtis, etc.

MT is better in these cases :

I 11.18 וַיָּבֹאוּ : καὶ ἦλθον G O L R = וַיָּבֹאוּ (BH).

14.12 וְיִשְׂרְפוּ : κατακαῦσαι G O (R) = וְיִשְׂרְפוּ (Rehm, p. 21).

20.4 וַיִּכְנַע : καὶ ἐταπείνωσεν αὐτόν G O L (in doublet) R = וַיַּכְנִעוּ
(Rehm, p. 58). BH wrongly posits וַיַּכְנִיעוּ. Rudolph notes that the
verb is too far from הכה for Par to be correct.

28.18 לִפְרֻשִׂים : τῶν διαπεπετασμένων G O L R = לִפְרֻשִׂים.

MT may be adequately explained by an ellipse of the natural
object.[2]

II 15.4 וְיָשֵׁב : καὶ ἐπιστρέψει (αὐτούς) G O L (in doublet) R =
וְיָשֻׁב. Goettsberger and Rudolph note that Par wrongly takes vv. 3ff.
as prophecy.

v. 6 וְכִתַּתּוּ : καὶ πολεμήσει G O L R = וְכִתֻּתּוּ (so nine de Rossi
mss.) Rudolph rightly calls the change unnecessary.

20.7 אֹהֲבֶךָ : τῷ ἠγαπημένῳ G O R = אֲהֵבְךָ.[3]

v. 34 הֶעֱלָה : κατέγραψεν G O L R = הֶעֱלָה. Cf. Part I, ch. iv, for
the rendering.[4]

29.10 וְיָשֹׁב : καὶ ἀπέστρεψεν (τήν) G (= B; κ. ἀποστρέψει c₂ = O L R)
= וְיָשֻׁב.

30.8 וְיָשֹׁב : καὶ ἀποστρέψει (... θυμόν) G O L R = וְיָשֻׁב (BH).

(xiii) *Change of mood*

MT is preferable in every case.

---

[1] *Genesius' Hebrew Grammar*, section 63n, calls MT "unintelligible". BDB lists under
Niphal; Köhler, *Lexicon*, repoints as Piel.

[2] Cf. BDB, p. 831a.

[3] cf. Part I, p. 123.

[4] p. 43.

I 16.31   מֶלֶךְ : βασιλεύων G R = מָלַךְ.

28.19   עָלָי הַשְׂכִּיל כֹּל מלאכות : κατὰ τὴν περιγενηθεῖσαν αὐτῷ σύνεσιν
τῆς κατεργασίας "according to his superlative understanding of the
work" G O L (in doublet) (R) = עָלָי הַשְׂכִּיל כֹּל מלאכת. BH annotates
"G aliter". Rothstein invokes a *Vorlage* עַל־הַשְׂכִּילוֹ למ׳ by a כ/ו error.
But in fact the old form of the preposition was seen here, and כל was
paraphrased; αὐτῷ renders the implicit subject of the infinitive and
does not represent a reading עליו *contra* Goettsberger. J.A. Bewer
reconstructs the *Vorlage* as עַל הַשְׂכִּיל : he rightly sees an infinitive
behind the Gk.[1]

II 10.15   הֵקִים : ἀνέστησεν G O R = הֻקַם, after reading לאמר before.

25.8   חֵזָק : κατισχῦσαι G O (L) R = חֲזַק, after reading אתעשת
earlier.[2]

29.27   הַחֵל (בעת) : (ἐν τῷ) ἄρξασθαι G O L R = הָחֵל (BH).

36.13   מָרַד : ἀθετῆσαι G O L R = מָרֹד.[3]

(xiv) *Change of person and/or number*

Par's interpretation is preferable in three cases :

II 14.6/7   דְּרַשְׁנוּ[2] : ἐξεζήτησεν ἥμας G O R = דְרַשָׁנוּ (BH), to be read
with Benzinger and Rudolph.[4]

22.9   וַיְמִיתֵהוּ : καὶ ἀπέκτεινεν αὐτόν G O L = וַיְמִיתֵהוּ (BH), to be
read with Kittel, *SBOT*, Curtis, BH and Rudolph, as more suitable to
the context.

23.7   וְהָיוּ : καὶ ἔσονται G O L R = וְהָיוּ (BH "1 c 9 MSS GVT" : so
Rudolph).

One instance is uncertain; Par's view is a distinct possibility :

I 13.9   שָׁמְטוּ : ἐξέκλινεν αὐτήν = שָׁמְטוּ (cf. BH). The same exegetical
tradition is found in the LXX of the parallel II Sam. 6.6 : περιέσπασεν
αὐτόν. Rehm, p. 111, would change the pointing, regarding the MT
of Sam and Chron as the influence of parallel texts.

In the last case MT is preferable :

II 25.27   וַיְמִיתֻהוּ : καὶ ἐθανάτωσεν αὐτόν G (= B, c₂ with O L R =
MT) = וַיְמִיתֻהוּ.

---

[1] *Bertholet Festschrift*, p. 76.

[2] See p. 115.

[3] cf. Soisalon-Soininen, *Die Infinitive*, pp. 125f., 154.

[4] Cf. p. 98.

(xv) *Confusion of strong and weak waw*

MT is preferable in all cases.

II 15.4 וַיִּמְצָא : καὶ εὑρεθήσεται G O L R = וימצא.[1]

24.8f. וַיִּתְּנוּ־קוֹל ... וַיִּתְּנֻהוּ ... וַיַּעֲשׂוּ : γενηθήτω ... καὶ τεθήτω ... καὶ κηρυξάτωσαν G O L R = וית׳ ... וית׳ ... ויע׳. In the first two cases an indirect command is made direct, and the indefinite third plural is rendered in the passive voice.

v. 11 וִישִׁיבֻהוּ ... וַיְעָרוּ : καὶ ἐξεκένωσαν G L R (G -σεν by inner-Gk error) ... καὶ κατέστησαν G O (L) R = וִישׁ׳ ... וַיְעׂ׳.

v. 20 וַיַּעֲזֹב : καὶ ἐγκαταλείψει G O L R = ויעזב. There is no need to posit וְעָזֹב with BH.

25.18 וַתַּעֲבֹר : καὶ ... ἐλεύσεται G O (L) R in doublet = ותעבר.[2]

32.5/4 וַיִּתְחַזֵּק : καὶ κατισχύσῃ G O L R in doublet = וית׳.[3]

(xvi) *The diacritical point*

II 6.22 וּנְשָׂא (BH) : καὶ λάβῃ G O L R = ונשא ("VarG" in BH) read by BDB, Goettsberger and Köhler, *Lexicon*. The same variants are found in MT at the parallel I Ki. 8.31, where Rg reads καὶ ἐὰν λάβῃ. Montgomery observed that "Akk. *nišu*, 'oath' (= Heb root נשא, used of 'lifting up' hands at an oath), suggests that נשא is here much more tenable".[4]

35.25 הַשָּׁרִים וְהַשָּׁרוֹת : οἱ ἄρχοντες καὶ αἱ ἄρχουσαι G O R = השרים והשרות, presupposed also by I Esdr. 1.30. MT is correct.

2. LACK OF VOWEL LETTERS

It is obvious from the evidence of Par that its *Vorlage* made much less use of vowel letters than MT. Transliterated names afford the best clues to such deficiency, but at times it may be detected in other words. Here is a list of cases where vowel letters present in MT were missing from the ms. which the translator used.

---

[1] See the comment on this verse in section xii (p. 73).

[2] See Part I, p. 164.

[3] See Part I, p. 164.

[4] *Kings, ad loc.*

I 2.18 אַרְדּוֹן : Oρνα G O, probably a familiar name derived from Oρδαν* = אַרְדָּן.

3.23f. אֱלִיעֵינִי : Eλειθανα G, Eλιθαιναν c₂ (Eλειθεναν B). The significance of these Gk readings may be most easily seen if the renderings of this name elsewhere in Par are cited.

4.36   Eλιωναι G L R

7.8   Eλειθαιναν B (Eλιθεναν c₂)

8.20   אֱלִיעֵנַי : Eλιωλιαα B (Eλιωαδ c₂)

26.3   אֱלִיהוֹעֵינַי : Eλιωναις G.

The form in 4.36 was most probably originally the standard one used throughout Par. In every case that form is preserved in L, and in 8.20 in R too. In 3.23f. and 7.8 -ⲱⲛⲀⲓ became -ⲐⲀⲓⲚ (via -ⲟⲚⲀⲓ?) before further adaptation. O has throughout the revised form Eλιωηναι which Rahlfs, *LXX*, strangely prefers in 4.36; 8.20; 26.3. The penultimate *yod* was doubtless missing in Par's *Vorlage*, as in 8.20 MT and in 7.8 "Varᴳ" (BH).

4.5   אָשְׁחוּר : Σαρα G, transposed from Aσαρ* or Aσααρ* = אַשְׁחֻר.

v. 11 שׁוּחָה : Aσχα G (O) R, transposed from Σαχα* = שֻׁחָה.

ibid. כְּלוּב : χαλεβ G O L R = כָּלֵב (BH: so "VS").

v. 12 בֵּית רָפָא ; Bαθραίαν G from Bαθραφαν* (Φ/P, cf. Bηθραφαν L) = בַּת רָ׳.

v. 14 מְעוֹנֹתִי : Mαναθει G O R = מְעֹנֹתִי.

v. 18 יְקוּתִיאֵל : Xετιηλ G from Iχετιηλ*[1] = יְקֻתִיאֵל.

v. 31 סוּסִים : -σεσοραμ G (= B*, σεωραμ c₂), transposed from -σεροσαμ* = סַרְסֹם (ר/ו).

v. 35 יוֹשְׁבִיָה : Iσαβια G O (R) = יָשְׁבִיָה.

6.59/74 עַבְדּוֹן : Aβαραν = עַבְרָן (ר/ד).

v. 64/79 מֵיפַעַת : Mαεφαλ c₂ (Mαεφλα B), probably from Mαφαεθ* (θ/δ phonetic error, then Δ/Λ) = מֵפַעַת. Albright takes Mωφααθ O as original,[2] but this is in fact not the source of G but another attempt at transcription, reading ו for י.

7.18   אִישָׁהוֹד : Iσαδεκ B from Iσεαδ*? (κ by dittography) = אִישְׁחֹד.

v. 19 אַנִיעָם : Aλιαλειμ B, Eλιαμειν c₂ from Aναμ* and Eναμ* (N/ΛI; ending assimilated to Λακεειμ) = אַנְעָם.

v. 23 בְּרִיעָה : Bαργαα B (-γαδ c₂) transposed from Bαραγα* (Rahlfs, *LXX*) = בְּרָעָה. Contrast v. 30 Bεριγα.

9.42f. מוֹצָא : Mασ(σ)α G O R = מֹצָא.

---

[1] See Part I, p. 143.

[2] "List of Levitic Cities", pp. 65,73.

11.11; 27.32 חכמוני : $A\chi\alpha\mu\alpha\nu\iota$ G O L (R), $A\chi\alpha\mu\epsilon\iota$ G, shortened from $A\chi\alpha\mu\alpha\nu\iota$ O L = חכמני.

v. 33 בחרומי : $B\epsilon\epsilon\rho\mu\epsilon\iota$ c₂ (-$\mu\epsilon\iota\nu$ B S$^{c·a}$, -$\beta\epsilon\iota\nu$ S*) = בחרמי.

12.6/4f. אלעוזי : -$\epsilon\iota\mu$ $A\zeta\alpha\iota$ B (... $A\zeta\epsilon$ c₂, ... $A\zeta\epsilon\iota$ S) from $E\lambda\lambda\alpha\zeta\alpha\iota$* = אלעזי.

v. 8/7 יעאלה : $E\lambda\iota\alpha$ G from $I\epsilon\eta\lambda\alpha$* (haplography of *iota*, metathesis : cf. $I\omega\eta\lambda\alpha$ O L R) = יעאלה.

14.5 אלישוע : $E\kappa\tau\alpha\epsilon$ G, probably originally $E\lambda\iota\sigma\alpha\epsilon$* (Rahlfs) = אלישע. Rehm, p. 52, n. 1, posits $E\lambda(\iota)\sigma\alpha\epsilon$ by C/T, ⲗ/K errors! More probably the original name was assimilated to $\dot{\epsilon}\kappa\tau\epsilon\hat{\iota}\nu\alpha\iota$ 13.10 adjacent in the preceding column (11 lines away in BM) via a IC/K error.

15.7; 23.16; 26.24 גרשום : $\Gamma\eta\rho\sigma\alpha\mu$ G, G O L R, G O L R = גרשם (BH in 26.24).

v. 11 אוריאל : $A\rho\iota\eta\lambda$ G = אריאל.

v. 21 השמינית : $\alpha\mu\alpha\sigma\epsilon\nu\epsilon\iota\theta$ G (O R) = השמנית via $\alpha\sigma\alpha\mu$- (so Rothstein) or המשנית.

17.16 הביאתני : $\dot{\eta}\gamma\acute{\alpha}\pi\eta\sigma\acute{\alpha}\varsigma$ $\mu\epsilon$ G O L R = אהבתני transposed from הבאתני. Cf. the parallel II Rg.7.18 $\dot{\eta}\gamma\acute{\alpha}\pi\eta\kappa\acute{\alpha}\varsigma$ $\mu\epsilon$.

19.2ff. חנון : $A\nu\alpha\nu$ G O (L) R = חנן.

24.4f. ויחלקום : $\kappa\alpha\grave{\iota}$ $\delta\iota\epsilon\hat{\iota}\lambda\epsilon\nu$ $\alpha\dot{\upsilon}\tau\sigma\acute{\upsilon}\varsigma$ G O L R = ויחלקם with David as subject, as in v. 3.

25.4 ירימות : $A\mu\sigma\sigma\upsilon$ G (in doublet)[1] from $I\alpha\delta\alpha\mu\sigma\upsilon\theta$* (haplography of *iota* and ⲗ-shaped letters; θ/C; transposed under influence of $\Sigma\sigma\upsilon\beta\alpha\eta\lambda$) = ידמות (ר/ד). Cf. v. 22 ירמות.

ibid., 30 מחזיאות : $M\epsilon\alpha\zeta\omega\theta$ c₂ ($M\epsilon\lambda\gamma\omega\theta$ B) R, G = מחזאות.

v. 26 מלותי : $M\epsilon\theta\alpha\theta\epsilon\iota$ B (-$\theta\epsilon\iota\theta$ c₂) from $M\epsilon\lambda\alpha\theta\epsilon\iota$* by internal assimilation = מלתי. In BH's note "G" should read "G^L".

27.30 אוביל : $'A\beta\acute{\iota}\alpha\varsigma$ B ($A\dot{\iota}\beta\acute{\iota}\alpha\varsigma$ c₂) from $A\beta\iota\lambda$* (Λ/A), then assimilated to $'I\alpha\delta\acute{\iota}\alpha\varsigma$ = אביל.

28.19 מלאכות : $\tau\hat{\eta}\varsigma$ $\kappa\alpha\tau\epsilon\rho\gamma\alpha\sigma\acute{\iota}\alpha\varsigma$ G O L (R) = מלאכת.

II 2.3/4 בונה : $\dot{o}$ $\upsilon\dot{\iota}\grave{o}\varsigma$ $\alpha\dot{\upsilon}\tau\sigma\hat{\upsilon}$ $\sigma\dot{\iota}\kappa\sigma\delta\sigma\mu\hat{\omega}$ G O L R = בנה בֹנֶה בֹּנֶה (Rehm) p. 27) by dittography. According to Curtis and Rudolph בנו was added, but this is less feasible.

4.3 יצוקים : $\dot{\epsilon}\chi\acute{\omega}\nu\epsilon\upsilon\sigma\alpha\nu$ G O R = יֹצְקִים (Rehm, p. 21) rather than יָצַק ם (Benzinger).

---

[1] See Part I, p. 163.

v. 5 יכיל : ἐξετέλεσεν G O L R = יְכַל (Rehm, p. 59; cf. Curtis) rather than יְכַלֶּה (BH "frt").

v. 12f. כתרות ... גלות : γωλαθ ... χωθαρεθ G O R = כתרת ... גלת as in the parallel I Ki. 7.41f. Contrast μεχωνωθ in v. 14.

8.17; 26.2 אילות : Αιλαμ G O, a more familiar Gk name (= עילם) substituted for Αιλαθ L, III Rg. 9.26 (for Ki אֵלוֹת), Αιλαθ G O L R = אֵילַת (BH). In the second case the parallel II Ki. 14.22 reads אֵילַת. Rehm, pp. 71,84,111, would so read in both cases.

v. 18 ויביאו : καὶ ἦλθον G O R = וַיָּבֹאוּ (Rehm, p. 60).

9.4 עליתו : τὰ ὁλοκαυτώματα G O L R = עֹלֹתוֹ.[1]

v. 21 הלכות : ἐπορεύετο G O L R = הֹלֶכֶת.[2]

10.5 עוד : ἕως G O L R = III Rg. 12.5 = עַד (BH, etc.). The LXX is erroneous, as Rudolph and Montgomery, *Kings*, have observed.

20.2 חצצון : Ασαμ G from Ασασαν O L R (Rahlfs) by parablepsis and the influence of Θαμαρ = חצצן.

v. 16 הציץ : Ασας c₂ (Ασαε B by c/ε error — Wutz, p. 20) = הצץ.

22.5 רמות : Ραμα G = רמת (BH) : cf. v. 6 רמה. Curtis would so read.

23.14 ויוצא : καὶ ἐξῆλθεν G O L R = וַיֵּצֵא (Rehm, pp. 60,118).

25.8 אתה עשה : ὑπολάβῃς G O L R = אתעשת via אַתְּ עֹשֶׂה.[3]

28.17 עוד : ἐν τούτῳ ὅτι G O L (in doublet) R = ע' ד'.[4]

30.17 להקדיש : ἁγνισθῆναι G O L R = לְהַקְדֵּשׁ.

31.13 יוזבד : Εζαβαθ G from Ιεζαβαδ* (haplography of *iota*) = יוזבד.

35.3 הקדושים : τοῦ ἁγιασθῆναι αὐτούς G O L R = הַקְּדֹשִׁים rather than לְהַקְדִּישָׁם (Benzinger). I Esdr. 1.3 (ἁγιάσαι αὐτούς- better αὑτούς) read the same.

II Ki.23.36/36.5 רומה : Ραμα G O R = רמה (BH, Rehm, p. 48).

In all these cases the interpretation of Par, using a text with less vowel letters than MT, does not represent any substantial improvement. MT's interpretation is not invalidated by the absence or presence of *matres lectionis*. But there are a few more instances where vowel letters have been added wrongly in MT, and Par's text and interpretation are clearly correct :

---

[1] See Part I, p. 47.
[2] See Part I, p. 202.
[3] See p. 115.
[4] See p. 86.

I 7.32 שׁומר : Σαμηρ G R = שׁמר, read by Benzinger, Kittel, Rothstein, Noth, *Personennamen*, p. 259 : cf. v. 34 שֶׁמֶר.

17.18 לכבוד : τοῦ δοξάσαι G O L R = לְכַבֵּד (BH), to be read with Oettli and Rudolph in view of the following object.

II 18.34 מעמיד : ἦν ἑστηκώς G O L R = III Rg. 22.35 = מַעֲמָד with Ki (BH "l melius").

25.23 הפונה : γωνίας G O L R = הַפֹּנֶה, generally read with some Heb mss., the Versions and II Ki. 14.13. Cf. 26.9.

26.3 יכיליה Kethib : Χαλια c₂ (Χααια B) probably originally Ιχαλια* = יכליה Qere, the correct reading (Rehm, p. 71, Noth, p. 246) : cf. II Ki.15.2 יכליהו. In Rg KR reads Χαλεια, taking over Par (*contra* Rehm, p. 42), and L Ιεχελια.

The *Vorlage* of Par must have had far fewer vowel letters than MT. Par's evidence represents only the top of an orthographic iceberg, and it may be safely assumed that there were many cases which the translation cannot bring to light. But the ms. did use them to a certain extent, as is shown by the confusion between ר and ו in II 20.21 להדרת : ἐξομολογεῖσθαι = להדות and the reading ἐπί σοι = אליכה for אלהים in II 25.16.

The more defective writing of the *Vorlage* represents an earlier stage of the text of Chron than MT. Rudolph notes that numerous differences and false readings in the LXX of the Old Testament reveal that the Heb text was defectively written[1] and suggests that the greater use of *matres lectionis* in Chron MT go back not to the Chronicler himself but to later copyists.[2] P. Kahle reasonably maintained that the extreme *plene* script, as witnessed in 1Q Isᵃ written before the destruction of the Temple, was introduced after the Maccabean period as a device to aid the study of Heb.[3] This stage was followed by a more sparing use when the official Heb text was established, as e.g. ,in 1QIsᵇ. Thus the Heb text passed through at least three stages, involving first a comparatively sparing use of vowel letters, then a more liberal use, and subsequently less frequent use again. Chron MT, compared with MT of Sam and Ki which correspond to the third stage, has been left in the second stage of this development.[4] Par, translated about the

---

[1] *Chronikbücher*, p. iv.

[2] Cf. Driver, *Samuel*, p. xxxif.

[3] *Die hebräischen Handschriften aus der Höhle*, p. 76; *VT* i, p. 42f. Cf. F.M. Cross, *JBL* lxxiv, p. 165.

[4] Cf. Gerleman, *Synoptic Studies*, p. 13f.

middle of the 2nd century B.C., is based on a text substantially still at the first stage. But on Par's evidence Chron MT has in most cases remained true to the intended meaning of the Chronicler in its addition of *matres lectionis*.

CHAPTER FOUR

HEBREW TEXTUAL CHANGES

The aim of this chapter is to analyse those discrepancies between the reconstructed *Vorlage* of Par and the MT which may be explained in terms of common textual errors such as wrong word-division, confusion of Heb consonants and parablepsis. In most cases corruption will be seen to lie on the side of Par's text. But there are a number of instances where Par has indirectly preserved the correct text while MT has suffered corruption. This service which Par can perform for the textual criticism of Chron has been described thus by Oesterley and Robinson : "The value of the Septuagint [of Chron] lies in the large number of small details in which it has preserved the right reading of the MT".[1]

1. ABBREVIATION

It has often been noted that at times the rendering of the LXX betrays an awareness that Heb words could be abbreviated. Perhaps the best known is Jon 1.9 עברי : δοῦλος κυρίου.[2] Both the affirmation and the warning of B.J. Roberts deserve mention : "A fruitful source of error, but one which must be carefully scrutinised, is the result of abbreviations and their introduction into the text. The presence of abbreviations has sometimes been denied, but there is no other explanation which meets all cases".[3] Certain renderings in Par have been explained in terms of abbreviation, and a thorough test may profitably be applied to the two books as a whole. The results of such a test are here set out, along with a résumé of previous suggestions based upon the LXX of Chron.

---

[1] *Introduction to the Books of the OT*, p. 118.

[2] More notable exponents of the case for abbreviation have been F. Perles, *Analekten*, pp. 1-10, S.R. Driver, *Samuel*, p. lxviiif., and recently G.R. Driver, *Textus* i, pp. 112-131; iv, pp. 76-94. For abbreviation implied in LXX Isa see Seeligmann, *Isaiah*, p. 65f.

[3] *OT Text and Versions*, p. 97.

(i) Radical abbreviation of common nouns

בן and בית : BDB notes the possibility of the abbreviation of both words into ב.[1] Thackeray found evidence in the LXX of Ezekiel of בני and בית being abbreviated into ב.[2] G.R. Driver has observed that according to Hatch and Redpath, *Concordance*, the LXX has 'house' for 'sons' in some eleven places and *vice versa* in fifteen, and he has traced the divergence to a common abbreviation.[3] The examples from Chron, which are not explicitly cited by Driver, are I 2.10 בני : οἴκου G O L R = בית (BH) via ב'; 4.19 (בני נחם)[4] : Μαναημ B for מנחם via ב' נחם; 6.44/59 בית שמש : Βασαμυς G = שמש ב'; 7.35 בן הלם : Βαλααμ G, a familiar name replacing Βααλαμ* = הלם ב'; II 21.13 בית : υἱούς G O L R = בני (Curtis); 23.3 בני : οἶκον G O L R = בית. In the first case Rothstein notes that Num 2.3 supports MT. The case in ch. 6 Albright would ascribe to phonetic abbreviation rather than to scribal abbreviation.[5] In II 21.13 Curtis noted that Par's reading may be original, and indeed בית may have been wrongly written after the instance of the word five words before. At 23.3 Rehm, p. 60, assumes the unlikely error of ת/נ.

חצר : I 2.52 חצי : Εσειρ G; 4.31 חצר : ἥμισυ G O (R). חצי has apparently been wrongly taken as an abbreviated חצ' and *vice versa*.[6] It is to be noted that in ch. 4 חצר has already occurred in v. 28, and abbreviation of the repeated noun need cause no surprise, yet the translator was remarkably inattentive at this point.

מזבח and מזרקות : II 4.11 את־המזרקות : τὴν ἐσχάραν τοῦ θυσιαστηρίου G O L R = המזבח את via המז'. Rehm, p. 59, rightly saw that אח המזבח underlies the Gk, but how is the second noun to be explained? Misunderstood abbreviation is the cause. מזרקי has occurred in v. 8; here again a repeated word has been abbreviated. The translator's error was prompted by his desire to link this whole section with Exodus, here with the altar hearth of Exod. 38.4/24.

שמע : II 9.1 שמעה את־שמע ἤκουσεν τὸ ὄνομα G O L R as in the parallel III Rg.10.1. At first sight paraphrase is a possibility, but it is significant that in v. 6 the verb and noun are rendered literally. It

---

[1] pp. 110b, 122a.

[2] *Jewish Worship*, p. 123.

[3] *Textus* i, p. 121f.

[4] See p. 138f.

[5] "List of Levitic Cities", p. 69.

[6] For confusion of *yod* and a mark of abbreviation cf. Driver, *Textus* i, p. 129.

seems that the translator found an abbreviated form in his *Vorlage* at v. 1 and read שמ׳ as שֵׁם. Wutz noted six more such cases in the LXX.[1] He traced them back to Gk errors according to his theory of transcription, but all may be claimed as instances of a common Heb abbreviation.[2]

G.R. Driver suggested that in II 18.33 τοῦ πολέμου G O L R for המחנה represents המלחמה via המ׳ (so the parallel III Rg.22.34).[3] These are indeed two well known nouns which may have had a common abbreviation, but Par's propensity for paraphrase needs to be taken into account. πόλεμος renders צבא at 17.18 G O L R; 25.5 G O L R; 28.12 G O L R, and מחנה becomes δύναμις in I 12.23/22 G O R; II 14.12/13 G O L R. It is therefore quite unnecessary to assume that the translator did not have המחנה before him. The note in BH "l prb c GV המלחמה" is accordingly going too far. III Rg.22.34 is apparently a case of Gk assimilation to Par.

(ii) *The Tetragrammaton*

Many examples have been found of יהוה apparently being abbreviated to י׳ and ה׳.[4] Driver finds a single instance in Par at II 3.1 נראה: ὤφθη κύριος G O L R = נרא׳ ה׳, involving both the abbreviation of the final radical of a defective verb and the use of ה׳ for יהוה.[5]

At I 9.20 occurs another case: יהוה: καὶ οὗτοι G (O R in a doublet) = הם (cf. vv. 23, 17) or המה (Rothstein; cf. v. 22) via ה׳; καί has been added as often to separate coordinate clauses.

At II 25.4 τοῦ νόμου κυρίου G O L (R) for תורה apparently represents תור׳ה = תורת יהוה. In II Ki 23.26/35.19c θυμῷ κύριος G O L R for אפו probably implies אף י׳.

(iii) *Other names*

Driver has pointed out that names of persons or places will have

---

[1] *Transkriptionen*, p. 71.

[2] Frankel, *Einfluss*, p. 14 note c, accounted for the rendering by the strange supposition that שמע was unknown to many Alexandrian translators, and so they rendered by the familiar and similar-sounding שם. Yet these same translators obviously knew the verb.

[3] *Textus* iv, p. 81.

[4] E.g., cf. Perles, *op. cit.*, pp. 2-4; Driver, *Textus* i, p. 119f.; iv, p. 79. In the last reference Par is wrongly cited as support for reading יהוה in II 30.27.

[5] *Textus* iv, p. 90. Cf. BH "ins c G יהוה".

been abbreviated if they are well known or recently mentioned.[1] He suggests that יהודה/ישׂראל variants may be so explained. He cites one such case from Chron with direct support of Par : II 21.2 ישׂראל : Ιουδα G O L R. In MT ישׂראל is used theologically of the southern kingdom, as comprising the people of God (cf. Curtis, ad II 28.19), and the Gk is best explained as a simplifying change. BH's note "1 c Seb ca 40 mss GS יהודה" is a facile rejection of a harder yet credible reading. The change in Par can be explained without recourse to abbreviation, but it may well have been one factor in the change. There are in fact three other cases of interchange in Par : II 13.1; 29.21 יהודה : Ισραηλ G, G O L R ; 28.19 ישׂראל : Ιουδα G O L R.[2] The third is "obviously a correction" (Myers) ; BH rightly but inconsistently keeps MT despite much evidence for יהודה. The second is a misinterpretation, the coordinate הממלכה having been taken to refer to Judah (so Curtis, Rudolph). The change may also be due to the influence of v. 24 על־כל ישׂראל ; and to these two factors may be added the facilitating one of abbreviation.

Driver also claims as instance of abbreviation II 36. 14 שׂרי הכהנים : οἱ ἔνδοξοι Ιουδα καὶ οἱ ἱερεῖς G O L R = שׂר׳ י׳ והכהנים. MT is apparently a misreading of a double abbreviation, י׳ = יהודה and שׂר׳ = שׂרי.[3] BH and Rudolph urge the insertion of יהודה ו with Par, Rudolph comparing I Esdr. 1.7. Abbreviation affords a simple explanation for the omission of the name. Then the *waw* was naturally dropped. Confusion over abbreviation also seems to occur at I 10.7 נסו : ἔφυγεν Ισραηλ G O L R = נס׳ י׳. In the relation between Chron and Par variants based upon י/ו are legion. An explicit subject is not necessary, as Rudolph explains.

Examples of other names being abbreviated are as follows :
I 1.39 אחוח לוטן : Αιλαθ B from Α(α)ιθαλ* = אחית ל׳. לוטן has already occurred in this verse and in v. 38, and so abbreviation is not surprising. But it was not recognised by the translator.[4]
5.4 בנו[1] : Βαναια[5] = בניה, a common name in Chron. An abbreviation בני׳ has been wrongly assumed.

---

[1] *Textus* i, p. 121 ; iv, p. 79f.

[2] In *Textus* i, p. 121 "II Chron xxi, 19, 27" should presumably read "II Chron xxviii, 19,27".

[3] Cf. p. 88f.

[4] Wutz, p. 30, assumed an original Αχιαθ* by a X/Λ error; Podechard, *RB* xiii, p. 381, saw a corruption אילט נמנע for לוטן תמנע נמנע.

[5] See Part I, p. 162.

19.3 ‏המכבד דויד‏ : μὴ δοξάζων G. An explicit subject is essential. Apparently ‏ד׳‏ dropped out by haplography.

26.7 ‏שמעיה‏ : Σαμαι G = ‏שמעי׳‏. The name has already occurred in v. 6; abbreviation is therefore not surprising.

II 8.16 ‏שלם‏ : Σαλωμων G O L R : Benzinger, Kittel, *Komm.*, Curtis and BH prefer LXX, reading ‏כלת שלמה‏ for ‏כלתו שלם‏, but MT's suffix is more natural after ‏שלמה‏ earlier in v. 16.[1] More probably after wrongly regarding ‏שלם‏ as an abbreviation, Par omitted the now superfluous suffix.

II Ki.24.4/36.5d ‏וימלא‏ : Ιωακειμ ἐνέπλησεν G = (via ‏יו׳‏) ‏יהויקים מלא‏. Manasseh is the implicit subject of MT; the translator erroneously found an abbreviation here because the reign of Jehoiakim is the overall subject of the context.[2]

(iv) *Numeral stems*

Driver gives many examples of variants involving numerals which may be explained by assuming a system of abbreviation based upon the use of initial letters.[3] Instances cited from Chron and Par are I 5.13 ‏שבעה‏ : ὄκτω G = ‏שמנה‏ via ‏ש׳‏; II 11.21 ‏ששים‏ : τριάκοντα G = ‏שלשים‏; 23.1 ‏השבעית‏ : ὀγδόῳ G = ‏השמינית‏. There are two other cases, not mentioned by Driver : I 4.27 ‏שש‏ : τρεῖς G O = ‏שלש‏; II 29.17 ‏ששה‏ : τρισ- G = ‏שלשה‏. Rudolph sees in the last case a religious change whereby the work was finished before the passover.[4]

(v) *Particles*

Driver makes the general claim that particles such as ‏הוא‏, ‏זה‏ and ‏לא‏ must often have been abbreviated, and also gives examples of abbreviated demonstratives.[5] One relevant example is given : II 25.8 ‏בא‏ : ἐν τούτοις G O L R = ‏באלה‏ via ‏בא׳‏.[6] As he mentions, this explanation not only makes MT intelligible but has "the advantage of conforming to the consonantal text and so avoiding any elaborate reconstruction

---

[1] Cf. Rudolph : "viel schwächer als M".

[2] Although the form ‏יויקים‏ is not actually found applied to the king, the frequent interchange between ‏יהו-‏ and ‏יו-‏ accounts for this abbreviation. Cf. *Textus* iv, p. 80, where ‏יו׳‏ is claimed as an abbreviation of ‏יהויקים‏ in II 36.10.

[3] *Textus* i, pp. 125-128; iv, pp., 82-86.

[4] In II 28.2 τριακοσίας G O for ‏מאתים‏ may have arisen via ‏מאות ש׳‏ taken as ‏שלש מאות‏. Cf. Driver's similar explanation of variants 2000 and 3000 in *Textus* iv, p. 82f.

[5] *Textus* i, p. 122f.; iv, p. 79.

[6] *Textus* iv, p. 90.

of it such as Rudolph's (in which the *ductus literarum* is totally dis-regarded)". Rudolph, having rejected as graphically impossible BH's suggestion to read בזאת at the end of the clause, prefers בם for בא with Hitzig as cited by Bertheau; it should be noted that he adds that either בם, באלה or בזאת would be possible.

Thackeray found a case of לא abbreviated into ל in Ezek. 36.6.[1] Another such abbreviation possibly occurs at II 18.18 : לכן : οὐχ οὕτως G O L R = לא כן,[2] which BH reads with Kautzsch, Benzinger and Kittel. But this frequent LXX confusion, instances of which are listed by Wutz, p. 69f., may be simply a phonetic error committed by Ara-maic speaking copyists who pronounced the negative לָא. The parallel III Rg. 22.19 reads the same. MT is better : לכן שמעו is a regular prophetic formula (cf., e.g., Isa.28.14; Jer 6.18).

(vi) *Prepositions*

Driver lists no cases of prepositions being abbreviated, but at some points Par assumes such abbreviation.

למען : II 10.15 λέγων G O R = לאמר via ל'. Katz suggested that at Gen 39.14 the LXX misunderstood ל as an abbreviation for לאמר,[3] an error which was doubtless encouraged by the occurrence of לאמר eight times in vv. 1-14. Here apparently a similar mistake was made, whereas ל' actually represented another abbreviation. Rehm, p. 60, tortuously suggested consonantal changes of ר/ו and א/ע. Rogers, p. 26, imagines a deliberate change of the translator.

עד : I 5.10 על : ἕως G O. This reading does not fit the context. It is surely an error for ὡς* (= עד 4.27) under the influence of ἕως in vv. 9,11. This may well stand for עד ל via ע' ל rather than עד (Curtis, BH). עד ל is a frequent preposition in Chron. In v.16 ἕως G O R again presupposes, for עד ל, על, here the correct reading. עד is generally read, but again עד ל gives a better link with MT perhaps.

II 23.8 עם־יוצאי : ἕως ἐξόδου G O L R = עד־מוצאי via ע'.

על : II 28.17 עוד : ἐν τούτῳ ὅτι G O (L) R = על דבר via ע' ד'. The *Vorlage* apparently lacked the vowel letter. Compare B.J. Roberts' observation : "the apparent preposition עד is often an erroneous reading of an abbreviation of על דבר, e.g. Josh. 17.14."[4]

---

[1] *Jewish Worship*, p. 123.

[2] cf. the comment of Driver, *Samuel*, p. 44, on the similar case in I Rg. 3.14 : "... strangely treating לכן as though contracted from לא־כן".

[3] *JBL* lxv, p. 324.

[4] *OT Text and Versions*, p. 97.

(vii) *Radical abbreviation of verbs*

G.R. Driver mentions the suggestion that verbs with final א may at one stage have been written without it.[1] He might have cited I 2.24 בכלב : ἦλθεν Χαλεβ G O (L) R = כלב (for בא) 'ב. Wellhausen is generally followed in adopting the reading of Par and V.[2] Driver gives two examples of other final radical letters being omitted.[3] One may compare II 2.1/2, 16/17 ויספר : καὶ συνήγαγεν G O L R = 'ויסף taken as וַיִּסֶף, a form found in II Sam 6.1 for ויאסף. אסף regularly underlies συνάγειν : cf. Rehm, p. 59, and BH "G ויאסף". But it should be noted that Rudolph considers the rendering to be a paraphrase based upon I 22.2, while Rogers, p. 20, suggests that the translator eliminated the ominous connotation of David's disastrous census.

(viii) *Noun-endings*

P. Lagarde drew attention to the scribal omission of endings like ה, ים and ות.[4] G R. Driver has found many examples.[5] There are a number of places where divergences between Chron and Par may be so explained.

(a) ם *or* ים *of masculine plural or dual*

I 2.53 קרית יערים : πολ(ε)ις Ιαειρ G = 'קרית יער. In vv. 50,52 Καριαθιαρειμ appears. Evidently this third instance was found in an abbreviated form and not recognised as such.

15.22 במשא יסר במשא : ἄρχων τῶν ᾠδῶν G L (in doublet) R = probably 'במשאי שר with omission of 'במ[2] as superfluous.[6]

21.17; II 6.19 אלהי : ὁ θεός G O L R, G O R = 'אלהי. Similarly I 22.7, unless μου L R has dropped out after θεοῦ G O. Another instance is II 18.13 אלהי : ὁ θεός G O L R. It corresponds to יהוה in the parallel I Ki 22.14; therefore Curtis and Rehm, p. 71, read אלהים, but Rudolph notes in support of MT that יהוה is changed to אלהי in Num 22.18.

---

[1] *Textus* i, p. 118.

[2] *De Gentibus*, p. 14f.

[3] *Textus* iv, p. 80.

[4] *Anmerkungen*, p. 4, cited by S.R. Driver, *Samuel*, p. lxviii, and G.R. Driver, *Textus* i, p. 114.

[5] *Textus* i, p. 114f., iv, p. 78f.

[6] cf. Part I, p. 114.

22.18　בידי : ἐν χέρσιν B = בידי׳.

II 26.14　לאבני קלעים : σφενδόνας εἰς λίθους (transposed) G O (L) =
לאבני׳ קלעים.

33.19　חוזי : τῶν ὁρώντων G O L R = חוזי׳. Kautzsch, Benzinger
and Curtis follow Par and one Heb ms. which reads חוזים. So too does
BDB, p. 302b, regarding MT as a scribal error. But החוזים would
surely be expected as in v. 18. This must be why Goettsberger and
Rudolph read חוזיו, assuming haplography.

35.6　והתקדשו והכינו : καὶ ἑτοιμάσατε G L, καὶ τὰ ἅγια ἑτ. O, καὶ τὰ
ἅγ. καὶ ἑτ. R. Benzinger and BH counsel deletion of והתק׳ because
G L omit. But O R's readings have an original ring. R's phrase is
probably authentic : καὶ τὰ ἅγια fell out before καί. Gehman took O as
original and reconstructed as ואת קדשים הכינו.[1] But the use of את before
the indefinite object is unlikely. καὶ τὰς θυσίας ἑτ. in I Esdr 1.6
implies והקדשים הכינו by comparison with the rendering in v. 13 (Curtis)
and it is to this reading that O points in Par (Rudolph). R's text suggests
והק׳ והכ׳. The second waw, shared by MT, is erroneous "since the
Levites did prepare *the holy offerings* for their brethren, the people
(v. 13)" (Curtis). It arose from a false association of והק׳ with הפסח
just before. How did והקדשים become והתקדשו? Probably והקדשים
was written in an abbreviated form as והקדשי׳, which was then taken
as a verb והתקדשו via a ו/י error (and והק׳ = והתק׳?).

(b)　י of masculine plural construct

בן is often rendered as plural, perhaps at some stage taken as
בני = בני׳. Wrong renderings occur at I 3.10 G O R (BH "3 MSS G S");
4.20 G O L R (Rudolph; Goettsberger so reads, assuming that names
have fallen out of MT); 9.8 G L (in doublet) (BH "nonn MSS G^{BL}"),
11 G (Rothstein); II 17.7 G O L R (BH wrongly cites as "G^L". Myers
reads with Par, but cf. Rudolph). In I 12. 8/7 υἱοί G O L R for מן
shows that בנ׳ was read as בני (BH). But Par's plural seems correct at
I 2.50 G O L R (generally read : BH "1 c G V"); 3.21 G O L R (BH
"1 c nonn MSS G S T", so Goettsberger and Rudolph), 23 G O L R
(generally read : BH "1 c Seb pl MSS G"); 4.17 G O L R (generally
read : BH "1 c pl MSS G V").[2]

---

[1] *VT* iv, p. 340.

[2] In 3.19 it is generally assumed that Par reads ובני rightly for ובן (e.g. BH "1 c
nonn MSS G S"). But the phrase containing ובן is missing in G by parablepsis and the
gap is filled by O L R.

In I 3.22 G O R wrongly have a singular for בני (BH "Seb G^{BL}"[sic]).¹

שר in I 27.5 is rendered ἄρχοντες in G O R because it is linked with v. 4 and read as שׂרי. The case in II 36.14 has already been considered.²

(c) ה *of feminine singular*

II 20.25 בהם : κτήνη G O L R = בהמה, which is generally read, via בהמ׳. Driver lists this example as an example of a misreading of an abbreviation in MT.³ It is possible, on the other hand, (but unlikely in the context) that המה- was taken as a long form of suffix and replaced by the more usual form.

(d) ת and ות *of feminine plural*

II 5.1 אצרות : θησαυρόν G O L R = אצר via אצר׳. Since elsewhere in Par this frequent word is uniformly rendered plural, it may be assumed that ות was not written in the *Vorlage*.

9.4 שלחנו : τῶν τραπεζῶν G O R = שלחנו׳.

(ix) *Suffixes*

Driver gives a number of examples, but none from Par.⁴ The following evidence may be adduced.

I 26.20 אחיה : ἀδελφοὶ αὐτῶν G O L R = אחיהם, which is usually read.

II 22.1 בערבים : ἐπ᾽ αὐτοὺς οἱ Ἄραβες G O R = (via ב׳) בהם ערבים. Benzinger and Curtis unnecessarily assume from Par that עליהם fell out of the text.

(x) *Medial abbreviation*

Driver notes a number of instances where one or more letters have been omitted.⁵ Since a similar practice is found in legends on coins he concludes that it is a standard type of abbreviation. It should however be stated that the cases may simply be due to carelessness. The list of instances of omitted letters to be given in the next chapter include some which may conceivably come under this category.⁶

---

¹ For 24.24 see p. 48.

² p. 84.

³ "2 Chron. 10.25" is a misprint for 2 Chron. 20.25 in *Textus* iv, p. 78.

⁴ *Textus* i, p. 117; iv, p. 79.

⁵ *Textus* iv, p. 80f.

⁶ pp. 155ff.

2. ASSIMILATION

Parallel assimilation in the *Vorlage* was seen in Part I, ch. ix to be a frequent phenomenon. But other types of assimilation had also been at work. Both the context and similar places elsewhere had a potent effect, just as they did in the Gk tradition, but to a lesser degree. Where the context was concerned in Gk assimilation, it was noted in ch. i that not only verses before and after but also material on either side in adjacent columns could bend words into another shape. It will be seen that the same phenomenon has been at work in the Heb. By observation a column in the *Vorlage* itself or in its past history may be deduced to have contained material amounting to twenty five lines (an average page) of BH.

(i) *Substitution*

(a) The influence of the context upon the *Vorlage* may be observed in the following cases.

I 1.40 אונם : *Ωναν* G (L) = אונן (BH : so "1 MS"), assimilated to אונן (*Avvav* G O L R) 2.3.

2.9 כלובי : *Χαβελ* B h from *Χαλεβ* c₂ O R (Ra.) = כלב (BH), as in vv. 18ff. Rothstein so reads here, but Rudolph, following Praetorius, defends MT as a *Koseform*.

v. 31 ישעי¹,² : *Ισεμηλ* G = ישמעיאל under the influence of הישמעאלי (*ὁ Ισμαηλίτης* G O R) v.17.

4.37 שמעיה : *Συμεων* G = שמעון (Curtis, BH), which occurs in vv. 24,42. The Heb similarity, closer than the Gk would be, suggests a Heb error.

5.12 שפם : *Σαβατ* G = שבט for שפט (BH), which occurs three words later.

8.4 אבישוע : *Αβεισαμας* G = אבישמע (Rothstein). This is not simply a מ/ו error (Rothstein), but was probably miswritten under the influence of אלישמע (*Ελεμασαι* G) 7.26.

ibid. אחוח : *Αχια* G = אחיה (BH), as in v. 7. Noth[1] and Rudolph so read, but Rothstein compares the perhaps identical אחרה in v. 1 and regards Par's form as a ו/י error.

---

[1] *Personennamen*, p. 235.

v. 21 בראיה : $B\epsilon\rho\iota\gamma a$ G (in doublet)[1] = בריעה, assimilated to the name in 7.30 in the preceding column (25 lines away in BH).

v. 35 מלך : $M\epsilon\lambda\chi\eta\lambda$ G from $M\epsilon\lambda\chi\iota\eta\lambda$ L (ι lost before identical sounding η) = מלכיאל (Rothstein, BH), assimilated to the name in 7.31, the only place it occurs in Chron.

9.17 עקוב : $A\kappa o\nu\mu$ G = עקום, assimilated in ending to the preceding שלום ($\Sigma a\lambda\omega\mu$ G O).

12.3 ויזואל : $\kappa a\grave{\iota}\ I\omega\eta\lambda$ G = ויואל (BH : "nonn MSS^{Ken} G^B S"). It is probably a Heb error, assimilated to the name in 11.38.

v. 12/11 אליאל : $E\lambda\iota a\beta$ G = אליאב with three Heb. mss, conformed to the name in v. 10/9.

v. 19/18 לעזרך : $\tau o\hat{\iota}s\ \beta o\eta\theta o\hat{\iota}s\ \sigma o\nu$ G O L R = לעזריך (BH), mechanically assimilated to אלהיך. Curtis so reads, but Rothstein rightly calls the change unnecessary.

v. 22/21 גדוד : $\gamma\epsilon\delta\delta o\nu\rho$ G O L (in doublet) R = גדור,[2] read under the influence of הגדור in v. 8 (approx. 19 lines away in BH).

v. 37/36 לערך : $\tau o\hat{\nu}\ \beta o\eta\theta\hat{\eta}\sigma a\iota$ G O L R = לעדר, as in v. 34/33.

v. 39/38 עדרי מערכה : $\pi a\rho a\tau a\sigma\sigma\acute{o}\mu\epsilon\nu o\iota\ \pi a\rho\acute{a}\tau a\xi\iota\nu$ G O (L) R = ערכי מ׳, adopted by Kautzsch, Rothstein and BH ("c nonnn MSS^{Ken}"). But עזרי המלחמה in v. 1 justifies MT (Rudolph), which has the merit of being a harder reading. G. R. Driver calls ערכי "an obvious correction ... into a known phrase".[3] It may well be significant that Par omits ערכי in v. 34/33 : is this in MT a misplaced variant to עדרי here ? ערכי is due to the influence of both the following noun and ערכי in v. 36.

16.37 ויעזב : $\kappa a\grave{\iota}\ \kappa a\tau\acute{\epsilon}\lambda(\epsilon)\iota\pi o\nu$ G O - ^{A} L R = ויעזבו, mechanically assimilated to the previous plural verb in the *Vorlage*.

23.9 חזיאל : $E\iota\epsilon\iota\eta\lambda$ B, $I\eta\epsilon\iota\lambda$ c$_2$ = יחיאל (BH), influenced by that name in v. 8.

24.4 לבני איתמר : $\tau o\hat{\iota}s\ \nu\iota o\hat{\iota}s\ Aa\rho\omega\nu\ I\theta a\mu a\rho$ G. Doubtless אהרן was written under the influence of לבני אהרן in v. 1. The change was followed by the omission of שמנה as no longer relevant. At some stage the name has been corrected.

v. 6 אחד אחז ... ואחז אחז : $\epsilon\hat{\iota}s\ \epsilon\hat{\iota}s\ ...\ \kappa a\grave{\iota}\ \epsilon.\ \epsilon.$ G O (L) R = אחד throughout, which BH reads "c 8 MSS G^{BA} V S^A". But Rudolph rightly points out that this expedient contradicts v. 4 where the ratio

---

[1] See Part I, p. 162.

[2] See Part I, p. 62.

[3] *JBL* lv, p. 100.

is two to one. Most commentators correct ואחז to ואחד. This implies
that the lots were taken alternatively : cf. 25.2-4 with 25.9-31.

v. 11 לשכניהו : τῷ Ἰσχανια G = 'ליש (Rothstein, BH), assimilated
to the preceding לישוע.

v. 31 הראש : Ἀρααβ G (in doublet)[1] = הראב, read under the influence of אב(ות) twice before.

25.4 עזיאל : Ἀζαραηλ G = עזראל (BH), as in v. 18. MT has two
alternative forms (Rudolph).

26.2 זבדיהו : Ζαχαρίας G = זכריהו (Rothstein, BH : "nonn MSS
G^{BA[sic]}S"), assimilated to the name a little earlier.

v. 27 הקדישו : ἡγίασεν G O L R = הקדיש, assimilated to the singular
verb in vv. 26, 28.

v. 28 המקדיש (כל) : ὁ ἡγίασεν G R = ההקדיש (Rothstein), conformed
to כל הה/ at the beginning of the verse.

27.21 זכריהו : Ζαβδίου G O = זבדיהו (Rothstein, BH), assimilated to
the name in v. 7.

v. 30 המרנתי : ὁ ἐκ Μεραθων G (O) L (R) = המרתני. Was it assimilated
to the ending of הפרעתוני v. 14 in the preceding column (22 lines
away in BH)?

28.8 אלהיכם : (τοῦ) θεοῦ ἡμῶν G O L R = אלהינו (BH), assimilated
to the earlier word in a portion lost by oversight either of the translator
or of a Heb copyist.

v. 9 ואתה : καὶ νῦν G O L R = ועתה (Rothstein, BH), assimilated to
v. 8.

29.16 הכינונו : ἡτοίμακα G O R = הכינותי, which occurs in vv. 2, 3, 19.

II 3.5 עץ : ξύλοις G O L (in doublet) R = עצי (BH), read under the
influence of העצים 2.9 in the previous column (25 lines away in BH).

ibid., v. 8 טוב : καθαρῷ G O L R = טהור, read by many Heb mss,
conformed to זהב טהור in v. 4.

5.13 בית יהוה (מלא ענן) : δόξης κυρίου G O L R = 'כבוד י (BH),
under the influence of v. 14 כ'י מלא (Rudolph).

8.9 המה : ἰδού B = הנה (Ziegler, Beiträge, p. 94), probably under
the influence of והנה 9.6 in the next column (28 lines away in BH).
Rehm, p. 59, classifies as a מ/נ error.

v. 11 בבית (דויד) : ἐν πόλει G O R = בעיר (BH), assimilated to מעיר ד'
earlier.

14.9/10 ויערכו : καὶ παρετάξατο G O b R = ויערך, assimilated to
the preceding singular verb.

---

[1] See Part I, p. 163.

18.14 הנלך : εἰ πορευθῶ G O L R (cf. III Rg 22.15 εἰ ἀναβῶ) = האלך, probably assimilated to the form in v. 5 in the *Vorlage*,[1]

v. 25 אמון : Εμ(μ)ηρ G O (L) R (so III Rg 22.26 for אמן) = אמר. Stade, followed by Burney and Curtis, considered the name original, comparing especially Jer 20.1.[2] But more probably אמר was written by mechanical assimilation to the root אמר used frequently in the immediate context.

20.5 וירושלם : ἐν Ιερ. G O L R = בי׳ (BH : "9 MSS G S T"), assimilated to בקהל before and בבית immediately following. Rudolph observes that this would be a superfluous statement. Goettsberger notes the frequency of MT's phrase in the context and so its stylistic suitability.

v. 11 מירשתך : τῆς κληρονομίας ἡμῶν G O L R = מירשתנו (BH : "G T") under the influence of הורשתנו two words later and of לגרשנו just before.

v. 20 ויאמר : καὶ ἐβόησεν G (O L R in doublet) = ויקרא, conformed to that word (κ. ἐκήρυξαν/εν G O L R) in v. 3 in the preceding column (28 lines away in BH).

21.11 בהרי יהודה : ἐν πόλεσιν I. G O L (R) = בערי י׳ (BH : "1 prob c Seb pl MSS G V", so a few commentators noted in Curtis). Cf. v. 3 ערי ... ביהודה and the phrase in 20.4 ; 23.2. Wutz, p. 65, notes a similar confusion in Isa 66.20 LXX and the opposite error in IV Rg 18.11. "MT ist gut" (Rudolph).

v. 15 רבים : πονηρᾷ G O (L) R = רעים (BH : "pc MSS G V"), assimilated to v. 19 (Rudolph), probably in the *Vorlage*.

v. 17 יהואחז (אם-) : 'Οχοζείας G L = אחזיהו (so one Ken. ms., Pesh and Targ), influenced by אם אחזיהו 22.10 in the next column (25 lines away in BH). Goettsberger suggested the influence of 22.1.

22.9 מתחבא : ἰατρευόμενον G O L R = מתחבש.[3]

26.8 העמונים : οἱ Μιναῖοι G O L R = המעונים with "5 MSS" (BH), conformed to the word two words before in v. 7. The opposite error occurred in MT at 20.1.

28.12 ברכיהו : Ζαχαρίας G La = זכריהו (cf. זכריה BH), assimilated to that name in 29.1 in the next column (29 lines away in BH).

v. 16 מלכי אשור : βασιλέα Ασ. G O L R = מלך א׳ (BH : "1 frt c 1 MS G V T ..., sed cf. 32.4"). Curtis, etc., and Rudolph so read in view

[1] On which see Part I, p. 206.

[2] *ZAW* v, p. 175.

[3] See Part I, p. 55.

of the singular in v. 20 and its parallel II Ki 16.7. But 32.4 most probably confirms MT here, and it should be kept as the harder reading. The *Vorlage* had suffered assimilation to v. 20.

v. 23 מלכי־ארם : βασιλέως Συρίας G O L R = מלך א׳ with one Heb ms, influenced by the phrase in v. 5.

29.21 ויביאו : καὶ ἀνήνεγκεν G O (L R) = ויבא, assimilated to that form in v. 4 in the previous column (26 lines away in BH). The similarity of ויאסף v. 20 to ויאספם v. 4 encouraged the change.

31.15 שמעיהו : Σεμεει G O L R = שמעי (BH). It is surely significant that שמעי occurs in v. 12f.

32.4 (כל־)-(המעינות) : τὰ ὕδατα G O L R = מימי (BH), influenced by מימי העינות v. 3.

ibid. יבואו מלכי אשׁור ומצאו : ἔλθη βασιλεὺς Ασσουρ καὶ εὕρη G (O L) R = ומצא ... יבוא מלך. The singular noun has been influenced by מלך א׳ v. 7. then the verbs were made singular. The translator found the altered text.[1] For the plural in the MT compare 28.16; 30.6.

v. 15 יצילו : σώσει G O (L) R = יציל : "pl MSS G V S T ... cf 17" (BH). The verb with God as subject was made singular, as it is in v. 17.

34.4 (... את מזבחות) ויתצו : καὶ κατέσπασεν G (L R) = וינתץ by assimilation to v. 7 את־המז׳ וינתץ. In Par τὰ θυσιαστήρια appears later in v. 7, which makes a *Vorlage* variant more likely. Curtis claims that αὐτοῦ in v. 4 shows that the verb must originally have been plural, comparing κατέστρεψαν A. But τά G L before the preposition is in fact the translator's device to make the phrase fit a singular verb.

v. 27 יען רך : καὶ ἐνετράπη G O L R = ויכנע (Rehm, p. 61), influenced by תכנע two words later. The consonants are very similar.

II Ki 24.3/36.5c על־פי : θυμός G O L R = על־אף, read under the influence of Ki. 24.20 in the next column (26 lines away in BH). Rg had the same *Vorlage*.[2]

36.14 העם : ὁ λαὸς τῆς γῆς G O L R = עם הארץ (BH), conformed to the phrase in v. 1 in the preceding column (21 lines away in BH, but it would be more in Par's expanded *Vorlage*).

There also occurs assimilation to similar places elsewhere in Chron. I 8.36 יהועדה[1,2] : Ιαδα G[3] = יעדה (BH), assimilated to יעדה, to be read for MT יערה, in the parallel list in 9.42, where a shorter form is used (Rudolph).

---

[1] cf. Part I, p. 164.

[2] In Rg v. 20 L and KR read ἐπὶ τὸν θυμόν; in v. 3 KR so reads but L has θυμός, clearly by assimilation to Par.

[3] cf. Part I, p. 158.

9.38 שמאם : *Σαμαα* G O L R = שמאה (BH), as in 8.32 (*Σεμαα* G O R).

14.4 שמוע : *Σαμαα* G L R = שמעא (BH), as in the same list in 3.5.

26.9 (מררי ...) הקרתי : *Κααθ* G = (not קהת BH, but a loose rendering for) הקהתי, influenced by the linking of קהת and 'מ frequently elsewhere in Chron, as Rudolph suggests. He observes that v. 1 supports MT. On the other hand, Rothstein claimed that v. 1 had caused an error here in MT.

27.18 אליהו : *Ελιαβ* G O L = אליאב (BH : "1 c G"), often adopted. But Rudolph wisely questions the palaeographical development and suggests that this is Jesse's eighth son, not mentioned by name elsewhere. Then the *Vorlage* had suffered assimilation to 2.13, etc.

II 12.15 להתיחש : *καὶ πράξεις αὐτοῦ* G O L (in doublet) R = ודרכיו borrowed from 13.22 (Rudolph) as a more common expression. ומעשיו (Benzinger, Curtis, cf. Goettsberger) was not read : *ἔργα* renders it elsewhere in Par. *πράξεις* renders only דרכים in Par.

14.7/8 (מאתים) ושמונה : *πεντήκοντα* G O = וחמשים (BH). The number of Benjaminite archers had suffered partial assimilation to I 8.40 where מאה וחמשים Benjaminite archers are mentioned.

30.6 מכף מלכי אשור : *ἀπὸ χειρὸς βασιλέως Ασσουρ* G O (L) R = מכף מלך א', influenced by the phrase in 32.11 (*ἐκ χειρὸς* ...).

v. 10 בארץ־אפרים : *ἐν ὄρει E.* G O L R = בהר א', assimilated to the standard phrase elsewhere in Chron : I 6. 52/67; II 13.4; 15.8; 19.4.

35.24 בקברות אבתיו : *μετὰ τῶν πατέρων αὐτοῦ* G O L R = עם א' (BH). II Ki 23.30; I Esdr 1.29 support Chron. The *Vorlage* had been conformed to the frequent phrase, e.g., in 33.20. Rehm, pp. 22, apparently credits the translator with the change.

II Ki 23.33/36.2c ברבלה : *ἐν Δαβλαθα* G A = בדבלתה (ד/ר). This Heb reading is also attested by IV Rg *ἐν Δεβλαθα* L, to which O L R in Par are assimilated. It has come from II Ki. 25.21 where the same Gk represents ברבלה in a similar setting. There -לתה was read by assimilation to 25.20 רבלתה (*εἰς Δεβλαθα*).

Passages outside Chron are occasionally echoed.

II 14.10/11 אין־עמך לעזור בין רב לאין כח : *οὐκ ἀδυνατεῖ παρά σοι σῴζειν ἐν πόλλοις καὶ ἐν ὀλίγοις* G O R = אין מעצור עמך להושיע ברב ובמעט. This is a reminiscence of I Sam 14.6 (Benzinger, Curtis, Goettsberger) : אין ליהוה מעצור להושיע ברב או במעט. At what stage did it enter the text ? The translator apparently found the variant : that the rendering comes from his hand is suggested by the fact that *δυνάσθαι*, etc., is used for עצר elsewhere in the LXX only at II Chron

20.37 עצרו : ἐδυνάσθη. The rendering in Rg has significant differences. The reminiscence was doubtless encouraged by אל־יעצר עמך אנוש at the end of the verse.

28.4 גבעות : δωμάτων G O L R = גגות, as often in the LXX Old Testament. The rendering can hardly be a conjecture on the translator's part since גבעת becomes βουνοῦ in I 11.31. Sacrificing on housetops is mentioned in II Ki 23.12; Jer 19.13; 32.29; Zeph 1.5. The reading was doubtless inspired by a reminiscence of one or more of these passages.

(b) It is not only the *Vorlage* which was affected in this way. The influence of the context upon the MT may also be observed by comparison with Par.

I 1.7 תרשישה : Θαρσεις G O L R = תרשיש (BH : "l c G V Gn 10,4"). MT is assimilated to the preceding אלישה.[1]

3.6 אלישמע : Ελεισα G = אלישע (cf. BH "l prb c 2 MSS 14,5; 2 S 5, 15 אלישוע, G^B ..."), influenced by אלישמע v. 8 (Rehm, p. 69). It should be noted that Rahlfs, *LXX.* and Ziegler[2] considered G a corruption of Ελισαμα O L R.

5.18 וגדי : καὶ Γαδ G L R = וגד, read by Ehrlich, Rothstein, BH, Rudolph. MT would require the article; it has been influenced by ולגדי v. 26.

6.6/21 עדו : Αδει G, cf. Αδδι O R = עדי. Cf. the corresponding עדיה v. 26. MT is assimilated in ending to בנו before and after.

8.37 רפה : Ραφαι G from Ραφαια O (Ra.) = רפיה (BH so reads), as in 9.43. The MT is assimilated to ורפא ("Ec 1 ורפה " BH) 8.2 in the preceding column (26 lines away in BH).

11.14 ויתיצבו ... ויצילוה ויכו : καὶ ἔστη ... ἔσωσεν ... ἐπάταξεν G O L R = ויתיצב ... ויצילה ויך, as in the parallel II Sam 23.12, to be read with Benzinger, BH, Rudolph, etc. The plurals are a mechanical assimilation to נסו v. 13 (Curtis, Rehm, p. 69).

12.3 ברכה : Βερχεια G R = ברכיה to be read with BH, Noth, p. 240, and Rudolph. The ending has surely been influenced by הכה 11.23 in the preceding column (26 lines away in BH). It is significant that בני השמעה becomes υἱὸς Αμα G from ... Σαμα* = בן שמע. בן is often read with Heb mss. (Curtis, Rudolph, cf. BH). As for the name, Rudolph follows Curtis' suggestion to read השמע (cf. 3.18), dismissing

---

[1] Podechard, *RB* xiii, p. 376; Ehrlich, *Randglossen*, vii, *ad loc.*

[2] *Beiträge*, p. 77.

the final *he* as a dittograph. But the evidence of Par suggests that יה
is secondary. Was it intended as a correction of ה in ברכה ?

14.11 ויעלו : καὶ ἀνέβη G O L R = ויעל, read by two Chron mss.,
corresponding to ויבא in II Sam 5.20. The singular is rightly read by
Rothstein, Rehm, p. 69, and Rudolph to suit עלה in v. 10. Doubtless
the MT has suffered assimilation to ויעלו in v. 8.

16.15 זכרו : μνημονεύομεν G, grown out of μνημονεύων O L (Curtis,
Ra.) by a ω/οε error under the influence of ἡμῶν v. 14 = זְכָּ(ו)ר, to
be read with Psa 105.8 (BH. Rudolph). The MT is assimilated to
זכרו v. 12 (Rudolph).

v. 19 בהיותכם : ἐν τῷ γενέσθαι αὐτούς G O (L) R = בהיותם, as in
one de Rossi ms., Vulg and Psa 105.12, to be read with Curtis, Rothstein and BH. נחלתכם just before caused the error. Rudolph, admitting
this possibility, claims nevertheless that either reading is possible. But
ויתהלכו in v. 20 surely demands a preceding third person.

21.12 נספה : φεύγειν σε G (O) L R = נסכה, cf. II Sam 24.13 נסך.
Par is generally followed : the MT is unsuitable in the context. Rehm,
p. 69, calls this a כ/פ error, but note the סס sequence in vv. 2, 3, 5.

22.7 Kethib בנו : τέκνον (vocative) G O L R = Qere בני with
"18 MSS V T" (BH), as in v. 11. The Kethib has been influenced by
v. 6 (Rudolph).

27.24 במספר : ἐν βιβλίῳ G O L R = בספר, to be read with Curtis,
Rothstein, BH and Rudolph. The MT is assimilated to the preceding
המספר. Ehrlich insisted upon על ספר, comparing העלה על־ס' II 20.34
and the occasional use of ἐν to render על in the LXX. But it is perhaps
significant that עלה of anger can be used with ב (II 36.16) as well as על
(Eccles. 10.4).

28.17 והמזלגות (והמ' והק') : καὶ τῶν κρεαγρῶν G O L R, BH counsels
"1 c G וְלִ' (ter)". But "das notwendige (s. G V) ל ist nur beim ersten
Wort zu setzen (וְלִמְ'), da der Chronist 'die Neigung hat, Präpositionen
nur einmal zu setzen' (Kropat 43...); so erklärt sich der Fehler von
M leichter" (Rudolph).

II 7.20 ונתשתים : καὶ ἐξαρῶ ὑμᾶς G O L R = ונתשתיכם (BH, Rudolph
so read), necessary after the protasis with second plural verbs. The
MT probably goes back to ונתשתם, which arose by mechanical assimilation to the three preceding verbs ending in תם־. Rudolph explains
the error as due to להם.

8.16 עד־היום : ἀφ' ἧς ἡμέρας G O L R = מיום, generally read with
the other versions. The MT has been influenced by the following
עד (Rudolph), and probably too by עד־היום v. 8.

11.17 (בדרך) הלכו : ἐπορεύθη G O L R = הלך. BH and Rudolph refer to 12.1, which speaks of Rehoboam's forsaking the law, as the motive for the singular. But the singular is superior on stylistic grounds. To "walk in the way(s)" of a king is a frequent formula in Chron. In every other case the verb is singular. This fact suggests that in MT the plural number is due to the two plural verbs earlier in the sentence.

v. 18   Kethib בן : θυγατέρα G O L R = Qere בת, which is generally read. The Kethib was mechanically assimilated to בן two words later (Rudolph) and to the pattern "בן + name + את" in v. 17.

14.6/7 דרשנו : καθὼς (ἐξ)ἐζητήσαμεν G O L R = כְּדָרְשֵׁנוּ, to be read with Winckler,[1] Benzinger, Rudolph. MT has come under the spell of דרשנו later.

20.1 מהעמונים : ἐκ τῶν Μιναίων G O = מהמעונים, generally read since Ammon has just been mentioned and three groups of people feature in vv. 10,22f. The third group is linked with הר שעיר : Goettsberger notes that the מעונים are associated with that place in I 4.41f. The error in MT is mechanical assimilation to עמון ועמהם just before; in 26.8 the opposite error occurred in Par's *Vorlage*.

v. 25 ופגרים : καὶ σκῦλα G O L R, which does not fit this specific list which is meant to be defining σκῦλα. It is probably an error for στολάς*, marred by σκυλ- which occurs five times in this verse. *Vestium* La supports this suggestion. Then it stands for בגדים, generally read with a number of Heb mss. and Vulg. MT has been conformed to פגרים v. 24.

22.2 ארבעים : εἴκοσι G O L R = עשׂרים, as in II Ki 8.26, frequently adopted because according to 21.20 Ahaziah's father was only forty when he died. Rudolph suggests the influence of ערבים v. 1. Rehm, pp. 60, 71, finds a מ/כ error in numerical lettering. Myers makes the interesting suggestion that two readings, 20 and 22, have been conflated by addition.

v. 6 ועזריהו : καὶ Ὀχοζίας G O L R = ואחזיהו, generally read "c 15 MSS G V S 2 R 8, 29" (BH). Goettsberger and Rudolph suggest the influence of the repeated name in 23.1.

25.28 בעיר יהודה : ἐν πόλει Δαυιδ G O L R = בעיר דויד, generally read "c 12 MSS S 2 R 14, 20" (BH, omitting reference to Par and Vulg). The error surely came about by confusion with בערי יהודה v. 13 in the preceding column (29 lines away in BH). Rehm, p. 71,

---

[1] *Alttestamentliche Untersuchungen*, p. 187.

finds merely an error of ד/ה. Myers keeps MT on the ground that in the Babylonian Chronicle Jerusalem is called "city of Judah".

30.22 (את־המועד) ויאכלו : καὶ συνετέλεσαν G O L R = ויכלו, read by Kittel, BH, Goettsberger and Rudolph, because the object does not suit MT's verb. No doubt MT has been influenced by אכלו את־הפסח v. 18. It repeats v. 21, but Par's reading is a good preparation for v. 23. שבעת הימים is presumably then in apposition to המועד.

31.4 בתורת יהוה (יחזקו) : ἐν τῇ λειτουργίᾳ οἴκου κυρίου G O L R = בעבודת בית י. Curtis posits בשרת בית י. But although שרת as a noun is rendered λειτουργικά in 24.14, λειτουργία οἴκου in Par always implies עבודת בית י : I 9.13; 23.24; 28.13,20,21. It is significant that the preceding verse (31.3) ends with בתורת י. Has MT been conformed to it ? The clause in Par corresponds well to that used of Josiah concerning the priests in 35.2 ויחזקם לעב' בית י. But that clause is not similar enough to justify a claim of assimilation in Par's *Vorlage* to that place. The reading in Par fits the context well : Hezekiah urges that the priests and Levites be fed so that they may devote their energies to the *service* of the Temple instead of earning a living elsewhere.

In one case the influence of another passage in Chron may be seen in MT. II 13.2 מיכיהו : Μααχα G O R = מעכה, which is generally read since it is expected, as in 11.20 and I Ki 15.2. There hardly lurks behind Par assimilation to Ki[1] or to 11.20 since the different name of the father, Uriel, would surely have been changed to Absalom, as is found there. How did MT's error occur ? It may be suggested that after writing "Shemaiah the prophet and Iddo the seer" just before, in 12.15, a copyist's mind strayed to the prophet who was soon to feature in ch. 18.

(ii) *Addition*

(a) The *Vorlage* of Par evidently contained extra elements drawn from elsewhere. First the influence of the context will be considered.

I 1.32 ילדה : + αὐτῷ G O R = לו, borrowed from ילדה לו 2.4 in the next column (26 lines away in BH).

11.6 ויעל : + ἐπ' αὐτήν G O L R = עליה, added from 10.4 in the previous column (24 lines away in BH).

24.28 אלעזר : + καὶ Ιθαμαρ καὶ ἀπέθανεν Ελεαζαρ G. The first

---

[1] *Contra* Sperber, *JBL* lix, p. 286.

four words were added in the *Vorlage* according to the sequence
וימת : ואיתמר אל׳ in v. 1f. in the preceding column (26 lines away in
BH). The last word is an amplification added at some stage for clarity.
26.18 לפרבר : + v. 16 καὶ τῷ Ιοσσα ... v. 18 διαδεχομένους
G O R. The changes in the repeated portion, even allowing for Gk
errors, point to the translation of a dittograph already in the *Vorlage*.
In v. 16 לשנים (εἰς δεύτερον G L (in doublet) R) stood in place of
לשפים. After writing לפרבר : [שנים] שנים שפים ולאספים in v. 17f. a copyist's
eye strayed back to לשנים : האספים in v. 15f. and he wrote out the
intervening passage once again. Subsequently לכשת (τοῦ παστοφορίου
G O R), which was read for שלכת, was glossed שלשת (τρεῖς B O R), as
Torrey has noted.[1] This variant was incorporated into the Heb repeated
portion after לשכת and displaced במסלה העולה, which was reinserted
three words later.
27.21 לחצי : + φυλῆς G O R = שבט, read too by "pc MSS V" (BH,
overlooking Par) by assimilation to the phrase in v. 20.
29.3 וכסף : + καὶ ἰδού G O L R = והנה according to Rothstein and
BH who both urge its insertion into Chron. The resultant text would
certainly read better than MT, but it is very difficult to see how it
could have fallen out. More probably a copyist's eye slipped back to
the last occurrence of כסף in v. 2. He started copying והנחשת but
realised his error half way through. והנח was left and subsequently
adapted to והנה.
v. 10 דויד[1] : ὁ βασιλεὺς Δ. G O L R = ד׳ המלך, assimilated to the
phrase in v. 24 (Δ. τοῦ βασ. G) in the next column (24 lines away in
BH).
v. 24 דויד : + ... πατρὸς αὐτοῦ G O (L) R = ד׳ אביו, influenced by
ד׳ א׳ v. 23. The addition is probably not Gk since G puts τοῦ βασ.
between Δ and π. αὐτοῦ; it goes back to a Heb text with the same
order as MT.
v. 29 ודברי : οἱ δὲ λοίποι λόγοι G O (L) R = ד׳ יתר, assimilated
to the formula frequent in II Chron (Gk usually καὶ οἱ λ. λ.).
II 9.10 זהב : + τῷ Σαλωμων G (O) L (R) = לשלמה (BH), added
from the similar clause in v. 14 (τῷ βασ. Σ. G O L R).
v. 12 אל־המלך : + Σαλ. G O L R = שלמה, by assimilation to the
phrase המ׳ ש׳ (ὁ βασιλεὺς Σ.) earlier in the verse.
v. 21 תרשיש אניות : + τῷ βασιλεῖ G O L R. Probably למלך was

---

[1] "Apparatus for the Textual Criticism of Chron-Ezr-Neh", p. 100.

added under the influence of the earlier phrase אֲנִי לַמֶּלֶךְ (ναῦς, but πλοῖα later). The parallel III Rg 10.22 has the same addition in a slightly different position.

v. 30 שְׁלֹמֹה : + ὁ βασιλεύς G O L = הַמֶּלֶךְ, assimilated to the phrase in 10.2 (Σ. τοῦ βασ. G O L R).

12.13 שִׁבְטֵי יִשְׂרָאֵל (מִכֹּל) : φυλῶν υἱῶν Ισ. B (L) R. בְּנֵי was written under the influence of מִכָּל־בָּנָיו 11.23 in the previous column (24 lines away in BH). שִׁבְטֵי was inserted by way of correction.

18.2 לַעֲלוֹת : + μετ' αὐτοῦ G O L R = עִמּוֹ (BH) by vertical ditto-graphy of עִמּוֹ in the preceding line, assuming a line of thirteen letters.[1]

20.33 לֵאלֹהָי : πρὸς κύριον θεόν G O L R = לַיהוה אֱלֹהֵי, assimilated to the phrase in v. 19 in the preceding column (25 lines away in BH).

21.13 בְּדֶרֶךְ : ἐν ὁδοῖς G O L R = בִּדְרָכֵי with nine Heb mss., influenced by v. 12.

24.12 וִיהוֹיָדָע : + ὁ ἱερεύς G O L R = הַכֹּהֵן (so one de Rossi ms.), assimilated to הכ' v. 25 in the next column (25 lines away in BH).

v. 21 הַמֶּלֶךְ : Ιωας τοῦ βασ. G O L R = יואש המ', as in v. 22 (Ιωας G O R).

25.5 יְהוּדָה וּבְנְיָמִן : Ιουδα καὶ Ιερουσαλημ G O (R) = י' וִירוּשָׁלַם under the influence of the phrase in 24.18 in the previous column (25 lines away in BH).

26.18 מֵעֲלָת : + ἀπὸ κυρίου G O (L) R = בַּיהוה, added under the influence of וַיִּמְעַל בַּי' v. 16, which Par renders differently.

28.13 חֲרוֹן אָף : + κυρίου c₂ O L R.[2] Four Heb mss. add יהוה. ח' אף י' in v. 11 has influenced this phrase.

29.27 הָעוֹלָה : ἀναφέρειν τὴν ὁλοκαύτωσιν G O L R = לְהַעֲלוֹת הָע'. The infinitive was repeated from earlier in the verse (ἀνενέγκαι G O R).

30.12 לַעֲשׂוֹת : ἐλθεῖν τοῦ ποιῆσαι G O (L) R = לָבוֹא לַע', as in v. 5 (ἐλθόντες/ας ποι. G O R).

32.12 (לִיהוּדָה) וְלִירוּשָׁלַם : καὶ τοῖς κατοικοῦσιν (ἐν) I. G O L R = וּלְיֹשְׁבֵי י' (BH), assimilated to וְיֹ' יר' v. 33. Rehm, p. 22f., apparently attributes the addition to the translator.

34.3 לֵאלֹהֵי (דָּוִיד אָבִיו) : κύριον τὸν θεόν G O L R = לַיהוה אֱלֹ'. The sequence יהוה ... ד' אָב' in v. 2 suggested the introduction of יהוה here.

v. 9 יְהוּדָה : υἱῶν Ιουδα G O L R = בְּנֵי י'. A copyist started writing the next word (וּ)בִנְיָמִן and abandoned his error half-written.[3]

---

[1] See p. 133f.

[2] For B see p. 38.

[3] cf. I 15.18 on p. 103.

v. 18   ספר : + ὅ G = אשר, read under the influence of הספר אשר v. 21.

35.1   ליהוה : + θεῷ αὐτοῦ G O L R. After having written יהוה אלהי in the previous verse a copyist added אלהי here. It was adapted to אלהיו by dittography of the following ו.

v. 4   ובמכתב : + βασιλέως G A f h j = מלך, copied by vertical dittography from the line above, assuming a fourteen letter line.

Extra material also came in from similar passages elsewhere in Chron.

I 23.1   וימלך את־שלמה בנו : + ἀντ᾽ αὐτοῦ G O L (R) = תחתיו (BH) under the influence of וימ׳ ש׳ ב׳ ת׳ 29.28. The addition is probably Heb : the Gk is less similar.

26.27   מן : ἃ ἔλαβεν ἐκ G O (L) R = אשר נשא מן added from 18.11 (οὗ ... G O L R) which is set in a similar context.[1]

27.24   למנות : ἀριθμεῖν ἐν τῷ λαῷ G O L R = למ׳ בעם, assimilated to 21.17 (τοῦ ἀριθμῆσαι (ἐν) τῷ λ. G O L R).

28.18   לפרשׁים : τῶν διαπεπετασμένων ταῖς πτέρυξιν G O L R = לפ׳ כנפים (Rothstein), assimilated to II 5.8 פ׳ כ׳ (διαπεπετακότα τὰς π. αὐτῶν G O L R).

II 14.10/11   ההמון : + τὸ πολύ G O L R = הרב, from the similar context of 20.12. The addition was probably made before the Vorlage was assimilated to I Sam. 14.6, whereby לאין כח was replaced by ובמעט.

29.33   בקר שׁשׁ מאות ... אלפים : + πεντακόσια B* = חמש מאות, a misplaced gloss assimilating to the account of Josiah's passover in which בקר חמש מאות is mentioned in 35.9 (-κοσίους G O L R).

30.18   הפסח בלא ככתוב : τὸ φασεκ παρὰ τὴν γραφὴν τοῦτο B (L). The last word represents misplaced assimilation to 35.19 הפסח הזה, which occurred before the phrase was omitted in Par's Vorlage.[2]

34.9   ואפרים : + καὶ τῶν ἀρχόντων G O L R = והשׁרים, a gloss from 24.10, where השׁרים (ἄρχοντες) are among those who contributed to the similar fund of Joash. Curtis suggested that the addition was possibly a corruption of an earlier ושמעון. Rehm, p. 61, considers that רדים had grown out of (אפ)רים.

Sometimes material has been added from places outside Chron.

I 12.9/8   וכצבאים : καὶ κοῦφοι ὡς δορκάδες G O L R = וקלים כצ׳ (BH) in reminiscence of II Sam 2.18 כאחד הצבים ... קל.

29.11   והמתנשׂא לכל לראשׁ : + καὶ ἔθνος G O L (in doublet) R =

---

[1] Cf. Part I, p. 163.

[2] See Part I, p. 213f.

והמון. ἔθνος is used for המון only in II 32.7 G O L R in all the LXX.
The word is a corruption of יהמיון, an explanatory gloss by reminiscence
of Psa. 83.3 where נשאו ראש is in parallelism with יהמיון.[1] Rothstein considered that the addition represented וגויה corrupted into וגוי.

II 2.3/4 עלות : + διὰ παντός G O L R = תמיד (BH: "1 frt"). The
preceding מערכת תמיד suggested the technical term עלת תמיד, found,
e.g., in Exod 29.42; Ezra 3.5.

(b) The MT is not devoid of assimilating additions.

I 3.2 לאבשלום : G O L R omit ל, as the context requires (BH :
"20 MSS G ST"). לאביגיל in v. 1 caused the slip (Rudolph).

6.8/23 בנו[1] : G omits. As Curtis and Rudolph state, the omission is
necessary in view of Exod 6.24 : Elkanah and Abiasaph were brothers.
The pattern of name + בנו in the context led to the error. Other changes
in this and preceding verses are also necessary in MT, but Par's text
in other respects read like MT and was already partially corrupted.

v. 11/26 אלקנה (Qere בני ; Kethib בנו) : G O L R omit, as is generally
done "c nonn MSS G S" (BH). A copyist's eye dropped to בנו אלקנה
in v. 12 and אל' was written here by error. The Qere is an attempt
to make the error fit the context.

15.18 בן is omitted in G O R. BH and Rudolph omit with three
Heb mss. and Par. The latter plausibly explains the awkward word
as a partial writing of בניה which occurs later in the verse; the error
was abandoned half-written.

16.42 ועמהם : + הימן וידותון, omitted in G O R. The names have
come in from וע' ה' ויד' v. 41 (Kautzsch, Benzinger, Kittel, Curtis,
Ehrlich, Rothstein, BH).

II 4.12 והגלות להכתרות : καὶ ... γωλαθ τῇ χωθαρεθ G O R = וגלת
הכתרת, as in I Ki 7.41. This reading is generally adopted since שתים
later must qualify גלות (cf. 12b). As Rehm, p. 70, has explained, first
the conjunction was mechanically repeated, then the article was
inserted to balance the new coordinate.

18.19 אמר (ככה וזה אמר כ') is omitted in G O L R and in I Ki 22.20.
It is otiose and is generally taken as a false anticipation of what follows.

31.12 והמעשר : + והקדשים, omitted in G O L R. As Rudolph has

---

[1] For the corruption cf. Psa 65/64.8 והמון : ταραχθήσονται = יהמון or יהמיון.
However, it is possible that there is a link here with II 20.6, which is very similar to
I 29.12. Between ובידך כח וגבורה and ואתה מושל בכל in v. 12, II 20.6 inserts
ממלכות הגוים. Was this phrase added here and attached by error to (לראש) לכל
in v. 11 so that לראש was displaced ?

seen, it has been added from ומעשר קדשים v. 6 in the present state of
that verse, on which see Rudolph.

External influence has affected Chron MT in two places on Par's
evidence.

II 10.16 איש is missing from G O R and I Ki 12.16. Kittel and Curtis
suggested dittography of ישי. Rehm, p. 84, and Rudolph have a
better explanation : MT takes the word from Sheba's similar cry in
II Sam 20.1, but אלהיך here renders the addition unsuitable.

15.16 וידק is missing from G O L R and I Ki 15.13. As Rudolph
(cf. Curtis) suggests, the text has been assimilated to the similar
record of Josiah's destruction of the Asherah in II Ki 23.6. Rehm,
p. 95, held that καὶ κατεπάτησεν* had fallen out before καὶ κατέπαυσεν,
but Rudolph rightly objects that λεπτύνειν is Par's verb in 34.4
(cf. 34.7).

(iii) *Omission*

In a few cases the influence of the context or of a similar passage
has removed elements from Par's text.

I 28.8 (קהל־יהוה) (ישראל כל) (לעיני כל) is omitted in G O R probably by
analogy with 29.10 לעיני כל־הקהל (Par omits כל and renders the
preposition differently).

29.22 בשמחה גדולה : μετὰ χαρᾶς G O R = בשמחה by analogy with
v. 17 בש׳ (ἐν εὐφροσύνῃ).

II 18.4 (יהוה) דבר is missing in G O R and also in the parallel III Rg
22.5   The error in the *Vorlagen* was doubtless under the influence of
v. 7.

24.18 את־בית יהוה (ויעזבו) : τὸν κύριον G O. בית was omitted by
analogy with v. 20 עזבתם את־יהוה and v. 24 עזבו את־יהוה. Evidently
the missing word was put in the margin and then incorporated into
the next column : cf. 25.5 את־יהודה : τὸν οἶκον Ιουδα G O L R (25
lines away in BH).

34.27 מלפני אלהים : ἀπὸ προσώπου μου G O L R = חלפני, assimilated to לפני twice later in the verse. As a consequence of this change
דבריו became דברי. Curtis and Rehm, p. 72, consider דברי original
in view of II Ki 22.19 אשר דברתי, but the Chronicler may well have
used the third person to refer to אלהים.

In two cases the MT appears to have suffered an error of this kind.
II 10.14 אכביד : ὁ πατήρ μου ἐβάρυνεν G O L R = אבי הכביד,
generally read with many Heb mss. and Par. As Curtis remarks, "the

sense, the parallel and v. 10 require it". The error was caused by looking forward to וְאַנִי אָסִיף.

23.18 יהוה (לְהַעֲלוֹת עֹלֹת) : (τῷ) κυρίῳ G O L R = לַיהוה (BH : "pl MSS G V"). This is used in Chron's standard phrase in I 16.40; 23.31 ; 29.21 ; II 8.12. Was ל lost because of יהוה three words before ?

3. DIVISION OF WORDS

Würthwein states that "there is no real proof that *scriptio continua* was used for Hebrew".[1] But he adds . "In the square script it was customary, as may be seen from the newly found manuscripts, to leave a gap between words, though admittedly this was sometimes so small that it could become doubtful where one word ended and another began". Occasional differences in joining together and dividing words, in MT and in the text underlying Par, may be appreciated in the light of this last remark. Errors in Par's text will be considered first.

I 4.18 היהדיה : αὕτη Ἀδια G O (R) = הי(א) הדיה.

v. 31 ברַי וּבשערים : Βραουμσεωρειμ G from Βαρ- A N d (Ra.) = שׁערים בראום (ב/מ). Rothstein fancifully regarded בראום as an error for בראות, which in turn was an error for לבאות (Jos 19.6).

v. 36f./36 בניה וזיזא : υἱοὶ Ἀσοσαλ c₂ (Ἀωσαλ B) = בני הזוזא (ו/י). The conjunction was absent.

20.2 וימצא המ': וימצאה המשקל was read.[2]

II 6.31 ייראוך ללכת בדרכיך : φοβῶνται πάσας ὁδούς σου G = ייראו דרכיך כל (לכתב). After wrong division the incomprehensible לכתב was omitted. Rehm, p. 17, wrongly sees here a case of brief paraphrase, while Rogers, p. 23f., imagines that the translator simply omitted ללכת as anthropomorphic.

13.10f./10 ו : במלאכת : ἐν ταῖς ἐφημερίαις αὐτῶν G O L (in doublet) R = במלאכתו. BH posits במחלקתם. Curtis thought that Par possibly read במחלקתיו. The latter's view of the suffix was correct : it was taken *ad sensum* to refer to the Levites. ἐφημερία is used ten times in Par for מחלקת and four for משמרת, but it is significant that the translator used it periphrastically in I 9.33 for לשׁכת.

---

[1] *Text of the OT*, p. 73. A.R. Millard, *JSS* xv, pp. 2ff., has carefully examined the available evidence and concluded that *scriptio continua* was not a practice of early Heb scribes.

[2] See Part I, p. 49.

20.14 בן־יעיאל : τῶν υἰῶν Ελεαηλ B ın from ... Αιαηλ*[1] = בני עיאל.

v. 22 ברנתו ותהלה : ברנה תהלה was read.[2]

22.1 בערבים : ב׳ ערבים was read.[3]

23.8 עם יוצאי : ע׳ מוצאי was read.[4]

25.8 אתה עשׂה : אתעשׂת was read.[5]

30.24 ויתקדשׁו : καὶ τὰ ἅγια G O R = וית קדשׁי (ו/י). Gehman suggests ואת קדשׁי.[6] BH posits וקדשׁי. False word-division is the simple explanation : the Aramaic sign of the definite object was wrongly seen here.[7]

In some instances Par's *Vorlage* offers a better text.

I 2.24 בכלב : ἦλθεν Χαλεβ G O (L) R = ב(א) כלב, which has been generally read since Wellhausen.[8]

4.15 עירו אלה : Ηρ Αδαι G from ... Αλα O (Λ/Δ; ending assimilated to καί) = עיר [ו] אלה which is generally read.

15.22 במשׂאי׳ שׂר : במשׂא יסר was read.[9]

17.10 ואגד לך : καὶ αὐξήσω σε G O L R = וְאַגְדִּלְךָ. Most commentators, but notably not Curtis or Rudolph, so read. Seeligmann has recently examined the context in detail and concluded that Par's *Vorlage* is "the only reading which suits the continuity of the context".[10]

26.17 למזרח הלוים : πρὸς ἀνατολὰς ... τὴν ἡμέραν G (O) L (in doublet) (R) = למזרחה ליום, read by Goettsberger, Rudolph and Myers in accordance with the following phrases. BH changes only the second word and ignores the evidence of Par.

II 32.22 וינח להם : וינהלם was read.[11]

4. METATHESIS

Letters within words were sometimes in a different order in the

---

[1] See Part I, p. 159.

[2] See p. 115.

[3] See p. 89.

[4] See p. 86.

[5] See p. 115.

[6] *VT* iv, p. 340.

[7] cf. יתהון Dan 3.12.

[8] *De Gentibus*, p. 14f.

[9] See p. 87.

[10] *VT* xi, p. 208.

[11] See p. 116.

Vorlage of Par. Many examples are discussed in other sections, but the following may be cited here. Inferior readings are listed first.

I 2.55 מחמת : Μεσημα G from Μεθημα*? = מתמח.

4.20 שׁימון : Σεμιων B O = שׁמיון (Rothstein, BH).

v. 22 וישׁבי : καὶ ἀπέστρεφεν G O R = וישׁיב (abnormal *scriptio plena*).

ibid. הדברים : αβεδηρειν B (c₂ O R) = הבדרין. It was because the translator found this corrupted form that he transliterated.

5.1 בכרתו : εὐλογίαν αὐτοῦ G O R = ברכתו (BH, etc.). All except Rudolph keep MT : the context indicates that the birthright rather than blessing is in view (Benzinger). Rothstein notes that Par's reading is derived from ויברך Gen 48.15.

v. 2 הבכרה : ἡ εὐλογία G O R = הברכה (Curtis, etc.)

7.8 זמירה : זמריה was read.[1]

8.5 שׁפופן : Σωφαρφακ G from Σωφαφαν* (κ by dittography; ending assimilated to Γερα; ρ is misplaced and belongs to the next name) = שׁופפן.

9.8 מכרי : Μαχειρ G e₂ R = מכיר (BH).

15.21 השׁמינית : המשׁנית was probably read.[2]

17.16 הביאתני : אהבתני was read.[3]

18.9f. תעו : Θωα G e₂, G = תוע.

v. 17 הפלתי : Φαλτεια G = פלתיה.

21.6 נתעב : נבעת was read.[4]

26.16 שׁלכת : παστοφορίου G O L R = לשׁכת (Curtis). BH posits, and Curtis gives as an alternative, לשׁכה, but this is unnecessary. Curtis favours Par, but Rudolph rightly calls it a "tastende Deutungsversuche".

27.29 Kethib שׁטרי : Ασαρται c₂ (-αις B by dittography) from Σαρται* (beginning assimilated to Ασειδων) = Qere שׁרטי (BH, etc.).

II 28.21 חלק : ἔλαβεν G O L R = לקח (Wutz, p. 372).[5]

Errors of metathesis in MT on the evidence of Par are as follows :

I 3.24 Kethib הדיוהו : Οδολια G from Οδοαια* (Λ/Λ) = Qere הדויהו, read by Rudolph, who compares 5.24; 9.7 and Lachish Ostraka III 17.

23.16; 25.4 שׁבואל : Σουβαηλ G O R, G O L R = שׁובאל, generally read, e.g., by BH, Noth, p. 257, as in 24.20; 25.20.

---

[1] See p. 42.

[2] See p. 77.

[3] See p. 77.

[4] See p. 11.

[5] See p. 137.

II 17.8 Kethib שמרימות : Σαμειραμωθ B e₂ = Qere שמירמות, read
by Rudolph, who calls the Kethib a pure scribal error and refers to
I 15.18.

There is an interesting case in I 10.11 :

יביש : οἱ κατοικοῦντες G O L (in doublet) R = ישבי. ישבי יביש is generally read "c MS^Ros 593 S 1 S 31,11" (BH). MT has preserved one
half of the phrase and Par the other.

5. TRANSPOSITION

There are some clear cases of different order of words in Par's
Vorlage. First will be considered the cases where there seems to be no
reason for preferring Par's order.

II 12.10 מגני נחשת / תחתיהם G O. Since III Rg 14.27 has the same
order as Par but uses different Gk, the change goes back to Heb texts.
v. 11 (read as שמרים) הרצים/ונשאום G O L (in doublet) R. Cf. I Ki.
14.28 ישאום הר׳. Heb parallel assimilation may well have contributed
to the change.

25.27 וינס/(read as מיר׳) בירושלם G O R. As Rehm, p. 24, observed,
the change of reading was caused by the change of order.

29.10 ממנו/חרון אפו G O R. It was the fresh order in a Heb which
caused the omission of בני in v. 11.[1]

32.28 (ל)/עדרים אורות G O L R. Benzinger, Kittel, Curtis and BH
change according to Par, as the sense requires. But more probably
the phrase is to be deleted as a correcting and explanatory gloss on
ערים in v. 29 (Ehrlich, Rudolph).

There are two cases where Par's order is preferable to that of MT.

I 19.17 ארם .../דויד G. Par has here been conformed to the text of
the parallel II Rg. 10.17.[2] But the order is clearly right (Rehm, p. 100,
BH "frt", Goettsberger, Rudolph). דויד, as it stands in MT, is superfluous since the subject is the same as that of preceding verbs.

II 31.2 לשרת/(ו)להדות ולהלל G O L R. Benzinger, Curtis and Rudolph rightly change the order : the gates are hardly a suitable venue
for the choir. "Das Wort wurde von einem Abschreiber übersehen, dann
darübergeschrieben und geriet später an verkehrter Stelle in den
Text" (Rudolph). Curtis helpfully refers to the Levitical doorkeepers
of I Chron 26.

---

[1] See p. 133.

[2] See Part I, p. 196.

6. Confusion of consonants

Par provides much evidence of differences from MT which must be traced back to a *Vorlage* in which certain consonants were confused or to misreadings of similar letters on the translator's part. The range of differences to be covered in this chapter has been mostly discussed by such scholars as S.R. Driver, F. Delitzsch, B. J. Roberts and E. Würthwein.[1]

(i) ב, כ and מ

These are a group of letters which are commonly confused. S.R. Driver cites a number of examples from the evidence of Rg and other books of the LXX.[2]

(a) ב and מ

In the case of ב and (ן)מ one must reckon with the possibility of paraphrase, as much cases as I 18.8 בה : ἐξ αὐτοῦ G O L R and II 16.10 מן־העם : ἐν τῷ λαῷ G O L R prove. In II 15.17 מישראל : ἐν τῷ I. G O L R is to be so regarded *contra* Rehm, p. 60.[3] How about I 19.10 בישראל : ἐξ I. G R? Rehm, p. 58, rightly marks with a query his suggestion of ב/מ confusion.

Cases where the translator's reading is inferior to MT will be listed first.

I 3.22 בריח : Μαρει G (ending probably assimilated to Μανει v. 24) = 'מ.

v. 24 ועקום : καὶ Ιακουν B h from Ακουμ* via Ακουν b = ועקוב.

4.17 ישבח : Μαρεθ B transposed from Ιεθμα* (I/P, under the influence of Αρεθ v. 7, 12 lines away in BM?) from Ιεσμα* (c/Θ : cf. Ιεσβα O R) = ישמח.

v. 19 (בני נחם) : Μαναημ B = מנחם.[4]

v. 24 יריב : Ιαρειμ h c₂ (-ν B) = ירים.

v. 31 בית מככבות : Βαιθμαρειμωθ B from Βαιθμαρκ-*? (cf. h's mixed reading Βαιθμα καὶ Χαρωθ) = בי מוכמות.

6.16/31 ממנוח : ἐν τῇ καταπαύσει G O R = 'ב.

---

[1] Driver, *Samuel*; Delitzsch, *Die Lese- und Schreibfehler des AT*; Roberts, *OT Text and Versions*; Würthwein, *Text of the OT*.

[2] *Op. cit.*, p. lxvii.

[3] See Part I, p. 153.

[4] See p. 82.

v. 56/71   בְּבֹשֶׁן : ἐκ τῆς B. G O R = מ'.

9.10   יהוירב : Ιωαρειμ B R = יהוירים (BH).

11.21   בשנים : ὑπέρ τοὺς δύο G O L R = מ'. For מן : ὑπέρ see v. 22.

v. 33   עזמות : Αζβων G (ending according to- ωνει v. 31) = עזב'.

v. 43   המתני : ὁ Βαιθανει G = הב'.

12.2   מאחי : ἐν τοῖς ἀδελφοῖς B = בא'.[1]

v. 8/7   מן : υἱοί S c₂ O L R = בני'.[2]

13.3   בימי : ἀφ' ἡμερῶν G O L R = מי'.

24.5   מבני : ἐν τοῖς υἱοῖς G O L R = ב'.

v. 8   חרם : Χαρηβ B h R = חרב.

v. 9   מימן : Βενιαμειν G; II 31.15 מנימן : Βενιαμειν G O L R = בנימן (BH; in the second case "3 MSS^Ken G V S"). Geiger saw here a deliberate change.[3] R. de Vaux considers ב' original.[4]

v. 13   ישבאב : originally Ιεσβααμ*[5] = ישבאם. Rudolph notes that the name is found in an inscription contra Kittel who read ישבעל according to Ισβααλ O (L), which Rudolph explains as an error for Ισβααβ*. But surely Λ is a misreading of M.

25.4   רממתי : Ρωμ* (Ρωμει G, assimilated to -ει just before) υἱοί G = רם בני. רמבתי was divided and בתי changed into a more familiar בני.

26.7   סמכיהו : Ισβακωμ B (in doublet).[6]

27.1   בחדש : ἐκ μηνός G O L R = מ', unless this is paraphrase.[7]

28.4   ובבית : καὶ ἐξ οἴκου G O L R = ומ'.

II 6.21   ממקום : ἐν τῷ τόπῳ G O = ב' (Rehm, p. 59).

13.9   בפר : ἐκ μόσχων G = מ'.

14.7/8   ומבנימן ... מיהודה : ἐν γῇ Ιουδα ... καὶ ἐν γῇ B. G O (L) R = בי' ... ובב'.

18.24   בחדר : ἐκ ταμ(ι)είου G O L R = מ' (Rehm, p. 60). But is this rather paraphrase?[8]

21.10   לבנה : Λομνα B g m = למ'.

v. 12   מכתב : ἐν γραφῇ G O R = ב'.

23.20   שרי המאות ... מבית : τοὺς πατριάρχας G O R ... εἰς οἶκον

---

1 Cf. Part I, p. 162.

2 See p. 88.

3 Urschrift², p. 221 note 1.

4 RB xlv, pp. 400ff.

5 See p. 52.

6 See Part I, p. 163.

7, 8 cf. Liddell and Scott, Lexicon, pp. 770b, 498b.

G O L R = 'ב ... האבות שׂ' (Rehm, p. 60).

24.23   מעם : ἐν τῷ λαῷ G O = 'ב (Curtis).

25.13   מהם : ἐν αὐτοῖς B O L = 'ב.

v. 23   בחומת : ἀπὸ τοῦ τείχους G O L R = 'מ (Rehm, p. 61).

v. 27   מעת : ἐν τῷ καιρῷ G O L R = 'ב (BH, Rehm, p. 61).

ibid.   בירושלם : ἀπὸ Ιερ. G O R = 'מ (Rehm, p. 61) on account of transposition (id., p. 24).

29.12   בן⁵ : ἀπὸ τοῦ G = מן.

32.26   בגבה : ἀπὸ τοῦ ὕψους G O L R = 'מ (BH : "G T").

34.7   בכל : ἀπὸ πάσης G (O) L R = 'מ.

II Ki.23.31/36.2a   חמוטל : Αβειταλ G = חבי״.

Ki.33/2c Kethib   במלך : τοῦ μὴ βασιλεύειν G O L R = Qere 'מ.

36.23   בכם : ἐξ ὑμῶν G O L R = 'מ?

There are cases where Par has preserved the correct reading.

I 6.25/40   בעשׂיה : Μασια h L, Μαασαι B from Μαασια* (Ra.) = 'מ, generally read, e.g. by BH ("1 c nonn MSS Gᴮ S") and Noth, p. 239.

II 15.8   מהר : ἐν ὄρει G O = 'ב, read by Kittel, BH ("1 c Gᴮᴬ (S V)") and Myers. The earlier מן, 'מ caused the change in MT.

(b)   ב and כ

In this category κατά raises doubts. Does it always imply כ for ב? One would hardly think so in a case like   I 24.3   בעבדתם : κατὰ τὴν λειτουργίαν αὐτῶν G O L R.

I 4.9   בעצב : ὡς γαβης G O R = כעבץ.

6.62/77   תבור : Θαχχεια B from Θαχχειδ* (Δ/Λ)? = תכיד?

8.10   שכיה : Σαβια G (O R) = שביה (BH : "mlt MSS Gᴮᴬ T").

14.15   כשׁמעך : ἐν τῷ ἀκοῦσαί σε G O L R = 'ב (BH : "G 2 S 5,24").

15.13   כמשׁפט : ἐν κρίματι G O L (R) = 'ב.

v. 15   כדבר : ἐν λόγῳ G O L R = 'ב (BH).

23.14,31   במספר : κατὰ (τὸν) ἀριθμόν G O L R = 'כ?

27.27   זבדי : Ζαχρει G = זכרי (Rothstein, BH).

II 3.8   לככרים : εἰς χερουβειν εἰς τάλαντα G O R = 'לכרבים לכ (Rehm, p. 27). The mistake, under the influence of the word in v. 7, was corrected at some stage, probably already in the Vorlage.

20.37   בהתחברך : ὡς ἐφιλίασας G O L R = 'כ.

28.2   בדרכי : κατὰ τοὺς ὁδούς G O L R = 'כ (Rehm, p. 61).

29.25   במצות : κατὰ τὴν ἐντολήν G O L R = כמ' (BH)?

35.4   בכתב : κατὰ τὴν γραφήν = ככתב? Kittel and BH ("pc MSS GVS") so read. The parallel I Esdr 1.4 reads as Par.

v. 9 (Kethib; וכנ׳ Qere) וכוכניהו : καὶ Βαναίας G O R in doublet[1] = ובניהו.

II Ki 23.36/36.5 (Qere; זבידה Kethib) זבודה : Ζεχωρα G (O) R = זכורה (BH).

II Ki. 24.3/36.5c ככל : ἐν πᾶσιν G O L R = בכל (Rehm, p. 48).

There is one case of error in MT.

I 17.20 בכל : κατὰ πάντα G O L R = ככל (BH : "1 c mlt MSS G S T 2 S 7, 22"; so Rothstein, Rehm, p. 69).

(c) כ and מ

II 6.18 אף כי : καὶ τίς G O L (in doublet) R = אף מי (Rehm, p. 59).

13.9 כעמי : ἐκ τοῦ λαοῦ G O L (in doublet) R = מ׳.

25.16 אלהים : ἐπί σοι G O R = אליכה.

33.2 כתועבות : ἀπὸ ... τῶν βδελυγμάτων G O R = מ׳ (Rehm, p. 61).

Par's reading is superior in one case.

II 22.6 כי : ἀπό G O L R = מן, generally read (BH : "c Ec l ca 12 MSS G S 2 R 8,29"; Rehm, p. 71, etc.). Rudolph is at a loss to see how such a reading could have arisen. Was the development כי/כ/מ/מן ?

(ii) ד and ר

The confusion of these two letters is a hardy perennial in Heb textual criticism.

I 2.18 יריעות : Ελιωθ [2] = ידיעות.

v. 24 אשחור : Ασχω B, Ασδωδ O, Ασδωμ R (Δ/M) together point to an original Ασχωδ* (Ra.) = אשחוד.

v. 44 ירקעם : Ιεκλαν c₂ (Ια - B) for Ιεκδαν* (Goettsberger) = יקדעם, which Goettsberger reads according to Jos 15.56 (BH : "1 frt"). Rudolph makes the pertinent point that since the place or places are unknown there is hardly reason to change. It is interesting to note that in Jos B reads Ιαρεικαμ = Chron MT.

v. 49 מדמנה : Μαρμηνα G = מר׳.

v. 53 היתרי : Αιθαλειμ G O for Αιθαδειμ* = היתדים.

3.22f.; 4.42 נעריה : Νωαδια G O (R) = נעדיה (Rothstein).

4.5f. נערה : Αωδα(ς) G (the name is transposed in v. 5) from Νοοδα* = נעדה.

v. 6 חפר : Ηφαδ c₂ O R (-λ B A) = חפד.

v. 10 מרעה : γνῶσιν G O L R = מדעה (Curtis). BH posits מדע.

---

[1] See Part I, p. 164.

[2] See Part I, p. 143.

v. 14 גיא חרשים : $A\gamma\epsilon\alpha\delta\delta\alpha\epsilon\iota\rho$ B from $\Gamma\alpha\iota\alpha\delta\delta\alpha\sigma\epsilon\iota\mu$* (ג by ditto-graphy, ς lost before ε, ending assimilated to $M\alpha\chi\epsilon\iota\rho$ v. 11) = ג' חדשים.

5.13; 8.12 עבר : $\Omega\beta\eta\delta$ G (O) R, G O R = עבד (BH : "9 MSS*", "15 MSS ... S").

v. 27/6.1; 23.6 גרשון : $\Gamma\epsilon\delta\sigma\omega\nu$ G L = גד'.

6.12/27,19/34 ירחם : $I\delta\alpha\epsilon\rho$ G,[1] $H\alpha\alpha\lambda$ B, $H\delta\alpha\delta$ c₂ from $I\delta\alpha\alpha\mu$* = יר'.

v. 58/73 ראמות : $\Delta\alpha\beta\omega\rho$ G, influenced by the consonants of $\Delta\epsilon\beta\epsilon\rho\epsilon\iota$ (Albright, "List of Levitic Cities", p. 70) from $\Delta\alpha\beta\omega\theta$* = יר'. Frankel[2] and Gilbert[3] wrongly took $\Delta\epsilon\beta$. and $\Delta\alpha\beta$. as a doublet for דברת in v. 57/72.

v. 59/74 עבדון : $A\beta\alpha\rho\alpha\nu$ = עברן.[4]

7.10f. ידיעאל : $A\rho\iota\eta\lambda$ G from $I\alpha\rho\iota\eta\lambda$* by haplography = יר'.

v. 19 שמידע : $\Sigma\epsilon\mu\epsilon\iota\rho\alpha$ G O R = שמירע (Rothstein, BH).

v. 37 בצר : $\Sigma o\beta\alpha\lambda$ G from $\beta\alpha\sigma\alpha\delta$* ($\Delta/\Lambda$; cf. $B\alpha\sigma\alpha\nu$ R) via $\Sigma\alpha\beta\alpha\lambda$*, assimilated to the original $\Sigma o\upsilon\alpha\lambda$ v. 36 = בצד. Rothstein wrongly asks whether ר was read as part of ל. But "manchmal ist $\Delta = $ ד (statt ר) zu Λ verlesen oder verschrieben worden".[5]

ibid. בארא : $B\alpha\iota\epsilon\lambda\alpha$ c₂ (-αιλα B) from $B\epsilon\epsilon\delta\alpha$* ($A/\Lambda$) = באדא.

8.8 בערא : $B\alpha\alpha\delta\alpha$ c₂[6] = בעדא (BH : so "1 MS").

v. 15 וערד ועדר : $\kappa\alpha\iota$ $\Omega\rho\eta\rho$ $\kappa\alpha\iota$ $\Omega\delta\eta\delta$ G = וערר ועדד.

v. 22 עבר : $\Omega\beta\delta\eta$ G from $\Omega\beta\delta\eta\delta$ O R (BH, Ra.) = עבד.

v. 25 יפדיה : $I\epsilon\phi\epsilon\rho\epsilon\iota\alpha$ G = יפריה (BH).

11.38 מבחר : $M\epsilon\beta\alpha\alpha\lambda$ G from $M\epsilon\beta\alpha\alpha\delta$* = מבחד. Rehm, p. 58, claims a ר/ל error.

12.13/12 אלזבד : $E\lambda\iota\alpha\zeta\alpha\rho$ B S from $E\lambda\zeta\alpha\beta\alpha\rho$*, changed into a familiar name under the influence of $E\lambda\iota\alpha\beta$ v. 11 = אלזבר.

v. 22/21 הגדוד : $\tau o\nu$ $\gamma\epsilon\delta\delta o\upsilon\rho$ G O L (in doublet) R = הגדור.[7]

14.15 הצעדה : $\tau o\upsilon$ $\sigma\upsilon\nu\sigma\epsilon\iota\sigma\mu o\upsilon$ G O (L R) = הסערה (Wutz, p. 76). So reads the parallel II Rg 5.24 ($\sigma\upsilon\nu\kappa\lambda\epsilon\iota\sigma\mu o\upsilon$ B A).

17.21 אחד : $\epsilon\tau\iota$ G O L R = אחר. In II Rg 7.23 $\alpha\lambda\lambda o$ implies the same *Vorlage*. BH and Rehm, p. 111, so read.

18.3ff.; 19.16,19 הדדעזר : $A\delta\rho\alpha(\alpha)\zeta\alpha\rho$ G O L R = הדרעזר, so Heb mss. (BH). II Rg 8.3; 10.16,19 read the same.[8]

---

[1] See Part I, p. 162.

[2] *Vorstudien*, p. 75.

[3] *AJSL* xiii, p. 297 note 1.

[4] See p. 76 for the defective writing.

[5] Ziegler, *Beiträge*, p. 61.

[6] See Part I, p. 143 for B.

[7] Cf. Part I, p. 62.

[8] See Driver, *Samuel, ad loc.*

23.9 הרן : $E\delta a\nu$ c$_2$ ($A\iota\delta a\nu$ B* m) = הדן.

v. 19 יריהו : $I\delta o\upsilon\delta$ B from $I\delta o\upsilon a$* = ידוהו.

ibid.; 24.23 אמריה : $A\mu a\delta\iota a$ G R = אמדיה.

v. 23 עדר : $A\iota\delta a\theta$ G from $E\delta a\delta$* (δ/θ) = עדד. Cf. 24.30 below.

24.23 יריהו : $I\delta\iota\mu o\upsilon$ c$_2$, $I\eta\delta\epsilon\iota\mu o\upsilon$ B = ידימו (ה/מ).

v. 30 עדר : $Ha\lambda a$ c$_2$, $H\lambda a$ B from $H\delta a\delta$* = עדד.

25.2 זכור : $\Sigma a\kappa\chi o\upsilon s$ B from -$o\upsilon\delta$* via -$o\upsilon\theta$* = זכוד. Wutz, p. 20, claims a ρ/s error. See the instance in v. 10 below.

v. 4 ירימות : $A\mu\sigma o\upsilon$.[1]

ibid., 31 עזר : $\Omega\delta$ G, -$\omega\theta$ B$^{ab\ vid}$ c$_2$ from -$\omega\delta$* (Ra.) = עוד.

v. 10 זכור : $Za\kappa\kappa o\upsilon\theta$ B from $Za\kappa\kappa o\upsilon\delta$* = זכוד.

26.31 יריה : $To\upsilon\delta\epsilon\iota as$ G from $'Io\upsilon\delta\epsilon\iota as$* (BH, wrongly citing as "G^B", Ra.) = ידיה.

27.9 עירא : $'O\delta o\upsilon\iota as$ G (L R) = עדיא (Rehm, p. 59).

v. 29 בשרון : $\epsilon\nu\ \tau\hat{\omega}\ A\sigma\epsilon\iota\delta\omega\nu$ G probably from ... $\Sigma\epsilon\iota\delta\omega\nu$*, assimilated to $A\sigma\epsilon\iota\eta\rho$ v. 21 (11 lines away in BM) = בשדון.

II 14.12f./13f. גרר : $\Gamma\epsilon\delta\omega\rho$ G O R = גדר.

16.2,4 הדד : $A\delta\epsilon\rho$ G O L R (so III Rg 15. 18,20) = הדר with "Var^G" (BH). Heb mss. so read in Ki.[2]

28.12 עזריהו : $O\upsilon\delta\epsilon\iota a$ B = עודיהו.

29.12 גרשני : $\Gamma\epsilon\delta\sigma\omega\nu\epsilon\iota$ G (O L) R = גד'.

31.15 בערי : $\delta\iota\grave{a}\ \chi\epsilon\iota\rho\acute{o}s$ G O L (in doublet) R = בידי (Curtis) via בעדי. This is more likely than על-ידי (Benzinger, who so reads : see Rudolph) or על-יד (BH).

II Ki 23.24/35.19a (קדשים[3]) : $\kappa a\rho a\sigma\epsilon\iota\mu$ G = קר'.

Ki 33/36.2c רבלה : $\Delta a\beta\lambda a\theta a$.[4]

In a few cases Par's reading is superior to MT.

I 1.6 ודיפת : $\kappa a\grave{\iota}\ E\rho\epsilon\iota\phi a\theta$ G from κ. $I\epsilon\rho\epsilon\iota\phi a\theta$* = יריפת ($\kappa a\acute{\iota}$ is a subsequent addition), an error for וריפת, which is generally read "c ca 30 MSS G [sic] V Gn 10, 3" (BH).

4.39 גדר : $\Gamma\epsilon\rho a\rho a$ G O L = גררה. גרר is to be read with Kittel, Curtis, Myers (cf. Rudolph). Cf. the *Vorlage* error in II 14.12f./13f. above. Has MT been influenced by גדור v. 18 in the preceding column (22 lines away in BH)?

---

[1] See p. 77; Part I, p. 163.

[2] See Montgomery, *Kings*, ad loc.

[3] See Part I, p. 213.

[4] See p. 95.

8.12 שׁמד : $\Sigma\epsilon\mu\eta\rho$ c₂ ($\Sigma\eta$- B) = שׁמר (BH "Ec 1 mlt MSS G^{BA} S T"), to be read with Noth, p. 259.

9.42 יערה‚¹‚² : $Ia\delta a$ G O R = יעדה, to be read with Rudolph; cf. BH "1 c ca 15 MSS יעדה vel c 8,36 יהועדה".[1]

24.27 עברי : $A\beta ai$ G from $A\beta\delta\iota$* (Ra., = $A\beta\delta\eta$ g) = עבדי, to be read with Rothstein and Noth, p. 252, as in 6.29; II 29.12.

(iii) ה, ח and ת

I 2.29 אביהיל : $A\beta\epsilon\iota\chi aia$ G for $A\beta\epsilon\iota\chi ai\lambda$* (Rothstein, BH, Ra.) = אביחיל, read by Curtis, Rothstein, BH "c mlt MSS ... S T". But MT is explicable, as Rudolph observes, referring to Noth, p. 39f.

4.5 חלאה : $\Theta oa\delta a$ (transposed) B for $\Theta o\lambda aa$* = תלאה.

v. 22 לחם : $a\vec{v}\tau o\acute{v}s$ G O R = להם.

6.45/60 ענתות : $A\gamma\chi\omega\chi$ G by internal assimilation from $A\gamma\chi\omega\theta$ g (Albright, "List of Levitic Cities", p. 67) = ענחות. Albright considers -$\gamma\chi$- a change by phonetic dissimilation from $Av\theta\omega\theta$*, but Par has the standard $Ava\theta\omega\theta$ in 7.8. More probably the *Vorlage* read otherwise.

7.24 ובתו שׁארה : κai $\vec{\epsilon}v$ $\vec{\epsilon}\kappa\epsilon\acute{\iota}voi s$ $\tau o\hat{\iota} s$ $\kappa a\tau a\lambda o\acute{\iota}\pi oi s$ G = ש'(א)ובהי. Frankel supposed that בתו' = בתוך was read, but then had to assume that $\vec{\epsilon}\kappa$. was secondary.[2]

11.8 יחיה : κai $\vec{\epsilon}\lambda a\beta\epsilon v$.[3]

12.41/40 לחם : $a\vec{v}\tau o\hat{\iota} s$ G O L R = להם (BH : "Ec 1 G"). Ziegler[4] and Rudolph so read.

21.29 בבמה : $\vec{\epsilon}v$ $Ba\mu\omega\theta$ B = בבמת (BH בבמות).

II 4.11 את־ : $\tau\grave{\eta}v$ $\vec{\epsilon}\sigma\chi\acute{a}\rho av$ G O L R = אח (Rehm, p. 59).

8.6 בעלת : $Ba\lambda aa$ B from $Baa\lambda a$* (Rehm, p. 59) = בעלה (Rehm).

20.22 ברנה ותהלה : $\tau\hat{\eta} s$ $ai v\acute{\epsilon}\sigma\epsilon\omega s$ $a\vec{v}\tau o\hat{v}$ $\tau\hat{\eta} s$ $\vec{\epsilon}\xi o\mu o\lambda o\gamma\acute{\eta}\sigma\epsilon\omega s$ G O = ברנתו תהלה.

24.27 המשׁא : $\pi\acute{\epsilon}v\tau\epsilon$, oi $\pi\acute{\epsilon}v\tau\epsilon$ [5] = חמשׁה.

25.8 אתה עשׁה חזק : $\vec{v}\pi o\lambda\acute{a}\beta\eta s$ ($\tau o\hat{v}$) $\kappa a\tau i\sigma\chi\hat{v}\sigma ai$ G O L R = אתעשׁת חזק (via אַת עשׂה). Cf. Ecclus 3.24 עשׁתוני : $\vec{v}\pi\acute{o}\lambda\eta\psi i s$. Oettli assumed and accepted תאמר ... אחזק on the basis of Par. BH reads "c G L V" אתה תחשׁב לחזק. Rudolph rightly condemns this proposal as graphically impossible and considers plausible Hitzig's suggestion

---

[1] See p. 94.

[2] *Vorstudien*, p. 215.

[3] See Part I, p. 129.

[4] *Beiträge*, p. 57.

[5] See Part I, p. 148.

אתה עשׂה חֹזק. G.R. Driver agrees and regards Par as confirmation.[1] In a private communication he renders the revised Heb "if you are assuming strength" and notes that "ὑπολαμβάνειν is commonly used of assuming something, esp. something false, in an argument". He thus regards the Gk as a paraphrase, but this is less likely than the suggestion above. So far as the Heb is concerned, a better solution than Hitzig's has not been found, but it labours under the difficulty that חֹזק does not appear to be a military term at all and is not used in Chron.

28.22 (המלך) הוא : καὶ εἶπεν G O L R = חוא(ו). cf. Dan 2.10 להחויה : εἰπεῖν (LXX). According to Curtis Par read אמר for אחז which follows המ׳, but both the order of words and the palaeographical difference run counter to his suggestion.

29.12 זמה : Ζεμμαθ G O = זמת.

II Ki 24.4/36.5d לסלח : τοῦ ἐξολεθρεῦσαι αὐτούς G O L R = לסלח. Cf. Lam. 1.15 סלה : ἐξῆρεν. The meaning is completely reversed : God's mercy is substituted for wrath. Rehm, p. 58, posits לכלותם.

In one case Par has preserved the correct reading.

II 32.22 וינהלם : καὶ κατέπαυσεν αὐτούς G O L R = וינח להם, which is generally read. Wrong joining of words was probably the initial cause of the error. Curtis notes the frequency of the restored phrase in Chron.

(iv) ו and י

S.R. Driver gave numerous examples of this confusion in various parts of the LXX.[2]

I 1.39 אחות : Αιλαθ[3] from אחית.

2.25 בונה : Βαναια G = בניה (BH).

v. 47 יהדי : Ἰησοῦ G, probably from Ιαδου*, assimilated to Ἰησοῦν/οὖς v. 38 = יהדו.

v. 53 הפותי : Μειφειθειμ G O R from Ηφ.*[4] = הפיתים.

v. 55 Kethib ישבו : κατοικοῦντες G O (L) R = Qere ישבי.

3.21 בני[1-4]; 4.16; 7.12 : υἱὸς αὐτοῦ G O L R, G, G O L R = בנו (BH : "MS[Ken 207] G V"), (BH), (Rothstein, BH). In the third case Curtis and Rudolph follow Klostermann in reading בנו, emending the following אחר to אחד.

---

[1] *Textus* iv, p. 90.

[2] *Samuel*, p. lxv f.

[3] See p. 84.

[4] See Part I, p. 144.

ibid. ישעיה; 6.15/30 עשיה : $I\sigma\alpha\beta\alpha$ B = ישעוה, $A\sigma\alpha\beta\alpha$ B = עשוה.

4.2 אחומי : $A\chi\epsilon\iota\mu\epsilon\iota$ G ≐ אחימי (Rothstein, BH).

v. 8 הרום : $I\alpha\rho\epsilon\iota\mu$ B O[1] = הרים.

v. 17 מרים : $M\alpha\iota\omega\nu$ B A from $M\alpha\rho\omega\mu$ n (*P/I*, ending assimilated to $A\mu\omega\nu$) = מרום.

v. 20 Kethib תולון : $I\nu\omega\nu$ G from $\Theta\iota\lambda\omega\nu$ O (Ra.) = Qere תילון.

v. 30; 12.1,21/20 ציקלג : $\Omega\kappa\lambda\alpha$ G, $\Sigma\omega\kappa\lambda\alpha$ B S, $\Sigma\omega\kappa\alpha\gamma$ S* from $\Sigma\omega\kappa\lambda\alpha\gamma$* (Ra. in the last two cases only) = צוק'. In the first case c was lost before ω and the ending was influenced by $E\rho\mu\alpha$; Gilbert wrongly saw a צ/ע error.[2] In the second case the ending was influenced by $M\epsilon\iota\nu\alpha\beta\epsilon\iota\alpha$ 11.47.

5.1 בני : $\tau\hat{\omega}$ $\upsilon\hat{\iota}\hat{\omega}$ $\alpha\hat{\upsilon}\tau o\hat{\upsilon}$ G O = בנו (BH).

v. 4 בנו[1] : $B\alpha\nu\alpha\iota\alpha$ = בניה.[3]

v. 10 וישבו : $\kappa\alpha\tau o\iota\kappa o\hat{\upsilon}\nu\tau\epsilon\varsigma$ G O R = יושבי.

v. 13 זיע : $Zo\upsilon\epsilon$ G O = זוע (Rothstein, BH).

v. 14 יחדו : $I\delta\alpha\iota$ (transposed) G from $I\alpha\delta\alpha\iota$ O = יחדי. Note BH : "Ec l יחדי K, יחדו Q; B(omb.) יחדי".

v. 16 שרון : $\Gamma\epsilon\rho\iota\alpha\nu$ c_2 (-μ B) for $\Sigma\epsilon\rho\iota\alpha\nu$* (Kittel, Rothstein, BH : c/r) = שרין, adopted by Kittel, Benzinger and Curtis. But MT is to be retained.[4]

6.19/34 תוח : $\Theta\epsilon\iota\epsilon$ G = תיח (BH).

v. 60/75 חוקק : $I\kappa\alpha\kappa$ G b = חיקק. Albright, "List of Levitic Cities", p. 71, assumes from the Gk that the vowel letter is secondary, but this does not follow.

7.7 עירי : $O\upsilon\rho\epsilon\iota$ G O R = עורי (Rothstein, BH).

v. 17 בני : $\upsilon\hat{\iota}\hat{o}\varsigma$ $\alpha\hat{\upsilon}\tau o\hat{\upsilon}$ G O = בנו (Rothstein).

v. 20 בנו : $\upsilon\hat{\iota}o\hat{\iota}$ G = בני.

v. 23 בביתו : $\hat{\epsilon}\nu$ $o\check{\iota}\kappa\omega$ $\mu o\upsilon$ G O R = בביתי (Rothstein, BH).

v. 25 בנו ו[1,2] : $\upsilon\hat{\iota}o\hat{\iota}$ $\alpha\hat{\upsilon}\tau o\hat{\upsilon}$ G[5], G O R = בניו.

v. 26/26f. בנו[1,2,3] : $\upsilon\hat{\iota}o\hat{\iota}$ G O, G G = בני.[6]

v. 27 בנו[1] : $\upsilon\hat{\iota}o\hat{\iota}$ G = בני.

v. 29 מגדו : $M\alpha\gamma\epsilon\delta\delta\epsilon\iota$ B = מגדי.

v. 33 ובמהל : $I\mu\alpha\beta\alpha\eta\lambda$ B from $I\beta\alpha\mu\alpha\eta\lambda$* = יב'.

ibid. עשות : $A\sigma\epsilon\iota\theta$ G O = עשית (Rothstein, BH).

---

[1] See Part I, p. 161.

[2] *AJSL* xiii, p. 285.

[3] See p. 84; Part I, p. 162.

[4] See Rudolph, *ad loc.*; Simons, *Geographical Texts*, p. 123.

[5] For B* see Part I, p. 156.

[6] See Part I, p. 162.

v. 36   וחרנפר‎ : (ι) *Αναρφαρ*.[1]

8.1   ואחרח‎ : *Ιαφαηλ* G, influenced by *Ιαφαληλ* 7.33 = יא׳‎.

v. 36f.   מוצא‎ : *Μαισα* B O R = מיצא‎ (Rothstein).

v. 39   אולם‎ : *Αιλαμ* G R = אילם‎ (Rothstein, BH). So in v. 40 *Αιλειμ* G from *Αιλαμ* R (Ra.).

ibid.   יעוש‎ : *Ιαις* c₂ (*Γαγ* B for *Ιαι**) = יעיש‎.

9.6   יעואל‎ : *Ιειηλ* c₂ O R (*Επειηλ* B for *Ειιειηλ**) = יעיאל‎ (BH : "G T"). The forms are alternatives (Noth, p. 246).

v. 16   ידותון‎ : *Ιθων* c₂ (*Ιωθ-* B) from *Ιδιθων* c (Ra.) = ידיתון‎. So 16.41 *Ιδειθων* G, 42 *Ιδ.* B S (BH); 25.1,3 (thrice), 6 *Ιδ.* G (BH); II 29.14 *Εδειθωμ* B from *Ιδιθων** (Ra.) (BH). The forms are alternatives (Noth, p. 244).

v. 26   והיו‎ : *ἦσαν* G O R = probably יהיו‎. Then ו‎ is not omitted *contra* Curtis. Cf. יהיה‎ : *ἦσαν* G O v. 24, for which Rothstein unnecessarily posited היו‎.

v. 35   Kethib יעואל‎ : *Ιειηλ* c₂ O L (*Ιεηλ* S, *Ειιηλ* B) = Qere יעיאל‎ (BH : "Q Ec l G V T"). Rudolph so reads. See 9.6 above.

v. 36   צור‎ : *Ισειρ* G O from *Σιρ* R (Ra.) by dittography = ציר‎.

10.7   נסו‎ : *ἔφυγεν Ισραηλ* = נס י׳‎.[2]

11.6   יהיה‎ : *καὶ ἔσται* G O e₂ = והיה‎.

v. 28   עירא‎ : *Ωρα* c₂ R (-αι B O) = עורא‎.

v. 44   Kethib יעואל‎ : *Ιεια* G from *Ιειηλ* O L R (Ra.; Λ/Δ and η dropped after ει) = Qere יעיאל‎ (BH : "Q G V T"). Rothstein and Rudolph so read, comparing 9.35. See 9.6 above. Rothstein wrongly suggests יעיה‎ as the basis of G.

v. 46   בני‎ : *υἱοῦ αὐτοῦ* G O R = בנו‎ (BH).

14.4   ושובב‎ : *Ισοβααμ* S (-βοαμ B c₂) from *Ισοβαβ**, assimilated to *Σαμαα* = ישובב‎ (Rehm, p. 58). Goettsberger wrongly posits an initial איש‎.

15.17   קושיהו‎ : *Κεισαιου* G O R = קישיהו‎ (cf. BH "G קישיה ‎").

16.32   יעליץ‎ : *καὶ ξύλον*[3] G O L (in doublet) R = ועץ‎.

17.14   במלכותי‎ : *ἐν τῇ βασιλείᾳ αὐτοῦ* G O L R = במלכותו‎, influenced by מלכותו‎ v. 11.

20.4   ספי‎ : *Σαφουτ*[4] = ספו‎.

23.9   Kethib שלמות‎ : *Αλωθειμ* G from *Σαλωμειθ* O (Curtis, Ra.) =

---

[1] See p. 28.

[2] See p. 84.

[3] B omits καί : see p. 47.

[4] See Part I, p. 163.

Qere שְׁלמִית (BH : "Q G^{AL} V T"). Noth followed by Rudolph, regards the Kethib as correct, taking the Qere as the feminine form of שְׁלמה.[1]

24.27 וְשהם : *Ισοαμ* G (O) = יְשהם. BH's note "dl ו c G", followed by Rudolph, is ill-founded.

25.4 מלותי : *Μανθει* B from *Μαλιθι** (*ΛΙ/Ν*) = *Μαλλιθι* L = מְליתי.

25.28 הותיר : *Ηθηρ* c₂ (*Ηθει* B, influenced by -θει v. 29) = *Ηθιρ* R = היתיר.

26.2 יתניאל : *Ιενουηλ* G from *Ιθνουηλ** (*Θ/Ε*) = יתנואל.

v. 3 עילם : *Ιωλαμ* G = עולם (Rothstein; ι = ע).

v. 14 בנו : *υἱοί* B h R = בְּני.

27.21 ידו : *Ιαδδαι* B O L R = ידי.

v. 34 אחרי : *μετὰ τοῦτον*[2] = אֲחרן.

II 3.4 אולם : *αιλαμ* G O L R = אילם (BH), as in Ezek. 40.[3]

v. 7 קירותיו : *τὰ ὀροφώματα* G O L R = קור'.

6.19 תחנתו : *τὴν δέησίν μου* G O R, as III Rg 8.28 = תחנתי (Rehm, p. 38) probably in both *Vorlagen*.

12.11 והשבום : *καὶ οἱ ἐπιστρέφοντες* G O L (in doublet) R = והשבים (Rehm, p. 60).

18.12 דברי : *ἐλάλησαν* G O L R = דברו (BH); so read the *Vorlage* of III Rg 22.13 *λαλοῦσιν* (Rehm, p. 40).

20.16 ירואל : *Ιεριηλ* G O L R = יריאל (BH).

23.14 פקודי : *τοῖς ἀρχηγοῖς* G O R = פְקידי ? So claim and read Curtis and BH, but cf. not only פְּקדי֜ II Ki 11.15 but also פקודי החיל Num 31.14.

24.26 שמרית : *Σομαιωθ* B for *Σομαρωθ** (Ra., Rehm, p. 61) = שְׁמרות.

26.11; 29.13 Kethib יעואל : *Ιειηλ* B O L R, (B) O L R = Qere יעיאל (BH : "Q G V T"). See I 9.6 above.

29.14 Kethib יחואל : *Ιειηλ* B O L R = Qere יחיאל (BH : "Q G V T"). Rudolph so reads, but Noth, p. 206, explains as an alternative form.

30.9 נלשוב : *καὶ ἐπιστρέψει* G O L R = ולשיב. For the form cf. 31.10 below.

31.10 לביא : *φέρεσθαι* G O L R = לבוא ?

v. 15 על־ידו : *διὰ χειρός* G O L R = על־ידי.

35.13 ויריצו : *καὶ ἔδραμον* G O L R = וירוצו.

In certain cases Par's reading is superior to MT.

I 1.40 עלין : *Σωλαμ* G from *Γωλαν** (cf. *Γωλαμ* O, hardly a ע/צ

[1] *Op. cit.*, p. 165.

[2] See Part I, p. 163.

[3] See Montgomery, *Kings*, p. 147.

error, as Gilbert claimed ¹) = עוֹלִן, transposed from עֵלֹון, which is generally read "c mlt MSS G^L Gn 36, 23" (BH).

4.7   Kethib יצחר : καὶ Σααρ G O = Qere וצחר, generally read, e.g. by Noth, p. 255.

6.20/35   Kethib ציף : Σουφ G O (L) R = Qere ציף, read by Curtis and Rudolph : cf. צופי v. 11.

7.1   Kethib יָשִׁיב : Ιασσουρ B from Ιασουβ O L R (Ra.) = Qere יָשׁוב, read by Rudolph, comparing Num 26.24.

v. 10   Kethib יעיש : Ιαους B R = Qere יעוש, generally preferred as the usual form of name.

v. 31   Kethib ברזות : Βηζαιθ B from Βερζαιθ O (Ra.) via Βειζαιθ* (P/I, ει/η; hardly Βη[ρ]ζαιθ, as BH claims) = Qere ברזית, which is usually read.

v. 34   Kethib יחבה : καὶ Ωβαβ G from κ. Ωβα*² = Qere וחבה, which is usually read.

9.12   משלמית : Μασελμωθ G = משלמות, to be read with Neh 11.13 (Rudolph).

20.5   Kethib יעור : Ιαειρ N P L R = Qere יעיר, generally read. Cf. II Sam. 21.19 יערי in error for יעיר.

23.18; 26.28; II 11.20   שלמית : Σαλωμωθ G R, G O, Εμμωθ G from Σαλαμωθ*? = שלמות. See note on I 23.9 in previous list. Ziegler posits Ελεμωθ, Σελεμωθ in the last case.³

24.24   Kethib שמור : Σαμηρ G O R = Qere שמיר, to be read, e.g., with Curtis and Rudolph.

II 2.2   חורם : Χιραμ G O L R = חירם (BH : "nonn. MSS^Ken G V S"). So vv. 10-12/11-13; 4.11a, 16; 8.2,18; 9.21. Cf. I 14.1; II 4.11b; 9.10 where G O L R follow Kethib חירם, while the Qere is חור׳. Par's form is etymologically superior from a basic אחירם. Is MT's form, called "unexplained" by Montgomery,⁴ a ו/י error perpetuated by analogy with the name חור ?

12.1   כהכין : ὡς ἡτοιμάσθη G O L R = כהכון, to be read with Rudolph because of the word order and the lack of suffix or article with מלכות. Cf. BH "1 c V T", ignoring Par.

19.8   וישבו : τοὺς κατοικοῦντας G O L R = יושבי, usually read.

20.37   דדוהו : Ωδια G O from Δωδια R (Ra.) = דדיהו, to be read with Benzinger, Curtis, Noth, p. 240, and Rudolph.

---

¹ *AJSL* xiii, p. 297.

² See p. 27.

³ *Beiträge*, p. 72.

⁴ *Kings*, p. 138.

32.21 Kethib וּמִיצִיאוּ : καὶ τῶν ἐξελθόντων G O L (R) = Qere
וּמִיצִיאֵי, a necessary construct form.

35.3 Kethib מְבוּנִים : τοῖς δυνατοῖς[1] from Qere מְבִינִים, which is
generally read.

36.23 יְהוָה : ἔσται G O R = יִהְיֶה (BH). יְהִי is generally read with
Ezra 1.3; I Esdr 2.5 ἔστω.

(v) *Other errors of writing*

(a) ה *and* מ *or* ם

I 5.21 חֲמִשִּׁים : πεντακισ- G O R = חֲמִשָּׁה with one Heb ms. (BH). As
Rudolph observes, the larger number is more probable.

7.40 רָאשֵׁי הַנְּשִׂיאִם : ἄρχοντες ἡγούμενοι G O R = רָאשִׁים נ'.

12.21/20 אֱלִיהוּא : Ἐλιμουθ G. Rothstein posited אֱלִימוּת and BH
אֱלִיהוּד. The former's assumption of a מ/ה error is probably correct.
But two possibilities concerning θ are more probable. It may be a
corruption of c in a Hellenized form of name : cf. Ἐλίους for אֱלִיהוּא
Job 32.1, etc., and Φάλλους for פַלּוּא Exod 6.14; I Par 5.3. Alternatively
it may be a phonetic error for Δ, either corrupted in turn from A or
added by analogy with Αβιουδ for אֲבִיהוּא.

15.5 עֲשָׂרִים : δέκα G L (in doublet) = עֲשָׂרָה.

24.23 יְרִיהוּ : Ι(η)διμου G = יְדִימוֹ.[2]

II 5.5 אַתָּם : αὐτήν G O L R אֹתָהּ (Rehm, p. 59).

11.16 וְאַחֲרֵיהֶם : καὶ ἐξέβαλεν αὐτούς G O (L) R = probably וַאֲחֵרִמֵם.
Cf. the Talmudic Aphel of חרם in the sense "excommunicate". In
v. 14 ἐξέβαλλεν αὐτούς renders הַזְּנִיחַם, but the translator often uses
the same Gk verb for two adjacent Heb ones. חרם becomes in Par
ἀναθεματίζειν once and ἐξολεθρεύειν twice, but a different meaning
would obviously require a different translation.

(b) ו *and* ר

I 2.34f. יִרְחָע : Ιωχηλ G O, influenced by Ραμεηλ v. 33 = יוֹחָע (H.P.
Smith, *JBL* xxiv, p. 27).

3.20 יוֹשֵׁב חֶסֶד : Αροβασοκ B from Ιαροβαχοσοδ*? = יר'.

4.31 חֲצַר סוּסִים : Ημισυσεσοραμ from חֲצִי סְרְסָם.[3]

7.3 יוֹאֵל : Ραηλ G from Ιραηλ* before haplography = יְרָאֵל.

---

[1] See p. 32.

[2] See p. 114.

[3] See p. 76.

10.11   לְשָׁאוּל : τῷ Σαουλ καὶ τῷ Ισραηλ G O (L) R, going back to a reading לישראל, which was corrected at some stage.

11.8   ויואב : καὶ ἐπολέμησεν G O (in doublet) = ויארב.[1]

25.3,9   (ו)גדליה : Τουνα G from Γουλια* (Γ/Τ, ΛΙ/Ν) = גוליה (ד/ר/ו); Γαλουια G = גלויהו.

II 1.16   מקוא[1],[2] : ἡ τιμή G O L R = מִקְרָא (cf. Rehm, p. 59, מֶקַר); ἐμπορεύεσθαι[2] = מִקְרָא.

12.10   על־יד : ἐπ' αὐτόν G O L R = עליו (ד/ר/ו). III Rg 14.27 ἐπ' αὐτόν in a different exegetical setting implies the same *Vorlage*. Par paints an imaginative picture of Shishaq's setting guards to keep Rehoboam under close observation.

v. 11   ונשאום : οἱ φυλάσσοντες (transposed) G O L (in doublet) R = שמרים (Rehm, p. 60).

20.21   להדרת : ἐξομολογεῖσθαι G O L R = להדות, influenced by הודו later.

25.4   ככתוב : κατὰ τὴν διαθήκην ... καθὼς γέγραπται G O L R, implying a reading כברת which has been corrected at some stage.

(c)   ו *and* ז

The cases in I 25.4,31; II 28.12 have already been discussed.[3]

II 31.17   ואת : οὗτος G O L R = זאת, read by Kittel, BH. Rudolph rightly regards the *Vorlage* as a secondary simplification of the text.

(d)   ז *and* נ

I 2.26,28   אונם : Οζαμ G = אוזם (Wutz, p. 223).

8.7   עזא : Αανα c₂ (Ναανα B by dittography) = ענא.

23.10   זינא : Ζιζα G O L R = זיוא, generally read "c 1 MS ... cf. 11 et 4, 37" (BH).

ז and נ are confused in MT at I 6.43/57. חילן : Σελνα B (transposed), assimilated to Λαβνα[4] from Θαιλαν* (Θ/C)? = תילן (ח/ת)? חילן is read by "mlt MSS" (BH) and seems to be required by חיֿלן Jos 21.15.

(e)   נ *and* פ

I 3.7; 14.6   יפיע : Ιανουε G, Ιανουου G, probably from Ιανουε* (Rehm) = ינוע. These cases are mentioned by Rehm, pp. 58,92. On

---

[1] See Part I, p. 129.

[2] See Part I, p. 160.

[3] p. 114.

[4] Albright, "List of Levitic Cities", p. 66.

p. 52, note 1, he rightly derives II Rg.5.16 $Iava\theta(a)$ from $Iava\epsilon$*, implying a similar *Vorlage* יגע.

26.16 לשפים : εἰς δεύτερον G L (in doublet) R = לשנים.¹

II Ki 23.36/II 36.5 פדיה : Νηρείου G O R = נריה (BH, Rehm, pp. 48, 92).

(f) *Combination of letters*

וג and ת are twice confused, once in MT and once in Par.

I 1.39 תמנע : καὶ Ναμνα G = ונמנע.

II 14.9/10 צפתה : κατὰ βορρᾶν G O L R = צפונה (Rudolph). Wutz, p. 234, saw here a ת/ג error. צפ(ו)נה is often read, but only Rudolph has correctly specified the error.

(vi) *Phonetic errors*

(a) *Gutturals*

The instances in I 28.9; II 21.11 have been already mentioned.²

I 17.16 עד־הלם : ἕως αἰῶνος G O L R = עד עלם (BH), under the influence of ע/ע frequently in the context.

25.1 Qere הנבאים : τοὺς ἀποφθεγγομένους G O R = הנבעים. Cf. Psa 59/58.8 יביעון : ἀποφθέγξονται.

II 7.13 הארץ : τὸ ξύλον G O R = העץ.

9.25 אריות : θήλειαι G O L R = הריות, a form found in Hos 14.1. Cf. the parallel I Ki 5.6/III Rg 2. 46i ארות : τοκάδες = הרות. The *Vorlagen* were similar. It should be mentioned that Montgomery cites an Accadian verb *aru*, "to become pregnant" as the possible basis of both Rg and Par.³

---

¹ See p. 100.

² See p. 92f. The following notes in BH should be mentioned here: I 19.17 אליהם¹ : ἐπ' αὐτούς G O L R : " l c G עליהם; 2 S 10,17 חלאמה"; II 13.7 עליו : πρὸς αὐτόν G O L R : "l c pc MSS G V S T אליו"; 32.19 אל : ἐπί G O L R : "l c G על". BH assumes an unwarranted degree of literalistic consistency in Par. In the first case MT has a reading clearly linked with Sam and it is to be noted that for אל' 2 G e₂ render likewise, but it is unlikely that a different *Vorlage* underlies the rendering. In the second instance, it is significant that על later in the verse is also rendered πρός, again most probably depending upon the same Heb. V. 9 sheds interesting light upon the last case : ירושלימה is rendered ἐπὶ Ιερ., while על¹ becomes ἐπί and על² πρός. For all his lapses into literalism on occasions, the translator is no Aquila. His interpretations of אל and על may not be pressed to BH's conclusions.

³ *Kings, ad loc.*

(b) *Labials*

Although it is quite possible that confusion of ב and פ was a palaeo-graphical error, it may be listed for now as phonetic.

I 4.21 עבדת : *Εφραθ* G = עפרת. The translator doubtless found the corruption, and this is why he transliterated.

15.15 בכתפם : *κατὰ τὴν γραφήν* G O L (in doublet) R = בְּכְתָבָם (Wutz, p. 248, Rudolph). The latter complains that most commentators (e.g. Benzinger, Curtis, Rothstein, BH) assume that Par omits the Heb.

26.15 לבניו : *κατέναντι* G O L (in doublet) R = לפני (Rudolph *contra* Rothstein's לנגד) via לבנו. Rudolph notes that this rendering is frequent in Par. Its use not only here but also in v. 16 for לעמת is in keeping with the translator's technique.[1] For the error compare I Esdr 1.10 *ἔμπροσθεν* for לבני in II Chron 35.12.

28.1 השבטים : *τῶν κριτῶν* G O R = השפטים (BH).

II 20.25 פגרים : *σκῦλα*[2] from בגדים.

(c) *Sibilants*

I 14.15 הצעדה : *τοῦ συνσεισμοῦ* G O (L R) = הסערה.[3]

15.22 יסר : *ἄρχων* G O^mss L R = שר (Rothstein)[4] Cf. ישר read by eight Heb. mss.

II 33.3 מזבחות : *στήλας* G O L R = מצבות (Goettsberger, BH). There is a similar confusion in II Ki. 12.10.[5] The change here may be partly due to the frequent association of במות־מצבות־אשרים in the historical books.

(d) ה ... *and* י ...

II 26.11 עשה : *ποιοῦσαι* G O = עשי (BH : "B(omb.) 7 MSS G V S T עושי").

32.19 מעשה : *ἔργα* (G) O L R = מעשי (BH : "Hill 1 MS G T")

35.15 חוזה : *οἱ προφῆται* G O (L) R = חוזי (BH : "pc MSS G V S T"). I Esdr 1.14 *οἱ παρά* also implies this reading.

In some cases Par implies a reading superior to MT.

I 23.24 עשה : *ποιοῦντες* G O L R = עשי (BH : "1 c pl MSS G V T (S)").

---

[1] cf. Part I, p. 53.

[2] See p. 98.

[3] See p. 113.

[4] See p. 87.

[5] See Montgomery, *ad loc.*

II 24.12 עושה : τοῖς ποιοῦσιν G O L R = עושׂי (BH "1 c 14 MSS G V S T").

34.10 עשׂה : ποιούντων G O L R = עשׂי (BH "1 c pl MSS G V S V [sic]"). Cf. v. 10b and II Ki. 22.5.

v. 13 עשׂה : τῶν ποιούντων G O L R = עשׂי (BH : "1 c pl MSS G S T").

7. HAPLOGRAPHY AND DITTOGRAPHY

(i) The use of gaps between words in the Qumran literature rather suggests the demise of S.D.Luzzato's rule that copyists wrote a consonant only once when it ended one word and began the next. I.L. Seeligmann, however, cites J. Fischer's discovery of more than a hundred cases where the application of this ruling and hypercorrection underlies the LXX of the Pentateuch.[1] Würthwein still argues for this ruling from the form היהוה in the Lachish Ostraka, and suggests, albeit rather cautiously, that "it may well be that we should consider the many cases of haplography in the Old Testament in the light of this possibility".[2]

It is a fact, however it be explained, that Par presupposes over a hundred cases of this type of haplography and dittography, of which nearly twenty afford a text better than MT. First those instances will be listed in which Par's text is either inferior to, or offers no material improvement upon, MT.

I 2.25 (ו)אחיה : ἀδελφὸς αὐτοῦ G O R = אחיהו. BH posits אחיה.

v. 40 (ה)אלעשׂה : Εμας B from Ελαας* = אלעשׂ. This form then affected the name in v. 39. There was a ΛΑ/Μ error.

v. 55 יעבץ (Qere י) : Γαμες G = עמץ (מ/ב).

3.18 ומלכירם (ו) : no conjunction in G = מ'.

4.27 ולישמעי(ו) : no conjunction in G = לש'.

6.8/23 ואסיר (ו) : no conjunction G O L R = א'.

v. 9/24 ושׁאול (ו) : no conjunction in G O L R = שׁ'.

v. 13/28 ובני (ו) : no conjunction in G O R = ב'.

7.8 בני בכר[1,2] : υἱοὶ Αβαχει G, v. Αβαχειρ c₂ (Αμ. B, influenced by Μαχειρ vv. 14ff.), both forms from Ιαβαχειρ* = יבכר.

---

[1] *VT* xi, p. 210.

[2] *Text of the OT*, p. 72f.

ibid.   (ו) אביה : *Αβιουδ* B h = אביהו, as אביהוא is rendered in 5.29/6.3.[1] Rothstein wrongly posits אביהוד.

v. 20   ואלעדה (ו) : no conjunction in G O R = א'.

ibid.   ותחת (ו) : no conjunction in G O R = ת'.

v. 21   וזבד (ו) : no conjunction in G O R = ז'.

ibid.   ועזר (ו) : no conjunction in G O = ע'.

v. 25   ורשף (ו) : no conjunction in G R = ר'.

8.1   אשבל (ו) : καὶ ... G O L R = וא'.

v. 34   (י) בן : υἱοί G R = בני.

ibid.   מריב[1],[2] בעל : Μεριβααλ G O = מרי בעל (BH). So in 9.40a.

v. 39   יעוש (ו) : καὶ ... G O L R = וי'.

9.5   (ה) הבכור (ו) : πρωτότοκος αὐτοῦ G O L R = בכורו.

v. 19   (ב) קורא : Κωρηβ G = קוראב.

v. 32   (ה) בני : Βαναίας S O L R = בניה (BH).

v. 44   וישמעאל (ו) : no conjunction in G R = יש'.

11.19   (מ) מאלהי : ὁ θεός G O L R = מאלהים (Rehm, p. 58)? Rehm rightly marks with a query : μου may have fallen out before τοῦ.

v. 34   (ה) בני : Βενναίας B c₂ = בניה (Rehm, pp. 54, 115).

v. 41   (ה) אוריה : Ουρει G = אור' (Rehm, p. 58).

12.3   (ה) השמעה : (σ) Αμα G = שמע.[2] MT probably earlier had שמעה, a form found in II Sam. 13.3,32.

v. 18/17   (י) בכפי : χειρός G O L R = בכף.

15.6   (ה) עשיה : Ασαι G e₂ = עשי. Such short forms as זכרי for זכריה would encourage the retention of the error.

v. 21   ומקניהו (ו) : καὶ no conjunction in G = מ'.

16.9   זמרו (ו) : καὶ ... G O L R = וז'.

v. 10   מבקשי יהוה (י) : ζητοῦσα τὴν εὐδοκίαν αὐτοῦ G O L R = מבקש י'.[3]

18.5   דרמשק (מ) : ἐκ Δαμάσκου G O L R = מד' (Rehm, p. 58, with a query). Alternatively the preposition may have been added in translation.[4]

23.19   יהזיאל (י) : Οζιηλ G R = ח'. Curtis shows that it is unlikely that עזיאל was read, as Kittel, Rothstein and BH claim.

24.20   שובאל (י) : Ιωβαηλ G from Ισωβ.* = יש'. The note in BH is misplaced.

v. 25   (י) לבני : υἱός G = לבן.

---

[1] Cf. Part I, p. 136.

[2] See p. 96.

[3] See Part I, p. 121.

[4] Cf. Part I, p. 45.

v. 26   יעזיהו (י) : *Oζια* G O e₂ R = ע'. Rothstein and BH so read, but Rudolph, following Noth, shows that the change is unnecessary. The form in v. 27 was changed to match this one. It is conceivable that the error was Gk in both cases.

25.4   מתניהו עזיאל (ו) : καὶ … καί G O L R = ומ' וע'.

26.5   פעלתי (י) : *Iαφθοσαλαθει* c₂ (-σλααθι B) from *Iαφωαλαθι* * ? = יפ'.

26.22/21   (י) בני : *τοῦ υίοῦ* (B) c₂ = בן.[1]

v. 25   (ו) בנו : *υίός* G R = בן.

27.4   דודי (ה) : *Δωδεια* B * (c₂) = דודיה.

v. 7   אתריו (ו) : καὶ οἱ ἀδελφοί G O (L) R = ואחיו rather than ואחיהם (BH).

v. 15   חלדי (ה) : *Xολδια* B R = חלדיה.

II 1.9   עתה (ו) : καὶ νῦν G O L R = וע'.

v. 13   מלפני (מ) : πρὸ προσώπου G R = לפני (Rehm, p. 59).

4.16   אביו (ל) : (καὶ) ἀνήνεγκεν B O L = אביל. Rudolph, following Rehm, p. 59, and Goettsberger, assumes that ויבא was read. Orlinsky scoffs at this Wutzlike reasoning,[2] but offers no alternative solution. In support of the suggestion of the present writer, compare Isa 18.7 יובל : ἀνενεχθήσεται, and Jer 31/38.9 אובילם : ἀνάξω. MT evidently caused difficulty, as it did for O L R in 2.12/13. It is significant that Kittel and Goettsberger suggest reading אבי for אביו. Was this an ancient variant underlying the *Vorlage*, or did dittography displace ו?

6.23   ולהצדיק (ו) : *τοῦ δικαιῶσαι* G O = ל'.

v. 30   מכון (מ) : ἐξ ἑτοίμου G O L R = ממ', as in vv. 33.39 MT.

11.11   את־המצרות : αὐτὰς τειχήρεις G = מ' אתהם.

v. 23/22   ויבן (ו) : διενοεῖτο G O L R = יבן. This equivalent is found in Dan LXX 8-12. BH notes "ins c G V חשב", expressing a widely held opinion (see Curtis). Rudolph calls this "naiv" on grounds of improbable textual development, and inserts כונן earlier independently of Par. It may be that MT can stand as it is, as Kropat, p. 24, urges.

12.7   היה (ו) : καὶ … G O R = וה'.

13.10   ולא (ו) : conjunction omitted in G O L R = לא.

14.6/7   ויצליחו (ו) : καὶ εὐώδωσεν G O R = ויצלח.[3]

15.9   עמהם (מ) : μετ'αὐτοῦ G O L R = עמה.

17.6   דרכי (י) : ὁδῷ G O R = דרך.

v. 7   לבן (ו) : καὶ … G O L R = ול' (BH, wrongly citing merely "G^L").

---

[1] See Part I, p. 145.

[2] *JBL* lviii, p. 598.

[3] See Part I, p. 160.

19.2 (י) ‏ולשנאי‎ : ἦ μισουμένῳ G O L R = ‏ולשׂנא‎. BH wrongly posits ‏ולשׂנאי‎.

20.12 ‏אלהינו‎ (ו) : κύριε ὁ θεὸς ἡμῶν B O L R from καὶ*[1] ... = ‏וא'‎. The error was encouraged by the combination at vv. 6,19f.

v. 34; 21.6,13; 35.18 (י) ‏מלכי‎ : βασιλέως G O, G, G L, G L = ‏מלך‎ (BH and Rehm, p. 60, in second case).

21.11 ‏גם‎ (ו) : καὶ γάρ G O (L) R = ‏וגם‎.

v. 12 (י) ‏דככי‎ : ὁδῷ G O L R = ‏דרך‎.

23.13 ‏במבוא‎ (ו) : καὶ ... G O L R = ‏וב'‎ (BH, Rehm, p. 60), then the next ‏ו‎ was omitted.

ibid. (ו) ‏קשׁר‎ : ἐπιτίθεσθε G O R = ‏קשׁרו‎.

v. 17 ‏שׁברו‎ (ו) : καὶ ... G = ‏ושׁ'‎ (Rehm, p. 60).

25.4 ‏בתורה‎ (ב) : τοῦ νόμου G O L (R) = ‏ת'‎.

v. 22 (ו) ‏לאהליו‎ : εἰς τὸ σκήνωμα G Omss = ‏לאהל‎ via a defective ‏לאהלו‎ (Rehm, p. 61).

26.10 ‏ובשפלה‎ (ו) : no conjunction in G O L R = ‏בשׁ'‎.

28.5 (י) ‏מלך‎ : βασιλέων G p = ‏מלכי‎.

ibid. (ו) ‏נתן‎ : παρέδωκεν αὐτόν G O L R = ‏נתנו‎ (Benzinger, who so reads, Curtis).

v. 9 ‏נביא‎ (ה) : ὁ προφήτης G O = ‏הנ'‎.

29.1 ‏יחזקיהו‎(ו) : καὶ ... G O = ‏ויח'‎.

v. 3 ‏הוא‎ (ו) : καὶ ἐγένετο G O L R = ‏והוא‎.

v. 11 ‏עתה‎ (ממנו after ‏בני‎ was omitted in the Vorlage and after transposition) : καὶ νῦν G O L R = ‏וע'‎.

30.16 (מ) ‏הדם‎ : τὰ αἵματα G O L R = ‏הדמם‎. Contrast 29.22 ‏הדם‎ : τὸ αἵμα G O L R in a similar context.

31.6/5 ‏ובני‎ (ו) : no conjunction in G O L R = ‏בני‎ (BH).

v. 21 ‏עשׂה‎ (ו) : καὶ ... G L = ‏וע'‎.

34.22 (ה ‏שׁומר‎ : φυλάσσουσαν G O L R = ‏שׁומרה‎ (Rehm, p. 61).

36.6 ‏עליו‎ (ו) : καὶ ... G O L R = ‏וע'‎. The change occurred while ‏אלהיו‎ preceded as 'n MT, and so before material from Ki was added to the Vorlage.

v. 18 ‏הכל‎ (ו) : καὶ πάντα G = ‏והכל‎.

In a number of cases Par's reading is preferable to that of MT.

I 6.62/77 (ו) ‏רמונו‎ : Ρεμμων G O L R = ‏רמון‎, read by Benzinger, Kittel, Curtis, Rudolph : cf. Jos 19.13. But ‏דמנה‎ Jos 21.35, for which

---

[1] For this type of error via $\overline{κε}$ cf. Part I, p. 152.

BH reads רִמֹּנָה, may lend support to MT here as an orthographical variant.

9.13 מלאכת (ל) : εἰς ἐργασίαν G O R =: למ׳, read by Curtis, Rudolph, BH ("1 c V", ignoring Par) and Kropat, p. 58.

13.6 שם (ו) : ὄνομα αὐτοῦ G O (L) R = שמו, read by Rehm, p. 119, and Rudolph. Others read שמו עליו or שמו שם.

15.16 לשמחה (קול) : (φωνῇ) εὐφροσύνης G O R = ש׳ read by Curtis, Rothstein, BH.

v. 27 השר (ה) : ὁ ἄρχων (τῶν ῳᾠδῶν) G O L R = שׂר (BH). "Either the art. is to be omitted or read במשא instead of המשא, cf. v. 22" (Curtis).

17.11 כי מלאו : ὅταν πληρωθῶσιν G O L R = כי ימלאו, as in II Sam 7.12, read by BH, Rehm, p. 69. Rothstein considers MT original. The following ו with perfects probably requires an initial imperfect.

22.1 מזבח (ה) : τὸ θυσιαστήριον G O L R = המ׳, read by Rothstein and Rudolph.

25.3 חשביה (ו) : καὶ ... G O L R = וח׳, which is generally read. The error in MT occurred after the loss of ושמעי.[1]

29.11 לכל לראש : πᾶς βασιλεύς G O L (in doublet) R = לכל ראש (cf. BH : "8 MSS V (in 11b G frt aliter)"). Rudolph so reads on the evidence of the secondary version πάσης ἀρχῆς.[2] But the original rendering in Par also supports the change.

II 2.3/4 הנה (ו) : καὶ ἰδού G O L R = וה׳, read by Rehm, p. 70, comparing I Ki 5.19 והנני.

5.1 ואת (ו) : the conjunction is omitted in G O R = את, generally read (BH : "1 c G^{BA} V S 1 R 7, 51").

6.18 שמים (ה) : ὁ οὐρανός G O L R = הש׳, read by BH, Rehm, p. 71, with I Ki 8.27.

8.9 ושרי שלישיו : καὶ ἄρχοντες καὶ (οἱ) δυνατοί G O R = ושריו וש׳ which is usually read with I Ki 9.22. Rudolph notes that MT's phrase never occurs. As so often in Par the suffixes are omitted in translation.[3] Rehm, p. 70, explains MT as haplography of ו and a י/ו error in a defective script (ושרו read as ושרי). Compare the reading ושריו in Heb ms. Ken 530.

---

[1] See p. 138.

[2] See Part I, p. 152.

[3] Cf. Part I, p. 48.

11.4 (י) דברי : τοῦ λόγου G O L R = דבר, read by Rehm, p. 71, with I Ki 12.24. Cf. דבר in v. 2.

24.25 (י) בני : υἱοῦ G O R = בן, which is generally read. Cf. v. 22.

32.5 (ה) החומה : G O L R have no article = ח', read by Curtis and BH to suit אחרת.

34.21 (י) דבר : τῶν λόγων G O L R = דברי, read by Curtis and Rehm, p. 72, with II Ki 22.13. Eight Chron mss. so read.

(ii) Besides the special type of haplography and dittography involving the beginning and end of words there are also other kinds involving both single letters and words.

I 5.10 ההגראים : τοὺς παροίκους G O = הגרים (BH). Cf. ההגרים read by ms. Ken. 178

6.5/20 לבני : τῷ Λοβενι G O R = לל'.

7.26 לעדן : τῷ Λαδδαν B O (R) = לל'.

10.5 וימת is omitted in G by haplography (Curtis, Rothstein, BH; Benzinger followed Par).

v. 13 לשאול : ἐπηρώτησεν Σαουλ G O L R = לש' שאול.

11.31 בני בנימן : Βενιαμιν G O L R = בנימן (Rehm, p. 58).

15.21; 27.20; II 31.13 עוזיהו : 'Οζίας G O L R, 'Οζίου G O L, 'Οζίας G L ... עזיהו (BH : "1 c nonn MSS G"; "1 frt c nonn MSSKen G"; "nonn MSSKen GBL S A").

18.11 וממואב : καὶ Μωαβ G O L R = ומואב.

23.9 ללעדן : τῶν Εδαν G = לעדן. A supralinear ל became attached to the wrong word : ובני v. 10 is rendered καὶ τοῖς υἱοῖς G O R.

24.7 לידעיה : τῷ Αναιδεια G from τῷ Λαιδεια* = לל'. The name was corrupted into a Gk word "shamelessness".

27.21 לבנימן : τοῖς υἱοῖς Βεν. G O (L) R =: לבני בני.

v. 31 ההגרי : ὁ Γαρείτης G =: הג'.

28.3 לשמי : τοῦ ἐπονομάσαι τὸ ὄνομά μου ἐπ' αὐτῷ G O (L) R = לשם שמי עליו. Rothstein and BH falsely reconstruct as לקרא ש' ע'. Cf. II 12.13 לשום את־שמו : ἐπον. τὸ ὄν. αὐτοῦ G O L R.

II 2.3/4 בונה : ὁ υἱὸς αὐτοῦ οἰκοδομῶ G O L R = בֻּנֹה בנה.[1]

v. 8/9 להכין : πορεύσονται ἑτοιμάσαι G O L R = הלכין ל' by adapted dittography. BH posits ילכו ל'.

v. 13/14 בארגמן : καὶ ὑφαίνειν ἐν τῇ πορφύρᾳ G O L R. According to Curtis and Rehm, p. 59, לארג was read. What probably happened

---

[1] See p. 77.

was that after וּבְעֵצִים a copyist continued וּבָאֶרֶג but then realised his mistake and copied the word again correctly. The abandoned error was taken as an infinitive construct.

6.28 כֹל : κατὰ πᾶσαν G O L R = כֹּל (Rehm, p. 59).

13.12 יִשְׂרָאֵל אַל : Ἰσραηλ G O = יִשְׂ׳.

28.23 לָהֶם : αὐτοῖς τοίνυν G O (L R) = לָהֶן לָהֶם by adapted ditto-graphy. For confusion between the words cf. Ruth 1.13 הֲלָהֵן[1,2] : μὴ αὐτοὺς ... ἢ αὐτοῖς.

31.1 וּמְנַשֶּׁה : καὶ ἀπὸ Μαν. G O b R = וּממ׳.

v. 3 לְעֹלוֹת לְעֹלוֹת : εἰς τὰς ὁλοκαυτώσεις G O L (R) = לְעֹלוֹת. Curtis suggests dittography in MT, but this is less likely.

ibid., 35.26 כַּכָּתוּב : τὰς γεγραμμένας G O L, γεγραμμένα G O R = כָּתוּב according to Rehm, p. 61, with respect to the second case, but it is also possible that the translator is ignoring the preposition : cf. 34.32 כַּבְּרִית : διαθήκην G O R.

36.20 מֶלֶךְ is omitted before מַלְכוּת in G O L R.

In some cases Par's text is superior to MT.

I 8.31 καὶ Μακαλωθ G = וּמִקְלוֹת which fell out before the same word in v. 32 (Goettsberger, Rudolph, BH : "ins c G^BA V S 9, 37"). BH includes A by error.

II 1.13 לַבָּמָה : ἐκ Βαμα G O = מֵהַבָּמָה, which is usually read. Rudolph, following Ehrlich, explains the error as due to haplography of מה and a false supplementing with ל.

3.2 הַשֵּׁנִי בִּשְׁנַת : τῷ δευτέρῳ ἐν τῷ ἔτει G O L R = הַשֵּׁ׳ בִּשְׁנַת. בִּשְׁנִי is usually omitted "c 3 MSS G V S" (BH).

8.9 אֲשֶׁר, omitted in G O L R, is generally omitted "c 7 MSS G V S 1 R 9, 22" (BH). Goettsberger, Rehm, p. 70, and Rudolph regard it as a corrupted dittograph of יִשְׂרָאֵל.

v. 15 סָרוּ מִצְוֹת : παρῆλθον τὰς ἐντολάς G O L R = ממ׳ ס׳, which is generally read with three Heb MSS.

15.9 וּמְנַשֶּׁה : καὶ ἀπὸ Μαν. G O L R = וּממ׳, which seems required in the context "c Ec 14 + 2 MSS^Ken" (BH, ignoring Par).

25.4 כִּי is omitted before כ in G O L R. Kittel, *SBOT*, BH ("dl c G V 2 R 14, 6") and Rehm, p. 71, follow suit. Eissfeldt suggests that this is a "Worttorso" standing at the end of a line as a "custos" and mechanically incorporated by a copyist.[1]

30.11 וּמְנַשֶּׁה : καὶ ἀπὸ Μαν. G O R = וּממ׳, read by BH, without citing Par, and by Rudolph, as seems necessary in the context.

---

[1] *VT* ii, p. 89, cited by Rudolph.

8. Parablepsis

(i) *Omission in the* Vorlage *or by oversight of the translator*

In many cases the evidence of Par points either to a defective *Vorlage* or to carelessness on the translator's part whereby material was skipped over by homoeoteleuton or -arcton, or by loss of a line or lines.

(a) *Omission of syllables and single words*

I 9.4   בני מן־בני בן־בני : υἱοὶ υἱῶν B (c₂) = בני בני.

v. 9   כל־אלה אנשים : πάντες οἱ ἄνδρες G O = כל־האנ׳.

v. 26   (מ) הם (הל׳) G O R.

v. 32   מן (בני) G O L R, lost by pseudo-haplography. Rudolph follows Par.

12.32/31   לבוא (להמליך) G O R.

17.3   לאמר (לך ואמרת) G (except c₂}.

19.2   אל־חנון (לנחמו) G O R. The absence of the whole phrase from II Sam 10.2 most probably has no bearing upon this partial omission.

22.5   נא (־נה) G O L R.

v. 16   ויהי יהוה : καὶ κύριος G O L R = ויהוה.

24.27   בני (בנו) G.[1]

25.9   השני הוא : (σ)Ηνια G O R in doublet[2] = שניהו.

26.11   טבליהו ה־ : Ταβλαι ὁ B R = טבלי ה־.

28.8   אחריכם (לבניכם) G.

29.14   וכי מי : καὶ τίς G O R = ומי.

II 4.22/21   והמזמרות (והמזרקות) G O L R. For confusion between the two words cf. Jer 52.19 מזרקות : μασμαρωθ.

9.15   יעלה (על־ה) G O in doublet.[3]

v. 30   בירושלם (שלמה) G O R (Rehm, p. 60, explains the omission as parablepsis).

17.8   וטוביהו (וטוב) G O.

19.1   בשלום (לירושלם) G R.

22.2   שתים (־ים). Rehm, p. 60, thinks in terms of alphabetic numeration and suggests that ב was lost after כ.

26.10   אכרים (וכרמים) G O R.

28.15   וישקום (ויסכום) G O R.

---

[1] Cf. p. 52 on v. 26.

[2] See Part I, p. 163.

[3] Cf. Part I, p. 202.

v. 22f. אחז : ויזבח : אחז : ἐκζητήσω G O La. According to Curtis אמר אדרש was read. But although ἐκζητεῖν usually renders דרש in Par, there is no obvious palaeographical bridge between the two readings. Moreover, Curtis ignores the word order : the earlier εἶπεν stands for הוא, taken as הוּא.[1] It is clear that the translator did not have the present text before him. Did he read אחזבה after a copyist's eye and pen had slipped from ז to ו ? And did he render this *vox nihili* with the aid of the sound אחז- ? Rogers, p. 36f., ascribes the changes to the translator to correspond to his "exalted idea of sacrifice and of monotheism".

29.11   בני (... ממנו) G O L R. ἀφ' ἡμῶν at the end of v. 11 in G O R stands for מ׳ transposed to the end of the verse in the *Vorlage*. The addition of τῶν υἱῶν[3] G O L in v. 12 probably signifies a misplaced subsequent restoration.

30.26   כי (מימי) G O L R.

33.17   זבחים (העם) G O. κύριος G O for ליהוה in the next phrase shows that the *Vorlage* lacked the word. Rogers, p. 40, assigned the omission to the translator because it was cultically distasteful.

36.15   עליהם (אבותיהם) G O L R.

(b)   *Omission of phrases and clauses*

Rothstein at two points makes the interesting suggestion that Heb line omission is the cause of gaps in Par compared with MT. In I 1.47ff. he suggests the loss of three lines of twenty letters, and in 4.26 the loss of a twenty three letter line. The idea raises a fascinating question for investigation. Do instances of omission in Par fall into regular numerical patterns of Heb consonants which would reasonably indicate lines of different length in the *Vorlage* and its predecessors ?

The answer is an affirmative one. Very many instances, either as units or multiples, comprise averages of twelve, fifteen, nineteen and twenty three letters.[2] Sometimes homoeoteleuton or the like is involved, and sometimes not. It is probable that lines of these dimensions were a feature of the Heb ms. history behind Par.

The instances which average twelve letters will be considered first.

---

[1] See p. 116.

[2] Orlinsky (*JBL* lxi, pp. 89ff.) examined the Heb mss. reproduced photographically in Kahle's *Masoreten des Ostens* and *des Westens* and found that many columns had 11-13/14 letters to a line, while wider columns had c. 17, c. 23, c. 25, c. 30, c. 35 letters. He claimed that in Gen. 39.14 a single line of 29 letters or a double line of the more usual line had caused vertical dittography: that in Gen. 39.17 a 15 letter line accidentally fell out of MT and perhaps a twelve letter one in 4.8 ; and that in Jud. 11.37 a 29 letter line or double lines was again the cause of error in MT.

I 3.19   (זרבבל) ושמעי ובן־זרבבל G (13).

4.36   ועדיאל וישימאל G (13).

6.30f./45f.   (אמציה) בן חלקיה : בן אמצי G R (13). Curtis sees homoeoteleuton here. Ἀμεσσεια B refers to אמ' v. 30 *contra* Rothstein and BH who take it as referring to the name in v. 31.

7.16   ובניו אולם ורקם (ובני) G O (13). BH marks the omission as אולם ... (אולם), but Rothstein apportions it as above with greater probability. It is more likely that υἱὸς αὐτοῦ G O stands for בני (= בנו) in v. 17 than for בניו in v. 16.

9.28   (יביאום) ובמספר יוציאום G (13).

17.19   יהוה בעבור עבדך G O (13). Rogers, p. 12, imagines that the translator omitted to enhance David's humility.

23.32   ואת משמרת הקדש (ומשמרת) G O (12). Rudolph (cf. Curtis) sees here homoeoteleuton.

25.2   על יד־אסף הנביא G O (12). BH observes that הנ' is missing, a misleading note.

29.23   יהוה למלך תחת G O (11).

II 1.4   (לו) דויד כי נטה לו G O (11). Curtis finds homoeoteleuton here. BH marks the omission wrongly. In the view of Rogers, p. 19, the translator omitted as undignified for such a sacred object.

3.12 is completely omitted in G. Curtis ascribes the omission to Gk homoeoteleuton because of his poor view of B. The cause is more likely to have been Heb (לכנף הכרוב האחר) ends vv. 11,12). Sixty six letters are involved, probably representing five lines of about thirteen letters each.

6.19   (התפלה) אשר עבדך מתפלל B* (12).

15.3   וללא כהן מורה (וללא) G (11).

28.5   ויביאו דרמשק G (11).

29.15   (יהוה) לטהר בית יהוה G (11).

The next average centres on the number fifteen. It may well be that a single Heb ms. behind Par had lines ranging in length from eleven to sixteen letters.

I 1.17   ולוד — 24 ושם is missing in G. Rothstein, Goettsberger, Noth[1] and Rudolph ascribe the omission to homoeoteleuton (ארפכשד occurs in both places). Curtis, prejudiced by his view of B, claims an inner-Gk error, but Rothstein thinks that the translator's eye strayed. 127 letters are involved; it may well be that eight Heb lines of about sixteen letters were lost.

---

[1] *Überlieferungsgeschichtliche Studien I*, p. 117.

6.55/70 ‏(ואת־מג׳) ואת־יבלעם ואת־מגרשיה‎ G (16). Albright, "List of Levitic Cities", p. 69, erroneously comments : "That this omission of Ιεβλααμ is due to the error of a copyist in the immediate ancestry of B is proved by its appearance in related MSS". This surprising statement is clarified by a later comment (p. 73) that e g are both related to the B group. Albright based his conclusion upon insufficient study of ms. groupings.

v. 58/73 ‏(ואת־מג׳) ואת־ענם ואת־מגרשיה‎ G (15).

v. 63/78 ‏(ואת־מג׳) ואת־יהצה ואת־מגרשיה‎ G (16).

7.15 ‏ותהינה לצלפחד בנות‎ G (16).

9.27/26 ‏(האל׳) וסביבות בית האלהים‎ G O R (16).

15.2 ‏(יהוה) לשאת את־ארון יהוה‎ G (14).

16.29 ‏הבו ליהוה כבוד שמו‎ G (15).

21.5 ‏חרב ... ויהודה (חרב)‎ G N (32). Goettsberger, Rehm, p. 58, and Rudolph blame homoeoteleuton for the omission. Did a copyist's eye slip two lines of sixteen letters ? Curtis claims a gloss in MT from the use of Israel for the whole kingdom in v. 4 and from the absence from Par. It is interesting to note that he here ignores the reading of A, regular champion of A though he is.

23.5 ‏(ואר׳ אל׳) וארבעים אלפים שערים‎ B * N i (16).

25.6 ‏לעבדת בית האלהים‎ G O (14).

26.21 ‏(ללעדן) ראשיהאבות ללעדן‎ (14).[1] Ms. Ken. 164 also omits.

28.1 ‏ולבניו עם־הסריסים‎ G O (15).

v. 8 ‏ובאזני אלהינו שמרו‎ G (16). One of BH's marks of omission is misplaced.

29.26f./26 ‏(מלך) על־כל ישראל ... מלך (על־ישראל)‎ G O (28). Rehm, p. 59, gives homoeoteleuton as the cause of the omission, but homoeoarcton also was doubtless a factor. Was another the omission of two fourteen letter lines ?

II 2.9/10 ‏(בתי עש׳ אלף) בתים עשרים אלף‎ B (16).

7.5 ‏(אלף) מאה ועשרים אלף‎ G (16). Four Heb mss. also omit. Rehm, p. 40, notes that III Rg 8.63 omits as well.

15.2 ‏(אסא) ויאמר לו שמעוני אסא‎ G (15). B's text has already been discussed.[2] παντί later, meant to be construed with ἀπάντησιν, shows that the omission had either already taken place in the *Vorlage* or was perpetrated by the translator.

25.17 ‏(וישלח) וישלח ... וישלח‎ G (48). Homoeoteleuton caused the omission,

---

[1] See Part I, p. 145.

[2] See p. 26.

as Goettsberger and Myers note. Probably three lines of sixteen letters each were lost.

28.18   ואת־תמנה ובנותיה (ובנ׳) G (14).

35.19f.   יאשיהו ... נעשׂה (יאשׁיהו) G O^mss (33).[1] Doubtless two lines of approximately sixteen letters were lost by oversight.

The next average number of letters to be omitted is nineteen.

I 1.43   לפני מלך־מלך לבני ישׂראל G (19).[2]

v. 47   וימלך — v. 49 שׁאול is placed after v. 51a. Clearly homoeoteleu-ton of וימ׳ was a factor of earlier omission, as Rudolph observes. Rothstein suggests that the translator's eye dropped three lines of twenty letters each. The omitted words were subsequently inserted after the second וימת הדד instead of the first.

17.19   הזאת להדיע את־ כל־הגדלות (הגדולה) G O (19). Benzinger and Rudolph have seen homoeoteleuton here; the latter notes that one of BH's omission marks is misplaced.

II 23.9   יהוידע הכהן לשׂרי המאות G O (19).

29.22   המזבחה ... וישׁחטו (המז׳²) G (37). Probably two lines of eighteen and nineteen letters were overlooked.

The last length of line to be considered is one of twenty three letters.

I 3.4   וימלך ... חדשׁים G (23).

4. 26   בנו ... ובני (בנו²) G (23). Rothstein suggested the omission of a line of this length.

II 9.16   שׁלשׁ ... האחת G (24).

17.11   ותישׁים ... מאות (מאות) G (23).

Rothstein's observations about line omission are strikingly confirmed by a mass of evidence throughout Par. The coincidence of omission of certain numbers of letters often locates the stage of the error as pre-Gk.

There remains to be listed a number of other cases of parablepsis which are most probably to be attributed to the content or treatment of the *Vorlage*.

I 7.21   ושׁותלח בנו (בנו) B*. c₂ O R have Σωθελε υἱὸς αὐτοῦ, but in view of the form in v. 20 the Gk is probably not original.[3]

9.4   בן אמרי (בן עמרי) G O R. Curtis suggested that the omission was deliberate because the transliteration would be the same as before, but the first vowel at least could have been varied.

---

[1] See Part I, p. 214.

[2] See p. 22 for the earlier words.

[3] See p. 51.

24.21 לבני רחביהו (לרח') G O R. Benzinger deleted with Par, but Curtis and Rudolph observe that the style in vv. 20, 22 supports MT.
II 14.11/12 אסא ולפני (לפני) G O L R.
20.14 בן־בניה (בן) G.
28.20f. לקח (קח), read for MT חלק (חלק) כי : לא חזקו (ו) G O L R. Winckler wrongly posited ויקח for καὶ ἔλαβεν.[1]
32.7 אל־תיראו ו(אל) G O. One might think at first of a Gk line omission of thirteen letters : μὴ φοβήθητε L R καί*. But the regular rendering in Par is μὴ φοβεῖσθε μηδέ (20.15,17; cf. I 22.13; 28.20); and so the error must be pre-Gk.

(ii) *Parablepsis in MT*

Par contains a number of additions which seem not only to go back to its *Vorlage* but also to represent material which has dropped out of MT.

(a) *Omission of syllables and single words*

I 4.17 ותהר : καὶ ἐγέννησεν Ιεθερ G O (L) R. The Gk verb hardly represents MT since this equivalent is found here only in the whole LXX. Rothstein and Rudolph read with Par וילד יתר, assuming parablepsis of the first word after וילון. Then presumably יתר was manipulated into a verb to suit the following את. MT's unusual construction (contrast 7.23) and lack of feminine antecedent (but note that some commentators, listed by Curtis, insert v. 18b) point to Par's *Vorlage* as correct. Benzinger and Kittel read ויתר הוליד for ויל' ות', but not only does this suggestion violate the word order in G O R, as Rothstein notes, but the Heb textual development cannot be explained so simply.
v. 19 הודיה : τῆς Ἰουδαίας c₂ O (Rothstein; τ. Ἰδουίας B) = היהודיה, read by Rothstein and Rudolph; cf. v. 18.
11.2 אתה : + ἦσθα G O L R = הייתה, as in II Sam 5. 2, which probably dropped out of Chron (Rothstein, BH, Rehm, p. 69). The later, contrasted ואתה תהיה seems to require it.
12.34/33 ולעדר : + τῷ Δαυιδ G O L R = דויד, overlooked after דר (Rudolph). BH inserts.
15.18 ויעיאל : + καὶ Ὀζίας G O L R, which stands for ועזזיהו in v. 21. Par's text apparently always had the shorter form עזיהו when

---

[1] *Alttestamentliche Untersuchungen*, p. 166.

MT has the longer one.[1] Rothstein and Rudolph (cf. BH) insert וְעֻזִּיָּהוּ to correspond with v. 21. It apparently fell out by homoeoarton.

25.3 וִישַׁעְיָהוּ : + καὶ Σεμει G O = וְשִׁמְעִי, which is generally read with one Heb ms. in accord with v. 17. This brings the number up to the stated six.

26.1 אָסָף : Αβια Σαφαρ G from Αβιασαφ* (Ra.). The original form was corrupted to -σαρ (Φ/P).[2] A correction was later incorporated into the text. Thus אֲבִיאָסָף is presupposed : either that or אֲבִיסָף is generally read.

29.22 וַיִּמְשְׁחוּ : καὶ ἔχρισαν αὐτόν G O L R = וַיִּמְשָׁחוּהוּ, read by Rudolph (BH : "frt 1").

II 4.10 מַכְתֵּף : + τοῦ οἴκου G O L R = הַבַּיִת, which is read by Benzinger, BH, Rehm, p. 70, Rudolph "c nonn MSS G 1 R 7, 39" (BH). It fell out before הֵימָנִית.

18.13 אֱלֹהָי : + πρός με G O L R = אֵלַי, which Benzinger, Curtis, Rehm, p. 71, and Rudolph insert with I Ki 22.14.

33.20 בֵיתוֹ : ἐν παραδείσῳ οἴκου αὐτοῦ G O L R = בְגַן בּ', as in II Ki 21.18 (Rg ἐν τῷ κήπῳ ...). בְגַן fell out by homoeoarcton (Rudolph). Benzinger, Kittel, Curtis and BH also insert. MT can hardly be right, as Rudolph notes, but Myers sees assimilation in Par. Rehm, p. 71, explains the omission of בְגַן in Par as due to pseudo-haplography of גַ/ת, but recourse to this unusual error is unnecessary.

34.22 וַאֲשֶׁר : + εἶπεν G O L R = אָמַר, which is added by Benzinger, Kittel, Curtis, Goettsberger, Rehm, p. 88, and Rudolph (cf. BH).

35.11 מִידָם : τὸ αἷμα ἐκ χειρὸς αὐτῶν G O L R = הַדָּם מִידָם, fallen out by homoeoteleuton (Rudolph). Then transposition has occurred in Par : de manus suas sanguinen La has preserved the correct order. An object is required : cf. 29.22 ; 30.16.

(b) *Omission of phrases and clauses*

I 1.4 נֹחַ : + υἱοὶ Νωε G O R = בְּנֵי נֹחַ, added by Podechard,[3] Rothstein and Rudolph (BH "ins ... ?"). Rudolph aptly refers to vv. 28,34.

4.19 נַחַם : + καὶ Δαλια (Δαλειλα B) πατὴρ Κεειλα καὶ Σεμείων (Σεμεγων G) πατὴρ Ιωμαν καὶ Μαναημ (B ; υἱοὶ Ναημ O) G O. BH suggests, without adopting, a *Vorlage* (דלי(ל)ה אבי קעילה ושמעון(-יון)ו)

[1] See p. 130.

[2] Cf. Fischer, *Das Alphabet der LXX-Vorlage im Pentateuch*, p. 12, concerning Exod 6.24.

[3] *RB* xiii, p. 376.

אבי י(ו)מן ובני נחם. Curtis states that the addition in Par, if original, fell out by homoeoteleuton, but apparently considers that the difficult double relationship of אבי קעילה rules out its originality. Rudolph accepts the plus in Par as going back to an original ... דליה אבי ושימון אבי יומן ובני נ' א' ק. He regards the first קעילה as an obvious miswriting and leaves a blank for the name. Σεμειων he links with the same name in v. 20.

The present writer would agree with Rudolph that the plus is basically original. Δαλειλα in B has clearly been assimilated to Κεειλα. שמעון, posited by Rothstein and BH is hardly right : Par uses the standard form Συμεων for that name, e.g., in v. 24. As in v. 20 שמיון was read for שימון.[1] Μαναημ has already been considered.[2] The plus has an original ring : Shimon provides a good link with v. 20. But the second אבי ק' presents a problem beyond that mentioned by Curtis. One expects simply ק' as the first in the list of Naham's sons. Surely אבי is a case of automatic assimilation to the previous pattern "X father of Y" and should be struck out. But even so Curtis' difficulty remains : Naham was the father of Keilah and not "Daliah". One may cut the knot with Rudolph. But is there not a way of untying it ?

The present writer suggests that דליה is in fact a corruption of ילדה, which was taken for the name of a son and mistaken for the name which occurs in 3.24 in the previous column at no great distance from this point (23 lines away in BH). ילדה is a gloss referring to a different tradition or interpretation, namely that Naham and Shimon were the woman's sons. This is in fact what one would expect from what follows. Mention of first Naham's sons in v. 19b, then of Shimon's in v. 20a would flow on more naturally if this were the case. Moreover, the *Vorlage* of Par (but not the translator) certainly equated אשתו הי' in v. 18 and אשת הוד' in v. 19, apparently taking אשת as an absolute, as it appears to be occasionally in the Heb Old Testament. These factors seem to have encouraged the view that v. 19a is a list of sons supplementary to the list in v. 18a. By an attempt to carry through this impression אחות was glossed ילדה, the same verb as in v. 18, with the message that Naham was not to be regarded as her brother, but rather "she gave birth" to him. The gloss was incorporated into the text a little later in an adapted form.

6.44/59 After the phrase concerning עשן, Par adds και την Ατταν

---

[1] See p. 107.

[2] See p. 82.

καὶ τὰ περισπόρια αὐτῆς G, which corresponds to Jos 21.16 ואת־יטה
ואת־מגרשיה. The question arises at what stage the phrase fell out.
Did the compiler of Chron overlook it and a Heb reviser "restore" it?
There are a number of cases of Heb contamination from Jos 6. Or did
the Chronicler take over the phrase, which was subsequently lost in
MT? Probably the phrase is to be reinserted in Chron with Curtis,
Rothstein, BH ("יתה" is an error) and Rudolph. The Gk text has
suffered both revision and corruption. Ατταν goes back to an earlier
Ιατταν* before τήν was inserted.[1] The ending has been assimilated to
Ασαν, as Albright notes.[2] So originally Ιαττα* stood in Par.

v. 46/61 המטה (ממשפחת) : ἐκ τῆς φυλῆς G O R = ממטה. Cf. Jos
21.5 ממש' מטה for which BH reads למשפחתם ממטה (cf. Jos LXX
ἐκ τῆς φυλῆς for both words). BH reads ממטה in Chron and then
inserts אפרים וממטה דן ו from Jos. Was this material omitted from
Chron as a thirteen letter line? The omission occurred in both MT
and Par's text; but whereas in MT ממטה has been adapted to המטה
to fit the lacuna, Par's text had a non-adjusted ממטה. Moreover Δαν
G for גד in v. 63 seems to reflect an original דן present earlier in the
Vorlage's textual tradition, to which גד was assimilated.

25.9 הראשון : + υἱῶν αὐτοῦ καὶ ἀδελφῶν αὐτοῦ G O (L) R =
בניו ואחיו. Rudolph follows Oettli, Benzinger, Kittel and Curtis in in-
serting on the basis of Par ב' וא' שנים עשר after ליוסף. Curtis observes
that the number 288 in v. 7 and the analogy of the following verses
demand it. How is the position in Par's text to be accounted for? A
marginal note in a Heb ms. was apparently misplaced. The note was
doubtless abbreviated to fit into a little space, and was meant to
refer to the whole phrase. BH restores on the basis of Par הוא וא' וב' ש'
ע' according to v. 9b, but it is less easy to get this out of Par.

II 23.18 הלוים : + καὶ ἀνέστησεν τὰς ἐφημερίας τῶν ἱερέων καὶ
τῶν Λευιτῶν G O L R = ויעמד את־מחלקות הכהנים והלוים. The addition has much claim to originality. Curtis observes that it removes the
difficulty of חלק meaning "distribute" in the shorter text of MT and
that its vocabulary has the marks of the Chronicler. Rehm, p. 25,
notes that the relative clause does not make sense without it. Rudolph
compares the phraseology of 8.14 and states that Par's plus provides
a parallel with v. 19. It clearly fell out by homoeoteleuton.

---

[1] See Part I, p. 143.

[2] "List of Levitic Cities", p. 66.

CHAPTER FIVE

HEBREW TEXTUAL CHANGES (CONTINUED)

The purpose of this chapter is to put on record types of variants which are not so easily explained as those in the previous chapter. Finally the data concerning corruptions of letters in ch. iv will be used to estimate the kind of script in which the *Vorlage* was written, and various conclusions drawn earlier with regard to Par's Heb text will be gathered up.

1. Glosses

Variants in Par sometimes indicate the presence of correcting or explanatory glosses in the *Vorlage* or in MT.

(i) Vorlage *glosses*

I 4.12 נחש : + ἀδελφοῦ Εσελων (Αθθομ L, Σελων R) τοῦ Χενεζει (Κενεζι O, Κ(Χ)ενεζαίου L, Κενεζι καὶ Αχας R) G O L R. BH and Rudolph insert on the strength of Par אחי ... הקנזי, regretting that the name cannot be restored. Benzinger and Kittel also adopt as a connecting link with v. 13. Kittel recognised the difficulty of Εσ. being represented as the son of two fathers, Tehinnah and Kenaz, but he saw here a mixture of families.

Curtis considered that Εσ. is merely a corruption of Εσεθων = אשתון in v. 11, and that the phrase was an early gloss to connect with v. 13. But surely he has oversimplified matters. In v. 11 G O R read Ασ(σ)αθων for אשתון, and L Εσσαθων : it is significant that none of the groups identified the two names. May not the Heb name have been חצרון, misread as חצדון? Then ⲉⲥⲉⲗⲱⲛ* (cf. Εσερων G R for חצרון 2.18) was corrupted to ⲉⲥⲉⲗⲱⲛ.

Kittel's difficulty is a real one and casts doubt on the originality of the phrase. It may be suggested that it represents two misplaced, separate Heb glosses. They were meant to apply to v. 15, but entered the text at v. 12 because of the similarity of עירו אלה and עיר נחש אלה.

The second gloss gives כלב בן־יפנה the epithet הקנזי, as in Num. 32.12;
Jos 14.6,14, in order to link with the preceding verses (cf. Curtis'
remark : "The link connecting Caleb with Kenaz is apparently omitted
as well known"). The first gloss is an attempt to relate this Caleb to
כלב בן־חצרון of 2.18 : יפ׳, it claims, was the brother of חצ׳.

5.23 חרמון : + καὶ ἐν τῷ Λιβάνῳ G O L (R) = ובלבנון (Rothstein,
BH). Rothstein considered the addition original, claiming that המה רבו
hangs in the air without it (cf. BH "ins ?"). But Curtis termed it
"doubtless a gloss". It is significant that בעל חרמון occurs elsewhere in
the OT only at Jud 3.3, where it is said to be part of the Lebanon
range. That reference probably inspired a geographical gloss here,
which was later incorporated into the list. This led to the new clause
division found in Par and to the omission of בארץ as superfluous.
Theoretically it could have fallen out of MT by homoeoteleuton of יי,
but its originality is unlikely.

19.9 באו : + παρενέβαλον G O L R = חנו or ערכו according to
Rothstein. Probably this represents a misplaced gloss in the *Vorlage*.
In v. 6 (ובני עמון) חנון was read as חנן (*Avav* G O (L) R). It was glossed
חנון, but the gloss became attached to בני עמון in v. 9, and was inserted
as חנו at the most convenient place.

v. 15 מפני אבשי אחיו : ἀπὸ προσώπου Ιωαβ καὶ ἀ. π. ἀδελφοῦ αὐτοῦ
B S m. The repetition of the prepositional phrase suggests that the
variant is Heb in origin. It may be suggested that יואב was originally
an explanatory gloss on the suffix of אחיו (for a modern parallel cf.
Rudolph's suggestion to read אחי יואב for אחיו). The gloss came into
the text, displacing אבשי, ומפני was then inserted before אחיו since a
reference to Joab's brother is necessary as the opponent of Ammon.
BH suggests on the basis of Par that מפני יואב has dropped out of MT
earlier in the verse, but the textual development would not be so easy
to explain.

20.7 אחי : υἱὸς ἀδελφοῦ G = בן אחי. The Gk text reads as if the
phrase qualifies Jonathan. But the *Vorlage* contained an incorporated
gloss identifying שמעא with David's son of that name in 3.5 instead of
David's brother. Rehm, p. 19, wrongly claims a Gk addition.

24.3 בעבדתם : + κατ' οἴκους πατριῶν αὐτῶν G O = לבית אבותם
(Rothstein, BH). Rothstein observes that it may have dropped out of
MT. But it is surely rather a correcting gloss on לבית אבות in v. 4,
where BH notes "l c 5 MSS S אבותם". Rudolph explains the omission
of the suffix in v. 4 as a case of pseudo-haplography of מ/ש.

26.6 הממשלים : τοῦ πρωτοτόκου Ρωσαι G (O) R. The first term

represents הבכור, a misplaced gloss on בנו, derived from v. 4. The second term stands for ראשׁ, an abbreviation for ראשׁים,[1] an explanatory gloss on the rare המ׳, as BH notes. Because it was taken as a name, אבי(הם) becomes αὐτοῦ in G O.

v. 14 בשׁכל (יועץ) : τῷ Μελχία G O R. Curtis compared Targ. יועץ מליך, which suggests an Aramaic gloss in the *Vorlage*. This translating gloss evidently displaced בשׁ׳.

28.20 Par adds to the end of the verse a long plus which is related to v. 11f. But BH's note "G + vb nonn (= 11.12a)" oversimplifies the facts. The plus cannot be a case of straightforward dittography either in Par — the triple genitives in v. 11 become accusative here, τοῦ οἴκου becomes plural, and several words in v. 12 are omitted here — or in the Heb text of Par, for the last reason. Moreover, scribal error lacks motivation : the repetition of חזק ועשׂה (v. 10) in v. 20 would not be sufficient reason since the beginning of v. 11 would also have been repeated in that case. Torrey, followed by Curtis and Elmslie, hailed the addition as lost treasure : "Our Hebrew text has accidentally lost a considerable passage ... The necessity of this ... is apparent from v. 21 compared with vv. 11-13. The omission in the Heb of MT was caused by homoeoteleuton".[2] But there are two objections. First, Torrey argues from the text of O, which for him is superior to the other groups of mss. But καὶ ἰδού with which O R preface the addition is merely an attempt, inspired by v. 21, to integrate the new material into the context. Secondly, the similarity of v. 21 to v. 13 is superficial : in the former verse the rooms allocated to the divisions of cultic personnel are mentioned, but in v. 21 reference is made to the divisions themselves as having promised support for Solomon. Mention of buildings and rooms do not fit the later context. The plus actually goes back to an explanatory Heb gloss on (כל מלאכת) התבנית in v. 19. It became wrongly attached to כל מלאכת ... in v. 20. A Gk gloss seems to be ruled out : the pedantic repetition would surely have been more exact.

II 1.15 הארזים : + ἐν τῇ ’Ιουδαίᾳ G O L R = probably ביהודה, an explanatory gloss to make it clear that the cedars did not flourish in the city but in the open country.

3.9 למסמרות : +ὁλκή τοῦ ἑνός G O L R = משׁקל אחד according to Curtis. He saw a problem here : "a little less than 2 1b. of nails served

[1] Cf. p. 87.

[2] "Apparatus", p. 67.

to hold over 32 tons of gold in place''. He assumed that Par preserved in adapted form an original שֶׁקֶל אֶחָד. But Goettsberger and Rudolph have rightly seen that the verse as it stands in MT refers to the weight of gold used to *plate* iron nails (cf. I 22.3).

The addition in Par is apparently an explanatory gloss suggesting that each nail weighed 2 lb. But more may still be said about these giant nails. It may well be significant that a reading הָאֶחָד appears in "mlt MSS" (BH) for הָאַחֵר in v. 12. Perhaps the variant was misplaced in the history of Par's Heb text, and was taken to refer to v. 9; then it was enlarged into מ׳ הָאֶחָד.

15.18   אביו : Δαυιδ τοῦ πατρὸς αὐτοῦ G O R = דויד א׳, a false clarification. Cf. the similar gloss in MT at 17.3. The parallel I Ki 15.15 confirms MT here. The dedicated gifts were doubtless the spoils of Abijah's campaigns of 13.16ff. The addition reflects later veneration of David (cf. Rogers, p. 63f.), but hardly on the translator's part.

18.1   ליהושפט : + ἔτι G O L = probably עוד, a scribal notification that the clause has already occurred in 17.5.

21.2   עזריה : ἕξ G (O L R) = probably שׁשׁה, a gloss intended to preserve six names, including two Azariahs; but it displaced the first name. Curtis thought that it might be original, but this is unlikely : the number generally comes at the end of name-lists in Chron.

28.6   בן־רמליהו : + βασιλεὺς Ισραηλ G O L R = מלך ישראל, a misplaced marginal correction of מלכי יש׳ which the *Vorlage*, attested by G, read for מלך יש׳ in v. 5.

(ii) *Glosses in MT*[1]

I 12.40/39   להם : G omits. Is this a misplaced variant to לחם in v. 41/40, where BH presents the following evidence "Ec 1 G להם; T להם לחם" ?

17.24   אלהי ישראל אלהים לישראל : (ὁ) θεὸς Ισραηλ G O R. MT conflates two traditions (Rehm, p. 69, BH), of which the *Vorlage* apparently had only one. BH deletes the second as a gloss. Curtis deletes the first, noting that the parallel II Sam 7.26 has אלהים על־יש׳. Curtis is more likely to be right : parallel assimilation would have reproduced the exact phrase of Sam. The second phrase is probably Chron's adaptation of Sam, while the first is a standardising gloss. BH claims that Par omits the second, but it is impossible to tell which Par's text had.

27.4   ומחלקתו ומקלות הוגיד : G O omit. Rudolph is surely right in

---

[1] For I 12.34/33 ערכי see p. 91.

seeing here a marginal comment on v. 4a, prompted by comparison with 11.12. He relates מק׳ to the post-Biblical and Aramaic קלקל "corrupt", and renders : "Was seine Abteilung betrifft, so liegt Verderbnis (des Namens) des Führers vor".

29.22 שֵׁנִית : G omits, and so does Pesh. It is "doubtless a gloss intended to harmonise this verse with 23.1" (Curtis, following Benzinger and Kittel). Rudolph points out that the addition was due to a misunderstanding of the "Überschriftscharakter" of 23.1.

v. 25 עַל־יִשְׂרָאֵל : G O omit. Myers observes that the omission may be correct since there were only two kings over Israel before Solomon. Is the phrase a misplaced variant to עַל־כָל־שׂ׳ v. 26, according to עַל־יִשׂ׳ in v. 27 ?

II 5.9 מִן־הָאָרוֹן : ἐκ τῶν ἁγίων G O L (in doublet) R = I Ki 8.8 מִן־הַקֹדֶשׁ. This reading, shared by five mss. of Chron (BH), is generally adopted. MT is usually explained as the mistake of a thoughtless scribe (Rudolph) or possibly a clumsy change made by the Chronicler (Curtis). Goettsberger complains with cause that the textual change is difficult. Some further explanation is indeed desirable. MT is surely to be linked with וַיְהִי which is read in place of Ki וַיִּהְיוּ (Par καὶ ἦσαν). וַיִּהְיוּ is generally restored "c pl MSS G S T 1 R 8,8" (BH). The singular must have prompted the question "What was still there ?" A marginal note supplied the answer : הָאָרוֹן. The explanatory gloss displaced הַקֹדֶשׁ. It was no doubt the correct answer to the question about the singular. Since the ark is the overall subject in the context, a careless copyist, letting his eye roam ahead, assumed it to be the implicit subject here and wrote וַיְהִי.

17.3 בְּדַרְכֵי דָוִיד אָבִיו : G O omit דָוִיד. BH speaks for most in its note "dl דָוִיד c 6 MSS Gᴮᴬ, cf 16, 7 ss". The name is a false clarification, such as appears in Par in 15.18. Benzinger compares v. 4, which makes it clear that Asa is meant. Rudolph observes that Chron does not distinguish between good and bad periods in David's life.

20.8 לְךָ : G O R omit. BH notes "dl c Gᴮᴬ V S". It is probably an alternative to לִשְׁמֶךָ three words later.[1] Both בָנָה לַיהוה and בּ׳ לְשֵׁם are common. Was the following *paseq* intended to point out an incorporated variant ?

22.8 וּבְנֵי אֶחָי : G O L R omit בְנֵי, which is also absent from the parallel II Ki 10.13. It was probably inserted by a glossator who understood

---

[1] Cf. לִשְׁמִי in II Sam 7.13 and לִי in the parallel I Chron 17.12.

literally the previous death of Ahaziah's "brothers" in v. 1 (Rudolph, cf. Curtis).

26.7 בעל : καὶ ἐπί G O L R = ועל, which Benzinger (following Winckler), Curtis and Rudolph adopt. בעל is certainly difficult, but where has it come from ? It may be suggested that it arose as an explanatory gloss on אלהי אדום in 25.20. From the margin it crept into the wrong column, displacing the similar ועל. It is significant that the two places are twenty five lines apart in BH, which in ch. iv was observed so often to be the size of a column in a Heb text behind Par.[1]

30.18 מרבית העם רבת : (τὸ) πλεῖστον τοῦ λαοῦ G O L R. Curtis commented that 'ר may have come in from v. 17 or represent dittography of 'מר. Rudolph takes as an Aramaizing adverb in v. 17 and here. Talmon sees here alternative readings.[2] It is conceivable that Par has omitted to render 'ר as superfluous, but it is more likely that its absence reflects the *Vorlage*, and that its position in MT indicates that it is a misplaced gloss assimilating to v. 17.

v. 19 האלהים יהוה : κύριον G O L R. "G V S" (BH) omit 'הא : the *paseq* may again indicate secondary material. But the variant was perhaps no stranger to the *Vorlage*. In v. 8 κυρίῳ τῷ θεῷ stands for ליהוה in G O (L R). The two places are nineteen lines away in BH. Did האלהים once stand in the margin and then get attached to the wrong column in the *Vorlage* ?

2. Synonymous readings

Par attests a number of variants which may be so described. The *Vorlage* apparently contained some readings alternative to those found in MT but yielding the same sense.

(i) יהוה *and* אלהים

It was suggested in ch. i that the sporadic omission of a rendering for יהוה in G goes back to a careless copyist's neglecting to fill in gaps

---

[1] Cf. Wellhausen's suggestion, mentioned by Driver, *Samuel*, p. 234, that בעלי קשת was a gloss on פרשים in II Sam. 1.6 and בעלי found its way into v. 6 before 'פ, and קשת into v. 18, standing alongside v. 6 in the next column.

[2] *Textus* i, p. 168.

left in the Gk for the Heb Tetragrammaton to be inserted.[1] This phenomenon, if rightly explained, creates the impression that κύριος throughout Par is a replacement for Gentile Christians of the Heb form. It is reasonable to conclude that behind κύριος lies ultimately יהוה in the *Vorlage* and that it is never the translator's loose equivalent for אלהים.

In many places יהוה evidently stood in Par's Heb text in place of MT's (ה)אלהים and suffixed forms, and occasionally *vice versa*. Here is a list of such alternative forms, discounting the effect of parallel assimilation :

יהוה for אלהים : I 24.5 G O; 26.20 G O L R, v. 32 G R; 28.2 G O L R, v. 21 G; 29.1 G O L R, v. 7 G O L R, v. 13 G O L R, v. 17 G O L R; II 6.40 G O L (in doublet) R; 13.12 G O L R, v. 15 G O L R, v. 16 G O L R; 15.1 G O R; 19.3 G O L R; 20.7 G O R, v. 29 G O L R; 24.5 G O L (in doublet) R, v. 13 G O L R, v. 20 G O L R; 25.8 (twice) G O L R, v. 20 G O L R; 26.5 (thrice) G O L R, G O R, G O L (in doublet) (R), v. 7 G O L R; 28.24 G O L R; 30.12 G; 31.13 G O L R, v. 21 G O L R; 32.31 G O L R; 34.32 G O L ; 36.19 G O L R.

To these instances should be added the four cases of omission of אלהים cited in ch. i.[2]

אלהים for יהוה : I 10.13 G; 15.15 G O L (in doublet); 25.6 G; 26.27 G O R (in doublet); 29.21 G O R; II 7.12 G O R; 24.24 G O e2 R; 32.26 G.

It is very probable that most of these cases are to be traced back to a divergent *Vorlage*. In eight cases אלהים stood for יהוה, and in thirty eight *vice versa*. Rehm, p. 109, does not mention the former and gives a total of thirty four for the latter, unaware that in four other cases gaps attest יהוה. He cites W.W. Graf von Baudissin[3] to the effect that between the translation of Chron and the fixing of the received text יהוה was replaced by (ה)אלהים. But Rehm cautions that κύριος occurs for אל׳ frequently in combinations with οἶκος and in other common phrases, and in association with κύριος standing for יהוה.

The variants in MT at II 30.19, mentioned at the end of the last section, are germane to the present discussion. Par's evidence there suggests that the variants were known as early as its *Vorlage*. It is possible that there were two recensions of Chron circulating in the

[1] pp. 58f.

[2] p. 58.

[3] *Kyrios*, vol.i, pp. 151f., 343ff., 472ff.

second century B.C., one with a predilection for יהוה and the other with forms of אלהים in greater evidence. The parallel with the Elohistic Psalms is obvious, but not to be pressed since MT frequently uses יהוה, indeed in some cases where Par's text did not.

H.A. Redpath made the issue a criterion for determining the dates of the translation of the various books of the LXX.[1] He came to the interesting conclusion that Par was translated before the consonantal text was settled, and II Esdr after.

(ii) *Forms of names*

I 1.34   ישראל : Ιακωβ G O R = יעקב, adopted by Benzinger and Kittel. Rudolph pertinently remarks that Chron never uses the latter name.[2]

2.13   אישי : Ιεσσαι G O L R = ישי, as in v. 12, read by many Kennicott mss. MT's form is found only here.

4.17   עזרה : Εσρει G (O) R = עזרי.

v. 22   יוקים : Ιωακιμ G O L R = יויקים (Rothstein). For the validity of MT's form see Rudolph.

v. 37   שמרי : Σαμαρ G = שמר.

5.15   עבדיאל : Αβδεηλ G = עבדאל, as in Jer 36.26.

7.27   יהושע : Ιησουε G O = יֵשׁוּעַ.

8.34f.   מיכה : Μιχια G = מיכיה. According to Noth מיכה was the later customary shorter form :[3] cf. II Ki 22. 12 מיכיה, parallel to II Chron 34.20 מיכה.

12.7/6   עזראל : Οζρειηλ B S = עזריאל, with five Heb mss. (BH).

24.7   יהויריב : Ιαρειμ G = יריב via a מ/ב error. Rothstein suggested that Ιω may have been lost after τῷ.

25.2   אשראלה : Ερaηλ G from Εσεραηλ* by parablepsis = אשראל. As Noth, p. 238, suggests, the ending in MT may represent ־אלה, Aramaic for אל.

v. 12   נתניהו : Ναθαν G R = נתן (BH).

v. 14   אשראלה : Ισεριηλ B = אשריאל? See above on v. 2.

26.7   אלזבד : Ελγζαβαθ B = אליזבד?

27.19   ישמעיהו : Σαμαιας G O L R = שמעיהו (cf. BH).

v. 21   יעשיאל : Ασειρ B, -ηρ c₂ assimilated to Αβεννηρ from Ασιηλ O (Ra.) = עשיאל.

[1] *JTS* vii, pp. 606ff.

[2] I Chron 16.17, where Psa 105.10 is taken over, is an exception.

[3] *Personennamen*, p. 107.

II 10.18 הדרם : Aδωνιραμ G L R = אדנירם, read by Curtis and BH. But Rudolph explains MT as another expression for a shorter form אדדם.

17.8 עשׂהאל : Iασιηλ G O = עשׂיאל, if ι = ע or is read by Gk dittography, or יעשׂיאל.

23.1 זכרי : Zαχαρια G (O R) = זכריה (Kittel, SBOT, who so reads; Curtis).

28.20 תלגת פלנאסר : Θαλγαφελλαδαρ B from Θαλγαθφελλασαρ* (Ra.), cf. Θαλαφελλαζαρ c₂ = ת׳ פלאסר (BH : "1 MS G^{BL} S").

33.6 גי בן־הנם : Γε Βανε Εννομ G from Γαι* Βαναι* E. (Ra.) = גי בני־ה׳.

35.22 מגדו : Μαγεδων G O (L) = probably מגדון, as in Zech 12.11.

36.8f. יהויכין : Ἰεχονίας G O L R = יכניה (BH). But it is conceivable that the translator chose to render thus MT's form in order to avoid confusion with יהויקים : note the confusion in IV Rg 24f.

In II 11.7 Βαιθσουρα B (c₂ O) for בית־צור may well attest a misplaced ה, indicating a variant שׂוכה for the following שׂוכו.

(iii) ין- for ים

Par sometimes attests a plural ending of the Aramaic type.

I 4.22 הדברים עתיקים : αβεδηρειν αθουκιειν B. For the orthography of the second word cf. ים - in MT at I 1.11; 14.10; II 26.7; 36.17.

11.13 בפס דמים : originally ἐν Φασοδομιν.[1]

13.6 כרובים : χερουβιν B A N S c q t. Also 28.18 G b R; II 3.7 G b R, v. 10 G *b* R, v. 11 G b R, v. 13 G, v. 14 G *b* R; 5.7 G b R, v. 8 G b R.

14.11 פרצים[2] : Φαρισιν G.

21.20 מתחבאים : μεθαχαβειν B.

26.15,17 אספים : Εσεφειν B.

II 13.4 צמרים : Σομορων G O L R = צמרון via ין-.[2]

16.4 אבל מים : Αβελμαν G, assimilated to original Δαν, probably from -μαιν O R (Ra.).

II Ki 23.24/35.19a תרפים : θαραφειν G (R).

---

[1] See p. 56.

[2] Cf. Kittel, SBOT, ad loc., for ין/ון variants.

(iv) *Other synonyms*

I 4.40 בני חם : חם G O L R (BH).

8.30 ובנו : καὶ υἱὸς αὐτῆς B O R = ובנה (BH) via ובנֹה.

16.40 בני יש' : ישראל G O L (R) (BH).

18.3 חמם : חמתה G O R. Cf. the addition of ה *locale* in 4.39 גדר : Γεραρα G O L = גררה.

19.3,19 בני עמון : עמון G O, G.

23.28 בני אהרן : אהרן G O R.

29.6 בני : שבטי (ישראל) G O L R.

II 4.17 בין : ἐν οἴκῳ G O = בית (Rehm, p. 59). But this is not merely a ן/ת error *contra* Rehm. The Aramaic synonym has been carelessly substituted.

5.3 איש ישראל : ישראל G.

6.11; 31.1 בני ישראל : ישראל G O L R (BH in 6.11). In the first case בני was evidently put in the margin and became misplaced in the preceding column : לבני אסף G O L R stood for לאסף in 5.12 (22 lines away in BH).

9.29 הלא־הם : ἰδού G O R = הנם, according to the usual formula.

10.9 ונשיב : καὶ ἀποκριθήσομαι G O R = ואשיב (BH). ἀποκριθῶ in III Rg 12.9 reveals a common underlying Heb reading, a simplifying variant of the royal plural.

11.1 בית יהודה : יהודה G O L.

v. 17 בדרך : ἐν ταῖς ὁδοῖς G (O R) = בדרכי.

13.23/14.1 בימיו : ἐν ταῖς ἡμέραις Ασα G O L R = בימי אסא (BH), an explanatory change to avoid Abijah being taken as the subject.

21.8 בימיו : ἐν ταῖς ἡμέραις ἐκείναις G O L R = בימים ההם, changed to avoid David being taken as subject. For the variant cf. בימיו Jer 23.6, but בימם ההם in the parallel 33.16.

23.3 הקהל : ἐκκλησία Ιουδα G O R = probably קהל יהודה.

24.6 איש יהוה : עבד יהוה G O L R (v. 9 was not changed).

25.8 יש־כח : יש G O R.

31.5 הרבה ישראל : הרבו בני ישראל G.

32.4 ויקבצו ... ויסתמו : καὶ συνήγαγεν (= וַיִּקְבֹּץ) ... καὶ ἐνέφραξεν G O L R. Evidently the *Vorlage* had singular verbs in both cases, agreeing *ad formam* with the subject עם. But the translator took Hezekiah as the subject.

34.30 איש יהודה : יהודה G O L R.

35.14 (ואחר) הֵכִינוּ : ἑτοιμάσαι G O R = הֵכִין (Walde, *Esdrasbücher*, p. 23).

3. Substitution

There remain cases of variant readings, hitherto not considered, in which a different word or words apparently underlies Par.

I 3.19 פדיה : Σαλαθιηλ B O = שאלתיאל (BH), generally regarded as a correction according to Haggai 1.1; Ezra 3.2, etc. Curtis ascribed the change to the translator or to a Gk copyist, but it is of a piece with Heb glosses already noted.

3.22 יגאל : Ιωηλ G O R = יואל, substituting a more common name. For the change cf. יואל I 11.38 for יגאל II Sam 23.36.

4.3 אבי : υἱοί G O R = בני (BH), with some Heb mss. Kautzsch so reads, but it is usually assumed, e.g. by Curtis, Rothstein, BH and Rudolph, that some words have fallen out of MT. Par's text represents an attempt to make sense of the already corrupted text.

8.29; 9.35 ישבו : κατῴκησεν G O L R = ישב with one Ken. ms. and Pesh (BH, ignoring Par) in the first case and with Pesh in the second (BH). A simpler reading has been substituted.

11.30 בענה : Νοοζα G = נעזה? Gk corruption may have marred Par's form.

v. 39 נחרי : Ναχωρ G = נחור, a more common name.

v. 46 המחוים : ὁ Μιει G = ? MT is corrupt, but the Gk can give no help. Curtis claims that G's form is an error for ὁ Μαωειν A, but only one hotly contending for the primacy of A could so imagine.

15.6f. ועשרים ... ושלשים : πεντήκοντα G (O), G = וחמשים twice. As Rothstein observes, there seems to be no reason for the change.

v. 27 כניה : Ἰεχονίας G = יכניה (BH). For the change cf. II 35.9 וכוניהו : I Esdr 1.9 καὶ Ἰεχονίας.

16.38 ואחיהם : καὶ οἱ ἀδελφοὶ αὐτῶν G O L R = ואחיו, read by Benzinger and Rothstein. It is more likely that a name has dropped out earlier (Rudolph, cf. Curtis, BH) than that Par's text is original.

17.13 אשר היה : τῶν (ὄντων) G O L R = היו א׳. The reference is not restricted to Saul.

19.18 ישראל : Δαυιδ G O = דויד. The sense is little changed. Rogers, p. 54f., sees here the translator magnifying David.

29.21 ויזבחו ... ויעלו : καὶ ἔθυσεν Δαυιδ G O L R ... καὶ ἀνήνεγκεν G O b R = ויזבח דויד ... ויעל, centring attention on David, as in 19.18. Rogers, p. 61, again sees the translator's hand here.

II 13.2 גבעה : Γαβαων G O R = גבעון (BH).

v. 7 ויתאמצו ... לפניהם : καὶ ἀντέστη (G) O R ... κατὰ πρόσωπον αὐτοῦ G O L R = ויתאמץ ... לפניו, taking Jeroboam as the subject.

23.12 העם : τὸν βασιλέα G O L R = המלך, a copyist's slip.

24.24 עשׂוּ : ἐποίησεν G O L R = עשׂה, making God the subject. According to Rogers, p. 32, the translator is deliberately avoiding the idea of pagan collaboration in divine judgment.

25.20 דרשׁוּ ... תתם : παραδοῦναι αὐτὸν ... ἐξεζήτησεν G O L R = דרשׁ ... תתו, taking Amaziah as the subject.

26.5 ובימי דרשׁו : καὶ ἐν ταῖς ἡμέραις αὐτοῦ ἐζήτησεν G O (R) = ובימיו דרשׁ.

27.5 עליהם ... השׁיבו לו בני־עמון : ἐπ' αὐτὸν G O L ... ἔφερεν B O L R αὐτῷ βασιλεὺς Ἀμμων G O = עליו ... השׁיב לו מלך ע'.

30.6 וישׁב אל : καὶ ἐπιστρέψει τοὺς (G) O L R = וישׁב את (Curtis, BH).

32.18f. ויקראו ... וידברו : καὶ ἐβόησεν ... καὶ ἐλάλησεν G O R = וידבר ... ויקרא (so three Heb mss.), influenced by the singular verbs in v.17 (Curtis).

35.12 ויסירו : καὶ ἡτοίμασαν G O L R = ויכינו (BH, which so reads). This is an easier reading, and so secondary. Did it arise by adaptation of the variant ויכניהו in v. 9, attested by I Esdr (see I 15.27 above)?

v. 14 ולכהנים² : καὶ τοῖς ἀδελφοῖς αὐτῶν G O L R = ולאחיהם. Cf. I Esdr 1.13 τοῖς ἱερεῦσιν ἀδ. αὐτῶν = ולכ' אח'. In I Esdr's Vorlage was a gloss which had displaced לכ' in Par's text.

4. כל

Würthwein includes כל among a list of small, common words which were readily inserted into the text.[1] This freedom is reflected in its addition and omission in Par, which probably reflects the Vorlage in this respect.

כל was apparently omitted as follows :

I 12.39/38 G O L R

28.1 כל² G O R (so one Ken. ms.), כל³ G O L R

v. 8 G (was πάσας O L R omitted before τάς ?)

v. 12 G O R, 13 כל² (haplography before כל' ?) G O L R

29.3 G O L R, 10 G O L R

v. 24 כל¹ G O L R, כל² G

II 1.2 כל³ G O

2.13/14 כל¹ G O L R

---

[1] Text of the OT, p. 74.

4.4   G O L R

6.29   כל³ G

v. 30   G O L R : the parallel III Rg 8.39 also omits.

8.6   כל² G O L R (included in ὅσα ? But cf. πάντα ὅσα 9.1)

11.16   G O L (in doublet) R, 23 כל³ G O L R

13.15   G O L R

15.9   G O L R

17.9   G O L R

18.16   G O R

24.7   G O R

26.20   G O L R

27.7   G O L R

28.6   הכל G O L R, 26 G O L R

29.18   כל²,³ G O L R, G O R (haplography before כליו in both cases ?)

v. 28   הכל G O L R, 34 G O L R

30.4   G O R

32.15   יכל¹ G O L R : Curtis and BH raise the possibility of dittography in MT after יוכל.

v. 27   G O R (haplography before כלי ?), 31 G O L R

33.25   G O L R

34.29   G O L R

II Ki.23.24/25.19a G O L R

36.14   כל² G O L R, 19 יכל¹ G O L R

כל was apparently added as follows:

I 4.6   G O L R, 10 G O L R

7.40   G O R

II 5.4   G O L R : probably added after the pattern of verb + כל before.

9.12   G O L R

20.24   G O L R

26.5 B

30.9   G O L R

32.13   G O L R, unless πάσης τῆς γῆς was intended to represent הארצות

33.9   G O L R

36.18   G O L

It is significant that the number of omissions is far greater than that of additions. It is possible that some of these cases cancel each other out : they may at times represent misplacements. For instance, was

כל put by error before אצרות in II 36.18 instead of before ארמנותיה in v. 19?

5. THE CONJUNCTION

There are still very many cases of omission of ו and addition of καί in Par which have not yet been accounted for. Würthwein rightly includes it in his list of small elements and words dealt with casually by copyists.[1] It would not be worth the labour to sift through the evidence to try to assess the variation of the *Vorlage* in the use of the conjunction. But here is a list of cases where BH advises change on the basis of Par.[2]

I 4.15   קנז וקנז : קנז   G O L R : "pl MSS G V T om : 1 sic vel ins antea nom".

5.24   ועפר : עפר   G O L R : "dl ו c G V T". A name may have fallen out (Goettsberger, cf. Curtis and Rudolph).

15.18   ואל׳ : אליאב   G O L R (except d j) : "1 c 5 MSS^Ken G (cf. 20)".

26.7   ואל׳ ואח׳ : אלזבד ואחיו   G O L R (except d, 44) : "1 (cf. nonn MSS^Ken G)".

v. 26   לשרי : χιλίαρχοι B O L R. Only c₂ prefaces with καί. Yet BH states "1 c 2 MSS G V S et 29, 6 ושרי".

II 5.5   והל׳ : הלוים   G O L R : "1 c 24 MSS G S T".[3]

6.22   ואלה : אלה   G O L R : "1 c G ... vel באלה".

III Rg 8.31, rendered differently, also read ו in its *Vorlage*.

v. 26   ומח׳ : מחטאתם   G O L R : "1 c mlt MSS G V S T 1 R 8, 35".

v. 29   וכל : כל   G O L R : "1 c G".

11.23   ולכל²: לכל   G O L R : "1 c G^BAL V".

18.3   עמך : ועמך   G O R : "G^BA עמך, frt 1".

19.10   כל : וכל   B O L R (only c₂ prefaces with καί): "1 c G^BA G^MSS V".

23.18   והל׳ : הלוים   G O L R : "1 c pc MSS^Ken G V S".

24.7   ובניו : בניו   G O L R : "1 c G V".

30.6   כמ׳ : וכמצות   G O L R : "1 c 1 MS G V".

32.32   ועל : על   G O L R : "1 c G V S^A T".

---

[1] *Ibid.*

[2] It should also be noted that in I 23.29 Curtis, Rothstein and Rudolph delete וללחם) with Par.

[3] See Part I, p. 200.

6. Letters added or omitted

Variants involving addition and omission of א form a special category.[1] Some may be due to the misreading of the translator.

I 4.18 היהדיה : αὕτη Ἀδια G (OR) = היא הדיה.

v. 23 במלאכתו : ἐν τῇ βασιλείᾳ αὐτοῦ G O R = במלכתו, encouraged by המלך just before. Cf. II 8.9 below.

17.17 כתור : ὡς ὅρασις G O (L) R = כתו(ר)אר (BH², Rehm, p. 112). Benzinger and Rothstein posited and read כמראה without explaining the mystery as to how one reading could develop into the other. S. Marenof contended that כראות must be the basis of Par on the ground that תאר is nowhere else so rendered throughout the LXX.[2] But in Par itself there is nothing to compare. The noun is used in v. 15 for חזון; its use here is an instance of the translator's habit of using a Gk word twice for different Heb words.

19.6 התבאשו : ἠσχύνθη G O (L) R. Cf. the parallel II Rg 10.6 κατῃσχύν-θησαν for נבאשו. There is no need to posit a reading התבששו. P.R. Ackroyd has shown that the LXX knew of a second root באש synonymous with בוש.[3]

II 8.9 למלאכתו : τῇ βασιλείᾳ αὐτοῦ G O L (in doublet) R = למלכתו (Rehm, p. 59).

Other letters were omitted from the Heb text of Par, or overlooked by the translator, as follows :

I 4.6 תימני : Θαιμαν G O R = תימן.

v. 35 ויהוא : καὶ οὗτος G (R) = והוא (BH).

5.1 נתנה : ἔδωκεν G O R = נתן (BH). Or is a pointing נְתָנָהּ presupposed by Par, with omission of an anticipatory suffix in translation ? Cf. v. 26 ויגלם לראובני : καὶ μετῴκισεν τὸν Ρουβην G O (R), where BH posits ויגל.

9.1 ; 29.29 הנם : οὗτοι G O R, εἰσίν G O (R) = הם.

v. 10 באהליהם : ἐν σκηναῖς G O = באהלים.

13.3 דרשנהו : ἐζήτησαν αὐτήν G O R = דרשהו (BH ; Curtis posits דרשוהו). Rudolph suggests that the third person is an attempt to exonerate David, or that -σαν is an error for -σαμεν.

16.32 יעליץ : καὶ ξύλον G O R = ועץ. Is there a link here with

---

[1] A number of cases have been dealt with in ch iv : I 2.24 (p. 87) ; 5.2 (Part I, p. 161) ; 5.10 (p. 130) : 7.24 (p. 115) ; II 18.18 (p. 86) ; 30.22 (p. 99).

[2] AJSL liii, p. 47.

[3] JTS ii, pp. 31ff.

Justin's famous reading ἀπὸ τοῦ ξύλου in Psa 96/95.10 = I Chron 16.31 ? It may be suggested that וְעֵץ was placed in the margin of a Heb ms. beside the parallel v. 12 of the Psa, and subsequently found its way into the text at v. 10.

17.27 וּמְבֹרָךְ : καὶ εὐλόγησον G O R = וברך. Rehm, p. 58, merely assumes a repointing וּמְבֹרָךְ.

24.19 צוהו : ἐνετείλατο G O L R = צוה (BH) ?

26.11/10 חלקיהו : τῆς διαιρέσεως G (O R in doublet) = חֲלֻקָּה (cf. II 35.5).

v. 21f. יחיאלי : Ι(α)ειηλ G (O L) = יחיאל.

v. 23 עמרמי, יצהרי, חברוני, עזיאלי : Αμραμ G L, Ισααρ B L, Χεβρων G O L R, Οζιηλ G O L R, omitting the final letter.

27.4 האחוחי : ὁ Εκχωχ G (R) = האחוח.

v. 7 ואחריו : καὶ οἱ ἀδελφοί G O L (in doublet) R = ואחיו. BH posits ואחיהם.

II 7.13 הארץ : τὸ ξύλον G O R = העץ.

18.25 והשיבהו : καὶ ἀποστρέψατε G O L R (except g) = והשיבו ?

v. 29 בגדיך : τὸν ἱματισμόν μου G O L R = III Rg 22.30 = בגדי in the *Vorlage* of either or both. This is not necessarily a deliberate heightening of Ahab's deception *contra* Montgomery, Wevers[1] and Rogers, p. 80, but simply a misunderstanding : after mention of Ahab's disguising himself it was not expected that Jehoshaphat would wear his own clothes.

21.3 מגדנות : ὅπλα G O L R = מגנות.

23.13 מודיעים : ὑμνοῦντες G O L R = מודים (Rehm, p. 60, seeing here a phonetic error).

24.10 וישמחו : καὶ ἔδωκαν G O R = וישֹ(י)מו (so rendering in 23.15). Rudolph suggests that Par so reads because rejoicing over a religious tax was considered improbable !

v. 14 ויעשֹהו : καὶ ἐποίησαν G O R = ויעשֹו.

29.21 להעלות : τοῦ ἀναβαίνειν G O R = לעלות.

34.16 הם עשֹים : τῶν ποιούντων G O L R = העשֹים (Rehm, p. 61, seeing here pseudo-haplography).

v. 32 כברית : διαθήκην G O R = ברית.

35.15 והשערים : καὶ οἱ ἄρχοντες καὶ οἱ πυλωροί G O L R. והשֹרים was read once (Walde, *Esdrasbücher*, p. 23) and has been corrected

---

[1] *CBQ* xiv, p. 51.

at some stage. For the error cf. II Ki 7.10 שָׂעֵר : τοὺς στρατηγούς L in a doubt = שׂר according to Rahlfs.[1]

In three cases MT appears to have suffered the omission of a letter :

I 3.1 שֵׁנִי : ὁ δεύτερος G O L R = הַשֵּׁנִי, which is generally read. ה dropped out after ת (Rehm, p. 87).

II 26.5 בראת : ἐν φόβῳ G O R = ביראת, required "c nonn MSS G^BA S T A" (BH), and generally read.

30.23 שׂמחה : ἐν εὐφροσύνῃ G L R = בשׂמחה, to be read with Kittel and BH ("l c 20 MSS", ignoring Par), as in v. 21. The error is one of pseudo-haplography.

It is significant that letters are added seldom :

I 2.30f. אפים : Ἐφραιμ G = אפרים (BH). There is no need to change with BH. A more familiar name was substituted for "Big-nose" (Rudolph, following Noth).

v. 53 The six proper adjectives, collective singulars in MT, were plural in the *Vorlage* according to G O R.

16.29 ובאו : καὶ ἐνέγκατε G (O) R = והבא(ו)או (BH).

II 35.3 תנו : καὶ ἔθηκαν G O (L) (in doublet) R = ויתנו (Benzinger), presumably by pseudo-dittography of ה.

In two cases a letter in MT is superfluous :

I 14.16 ויכו : καὶ ἐπάταξεν G O L R = II Rg 5.25 = Sam ויך, rightly read by BH, Rothstein, Rehm, p. 69, and Rudolph : cf. v. 11 ויכם. Ms. Ken. 101 has ויכה.

II 31.10 והנותר : καὶ κατελίπομεν G (O L) = ונותר, which is usually read. MT has been influenced by והותר a few words before.

7. Omission

(i) *Words or phrases in apposition*

This type of omission represented in Par has already been discussed.[2] The case in II 30.24 was seen to be due to the translator, and it may well be that some of the following instances arose in the same way. Sometimes a name is involved, but usually an epithet.

I 6.8/23 בנו[1] G

18.11 המלך G O

---

[1] *LXX-Studien*, iii, p. 288.

[2] p. 119f.

22.18   אלהיכם   G O L R. Rogers, p. 16, suggests that the translator omitted to avoid implying that God was under obligation to the nation.

24.31   דויד   G O L R.

26.2f.   הששי – השני   G, 4f.   השמיני – השני   G, 11   הרבעי   G. Benzinger suggested that MT's numbering was not original.

v. 25   בנו²⁻⁵   G O R

28.2   המלך   G R

II 2.11/12   המ׳   B*

6.16   אבי   G. It is represented in v. 15

8.14   אביו   G O

9.22   המ׳   G O L R; it is also missing in the parallel III Rg 10.23.

10.18   המ׳   G.

11.3   מ׳ יהודה   G O

12.10,13   המ׳   G O R, G O.

20.35   מ׳ יהודה   G

22.11   בת המ׳¹   G, הכהן   B*

23.8   הכהן²   G O

24.22   המ׳   G O R

25.17   מ׳ יהודה   G O

26.20   עזריהו   G O

v. 22   בן־אמוץ   G O

28.16   המ׳   G O

29.6   אלהינו   G O

32.10   סנחריב   G

35.14   בני אהרן   G O R

(ii) *Prepositions and adverbial or prepositional words or phrases*

I 4.29   ב³   G O, 30   ב²,³   G O, G, 31   ב¹,²,³   G, G, O R, G O R. The fact that Chron lacks ב in three cases in v. 28 suggests *Vorlage* omission here.

v. 43; 14.12; II 32.21   שם   G

5.16   ובכל : וכל   G O R (BH)

v. 23   בארץ   G, superfluous after the redivision of clauses

6.65/80   ב(גלעד)   G O R

12.18/17   לעזרני   G O R. Rothstein suggested that it was perhaps an explanatory gloss on לשלום.

v. 23/22   לעזרו   G O R

v. 40/39   עם־דויד   G O

14.2   למלך   G O

17.4   לי B * S

29.16   לך G O R. It was evidently added in the margin and then attached to v. 14 : σοι is added to προθυμηθῆναι in G O L R. It was wrongly placed under the influence of להתנדב־לך v. 17.

v. 20   נא G O

II 1.3   עמו G

2.15/16   לך G O R

7.21   ככה G O. Cf. its omission in a similar question in III Rg. 1.6

10.10   אלהם G O R

13.5   לו G O L R

14.12/13   מאד G O L R

18.20   אליו G O L R. It was added instead after εἶπεν in B O L R in v. 23

19.5   בארץ G O L R

23.13   בחרב G

24.20   להם G O

25.8   למלחמה G O R

28.10   רק G O L R

29.29   אתו G O R

30.6   לכם G O R

v. 10   בם G O L R

34.6   עד G O L R

(iii) *Other omissions*

I 1.11-16   G. Rudolph observes that the omission is best explained by the assumption that the *Vorlage* lacked these verses, but that their absence cannot be explained in terms of homoeoteleuton or the like. Part of the genealogy of Ham is omitted, that concerning Egypt and Canaan. Did a nationalistically minded Jew delete the passage ?

v. 50   ושם אשתו ... זהב G. Twenty seven letters are involved.

5.26   והרא G O R

6.14/29   מררי מחלי B *

v. 44/59   ואת־מגרשיה² G

7.6   בלע G

11.25   הנו G O L R

14.16   דויד G O, a rather awkward omission

18.5   דויד G, again awkward

v. 13   את־דויד G. One suspects Gk omission in these three cases, but it is difficult to see how it could have occurred.

22.9 ²יהיה G O L R

24.1 בני אהרן G. It was wrongly restored at the end of v. 2 (B O L R), put before ויחלקם instead of after מחלקתם.

26.8 אלה G O R. It too was misplaced, in the similar place at v. 11 (οὗτοι O (L) R : B is corrupt)

II 3.13 האלה G O

4.12 שתי G O R

v. 13 שנים B*

8.16 שלמה G O R, ¹בית יהוה G O R

9.1 היה G O

v. 22 הארץ G O R

10.16 ²לא G O L R

11.3 ישראל ב G O, a simplification of the text

13.3 את־המלחמה G. Is it to be understood from v.2 ?

15.4 ויבקשהו G O R

16.7 ³מלך G O R

21.16 רוח G O L R

23.13 עומד G O. Rehm, p. 18, sees here a concise rendering.

24.26 אלה G O L R

32.5 (ו)יעל על ה G O L R

II Ki. 23.25/35.19b מלך G O L R

35.20 את־הבית G O^{mss}. I Esdr 1.23 also omits.[1]

8. ADDITION

(i) *Names as subject*

I 11.23 בניהו G O L R

29.21 דויד G O L R.[2]

II 11.15 ירבעם G O L R

12.10 שישק G O R

17.1 יהושפט G O L R (except d m)

---

[1] See Part I, p. 214.

[2] See p. 144.

(ii) *Prepositions*

I 2.23 בני : υἱῶν G O R = לבני. Rothstein, BH ("frt") and Myers so read, but Rudolph gives good reasons for retaining MT.

5.26 ונהר : καὶ ἐπὶ ... G O R = ועל־נ׳ ?

12.38/37 וחצי : καὶ ἀπὸ ... G O L R = ומח׳.

17.7 נגיד : εἰς ἡγούμενον B O L R = II Rg 7.8 = לנ׳ ?

18.10 הדדעזר : τῷ Αδρα(α)ζαρ G O L R = להד׳, read also by II Rg 8.10, simplifying the construction.

23.28 ומעשׂה : καὶ ἐπὶ ... G O L R = ועל־מ׳ (BH)

25.6 נבלים וכנרות : καὶ ἐν ... καὶ ἐν G O L R = ובנ׳ ובכ׳.

26.25 ואחיו : καὶ τῷ ἀδελφῷ αὐτοῦ G O L R = ולאחיו, adopted by Benzinger and Rothstein. But, as Rudolph states, there is no need to change.

v. 28 וכל : καὶ ἐπὶ = G O L R = ועל־כל.

27.6 ומחלקתו : καὶ ἐπὶ τῆς ... G O L R = ועל־מ׳, which is usually read.

v. 28 והשׂקמים : καὶ ἐπὶ τῶν ... G O L R = ועל־הש׳.

II 2.6/7 וכרמל ותכלת : καὶ ἐν τῷ ... καὶ ἐν τῇ ... (G)[1] O L R = ובכ׳ ובת׳, read by BH. But the reading may have been prompted by v. 13/14.

12.5 ושׂרי : καὶ πρὸς ... G O L R = ואל־שׂ׳.

24.14 ויהוידע : καὶ πρὸς ... G O L R = ולפני י׳.

v. 23 וירושׁלם : καὶ ἐπὶ ... G O L R (except d m) = ואל־יר׳.

34.3 והפסלים : καὶ ἀπὸ ... G O R = ומן־הפ׳.

Cf. II 12.13 העיר : ἐν τῇ πόλει G O L R = בעיר.

(iii) *Adverbial words and phrases*

I 10.12 + ἐκ Γαλααδ G O L (R) = מגלעד ? (Rothstein)

28.3 + ἐπ᾽ αὐτῷ G O L R = עליו (BH).[2]

29.4 + ἐν αὐτοῖς G O L R = בהם (Rothstein)

II 2.12/13 + σοι G O L R = לך (BH)

II Ki.24.1/36.5a + εἰς τὴν γῆν = אל־הארץ. Cf. IV Rg L ἐπὶ τὴν γῆν.

(iv) *Other additions*

I 3.21 + υἱὸς αὐτοῦ G O L R (except a d y) = בנו with "nonn MSS" (BH). The addition was necessitated by reading בני as בנו earlier.

---

1 For the partial parablepsis in G see p. 52.

2 See p. 130.

12.16/15 העמקים : τοὺς κατοικοῦντας αὐλῶνας G O (L R) = probably יושבי הע׳ since the other versions so render.

v. 19/18 + καὶ εἶπεν G O L R = ויאמר (BH "G V + לאמר").

16.7 + ᾠδή G (except S) Oᵐˢˢ = שיר ?

28.2 + ἐγένετο G O L R = היה. BH urges its insertion "c G S 22, 7".

II 2.3/4 + τοῦ ἀναφέρειν G O L R = להעלות (BH : "1 frt c G"). The verb was doubtless added because להקטיר was felt to be too far away. Rehm, p. 59, explains as dittography of עלות.

15.2 + καὶ εἶπεν G (O R) = ויאמר, supplied after Heb parablepsis involving ויאמר earlier.[1]

20.21 + καὶ αἰνεῖν G O L R (except m) = להלל (P.R. Ackroyd, *JTS* xvii, p. 396 note 2) after reading להדות earlier. The common association of the two verbs encouraged the addition. קדש becomes τὰ ἅγια G O R : Ackroyd posited הקדשים, but this is unnecessary in view of I 23.28 לכל־קדש : τῶν πάντων ἁγίων G O (L).

v. 27 בשמחה : + μεγάλη G O L R = גדולה.

30.26 + ἐγένετο G O L R = היתה. BH adds "c Varᴳ G V S T".

31.6 +ἤνεγκαν G O L R = הביאו (Curtis), repeated to aid comprehension. BH counsels its insertion in Chron, but it is difficult to see how it could have fallen out.

9. Script of the Vorlage

The work of J. Fischer in other books of the LXX is fundamental in this field. He described the script of the Pentateuchal *Vorlage* of the LXX as follows : "ein neuaramäisches Alphabet, welches sich aber in manchen Formen bereits der Quadratschrift näherte".[2] Later he gave a useful summary of his finds concerning major consonantal confusion : רד 36 times, מה 16 times, יו 11, and רו 9.[3]

When subsequently he turned to Isa he arrived at a slightly different result from the one concerning the Pentateuch, but a result which is not surprising. The LXX of Isa apparently used a ms. similar in script to those of the Pentateuch but with a stronger tendency towards the square script.[4] כב, יו and חה are more confused than in the Penta-

---

[1] See p. 135.

[2] *Das Alphabet der LXX-Vorlage im Pentateuch*, p. 115.

[3] *Zur LXX-Vorlage im Pentateuch*, p. 37.

[4] *In welcher Schrift lag das Buch Isaias den LXX vor?*

teuch. The chief errors are : רד 56 times, יו 27, כב 15, פב 7, פנ 6, רו 6, מה 6, תה 6 and נו 4. He drew similar conclusions from the LXX of Amos : מב, פב, כב, מכ, רד, רו and יו are especially prone to interchange.[1]

S.R. Driver called the character of the Heb text used for the LXX of Samuel "a transitional alphabet, probably a Palestinian one, of a type not greatly differing from that of Kefr-Bir'im ... In this alphabet not only are ו and י remarkably alike, but also ב and כ, and ב and מ (of which there are many clear cases of confusion in the LXX) : ה, ח and the final ם also approach each other. ד and ר resemble each other in most Semitic alphabets : so that from their confusion — next to that of ו and י the most common in the LXX — little can be inferred respecting the alphabet used".[2]

H.M. Orlinsky has struck a dissentient note. With regard to Job the Gk evidence has forced him to posit an Aramaic cursive script of about the third to second century B.C., in which יו, תחה, מכב are never confused but עד are alike.[3]

What of Par's Heb text ? Consonantal errors were listed in ch. iv. Apart from the indeterminate confusion of רד, מכב and יו were most common, then תחה and רו. מה and פנ should also be mentioned. פב should perhaps be included too as palaeographic rather than phonetic in the source of their confusion. It is clear that Orlinsky's conclusions concerning Job do not apply here. Driver's evidence concerning Sam and Fischer's concerning Isa and Amos are obviously analogous to these finds.

A problem arises in all work of this kind. Was the script of the *Vorlage* such that *all* these palaeographical errors could be made ? Or do some go back to an earlier stage in the history of the *Vorlage* and to an earlier script ? All that the frequency of errors can conclusively demonstrate is the latest type of script to which errors point : some letters must have been in the forms associated with the square script. But it may well be that misreadings of letters dissimilar in that script go back to the translator and so to similarity in the *Vorlage*.

In an invaluable study for the student of LXX *Vorlagen*, F. M. Cross has amassed and commented upon a large number of actual Heb scripts.[4] The present writer would single out the following scripts

---

[1] *TQ* cvi, p. 334f.

[2] *Samuel*, p. lxiv.

[3] *JQR* xxx, p. 37f.

[4] *The Bible and the Ancient Near East*, pp. 133ff.

as particularly relevant. Figure 1, is described as a formal script "trans-itional between the Archaic (proto-Jewish) and Hasmonaean periods (*ca.* 175-150 B.C.). From an unpublished exemplar of Deuteronomy from Qumran (4 Deut^a)". Figure 2, lines 1 and 2 comprise "an early Jewish semicursive, or mixed, hand from Egypt (*ca.* 150 B.C.). From the Nash Papyrus" and "a Jewish semicursive script from the Judaean wilderness (*ca.* 125-100 B.C.). From a Murabba'at ostracon". Finally, figure 3, is a Qumran semicursive script "from an unpublished manus-cript of the Twelve Minor Prophets (4Q XII^a). *Ca* 150-100 B.C." Cross explains the semicursive script as "an intermediate script formed by the crossing of formal script types and the developed cursives, especially those of the second century B.C. and later. It is an unstable type, in which much mixing of traditions occurs, and hence a source of 'infection' of both formal and cursive styles. Often it maintains common traits over considerable periods of time despite its great variety in individual styles".[1]

The *Vorlage* of Par is to be related to forms of letters found in the four scripts mentioned above.

רד are similar in all four;

כב are similar in all four, but their confusion with מ would be more likely in figure 1.

יִ are similar in figure 2, lines 1 and 2, and in figure 3.

תחה are most alike in figure 3.

רו are similar in figures 1 and 3.

מה and סה are very similar in figure 2, line 1.

פנ are very similar in figures 1, 2, line 1, and 3.

פב look alike in figures 1 and 3.

It may be tentatively concluded that Par's *Vorlage* was written in a semicursive script in which certain letters had a more formal character than in figures 2, lines 1 and 2, and 3. The palaeographical evidence does not conflict with Eupolemus' use of Par about 150 B.C.[2]

---

[1] *Op. cit.*, p. 146.

[2] It is unfortunate that the discoveries of Chron so far in the Qumran area are likely to shed little light on the LXX *Vorlage*. 4Q Chron is "leather lace with only four complete words legible" (Cross, *Ancient Library of Qumran*, p. 32, cited by Burchard, *Biblio-graphie zu den Handschriften vom Toten Meer*, 1965, p. 328).

Fig. 1

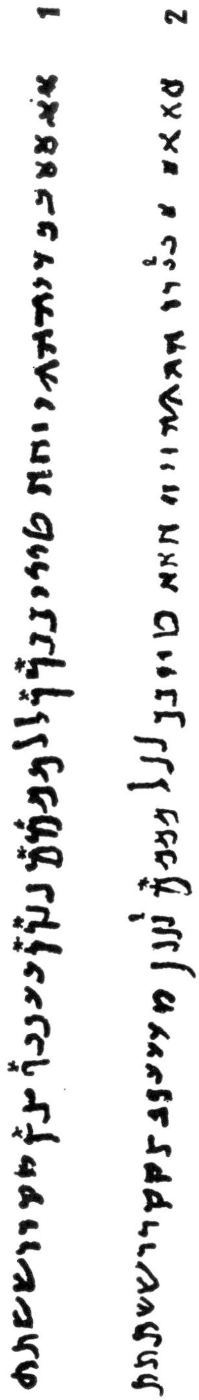

Fig. 2

Fig. 3

10. Condition of the Vorlage

W.A.L. Elmslie has commented on Par. "The text of Chronicles is in fairly good condition. Where it is faulty the LXX does not help; for it was made from a manuscript virtually identical with the present Hebrew text".[1] Elmslie was evidently referring to the A text of Par like Torrey his mentor, but his words contain more than a modicum of truth even where G is concerned. Certainly the prototype of G mirrored the Heb text upon which it was based more than many have imagined. Behind intensive Gk corruption, behind the idiosyncrasies of the translator lies a text which may in very many cases be easily related to MT. It is uncertain how many errors were committed by the translator in careless reading. It is unreasonable to assume that he had a text exactly like MT before him, if only because no ms. is an exact reproduction of another. But many variants may be simply restored to forms identical with those in MT, much more often than the apparatus in BH would have its readers believe.

R. Gordis[2] has agreed with Frankel[3] that Par mainly follows the Qere. Gordis claims in a table of LXX data that Par agrees with the Kethib in sixteen cases, of which thirteen are certain and three doubtful; and with the Qere in twenty nine cases, twenty seven being certain and two doubtful.[4] The author's totals are thirty six alignments with the Qere and sixteen with the Kethib. The bracketed material refers to Frankel's list.[5]

Par's text agreed with the Qere :

I 1.51 (*contra* Frankel)	9.4,33 (not listed), 35
2.55	11.20,44
3.24	20.5
4.7,20	22.7
6.20/35	23.9
7.1,10,31	24.24
v. 34 (twice, the first case not listed)	25.1 (not listed)

---

[1] *Interpreter's Bible*, vol. iii, p. 347.

[2] *The Biblical Text in the Making*, p. 60.

[3] *Vorstudien*, pp. 219-242.

[4] *Op. cit.*, p. 65.

[5] *Op. cit.*, p. 229f.

27.29 (not listed)   v. 21 (*contra* Frankel)
II 9.29   29.13 (not listed), 14
11.18   32.21 (not listed)
17.8   34.6
18.8 (not listed), 33   35.3 (not listed).
26.3,7 (neither listed), 11

Par's text agreed with the Kethib :

I 4.41   II 4.11
6.10/25   9.10
8.25 (*contra* Frankel)   13.19
11.11   24.27 (*contra* Frankel)
12.3 (not listed), 6 (*contra*   33.16
   Frankel)
v. 19   34.9
14.1   35.9 (not listed)
26.25

Since line omissions most frequently involve sixteen letters, it may be concluded that the *Vorlage* tended to have lines of that length : it is easier for a translator, juggling with intense mental activity as well as with scribal transmission, to overlook lines than for a copyist, who was anyway presumably more used to his work. But the translator obviously found a text with many omissions already perpetrated. One is reminded, in passing, of Allgeier's comment on the omissions in the Gk of II Esdr : "Nicht zu Θ passen die grossen Lücken."[1] This remains true whether a second century Theodotion or a first century one is postulated.

As to orthography, vowel letters were used much less than in Chron MT, the significance of which fact has been already discussed. A third masculine singular suffix in ה instead of ו was on occasions found or wrongly recognised, although Chron MT has no instances. S.R. Driver observed that in the Massoretic OT "there occur a number of instances in which ה has been suffered to remain, testifying ... to a previous general prevalence of this form".[2]

The *Vorlage* was evidently a popular text which had suffered a certain amount of assimilation to parallel sources, chiefly to Sam-Ki.

---

[1] *Biblica* xxii, p. 249.

[2] *Samuel*, p. xxxii.

Chapters describing well-known incidents were adapted, sometimes quite extensively; the end of II Chron was practically abandoned at many points in favour of material from Ki. Therefore Par's agreement with the parallel, even when traced back to the *Vorlage*, rarely has the worth of an independent witness. The changes made in Par's Heb ms. towards the present text of Sam-Ki are most probably to be related to the proto-Massoretic text, which was apparently used as the basis of the later *kaige* recension. It would be naive to conclude that the proto-Massoretic text must therefore be only slightly older than that recension. There appears to be little evidence available to clarify the previous history of this textform. F. M. Cross has described it as a Babylonian text "re-introduced into Palestine, perhaps in the Maccabean era ..., or perhaps later in the second or first century B.C."[1]

At some stage in its history Par's Heb text had evidently been annotated with marginal corrections, comments and other glosses, including material from similar, non-parallel sources.

A glance through the apparatus of BH to see where Par is not cited reveals that the *Vorlage* contained many of MT's errors, which must therefore have been perpetrated no later than the second century B.C. But it has been observed that it not infrequently preserved the correct text. Used with care, Par provides as it were in refrigerated form a Heb text which is a valuable witness to the state of the text of Chron in second century B.C. Egypt.

---

[1] *IEJ* xvi, p. 94.

INDEX OF BIBLICAL PASSAGES

A. CHRONICLES/PARALIPOMENA

Asterisks refer to criticism of the apparatus of BH[3]

I		2.39	125	2.53	16, 18, 87, 112,
		2.13	95, 148		116, 157
1.4	138	2.14	3	2.54	23
1.5	34	2.16	34, 51	2.55	41, 56, 107, 116,
1.6	114	2.17	34, 51, 90		125, 166
1.7	96	2.18ff.	90	3.1	3, 14, 29, 30,
1.8	34	2.18	3, 35, 45, 76		34, 51, 103, 157
1.9	34		112, 141	3.2	16, 18, 103
1.11-16	159	2.21f.	29	3.3	27, 38, 57
1.11	149	2.22	19, 38	3.4	136
1.17-24	134	2.23	3, 38, 161	3.5	3, 95, 142
1.27	63	2.24	87, 106, 112, 155	3.6	42, 96
1.28	64, 138	2.25	3, 34, 116, 125*	3.7	3, 35, 122
1.32	26, 34, 64, 99	2.26	122	3.8	42
1.33	27	2.27	34	3.10	88
1.34	64, 138, 148	2.28	122	3.11	46
1.35	3, 47	2.29	3, 57, 115*	3.12	3
1.37	18, 24	2.30f.	157*	3.13	3
1.38	63, 84	2.30	45	3.14	14
1.39	84, 116, 123	2.31	7, 17, 45, 90	3.15	3
1.40	3, 7, 18, 63	2.33	3, 7, 42, 121	3.17	3
	90, 119	2.34f.	121	3.18	3, 34, 96, 125
1.41	20	2.34	7	3.19	3, 88, 134, 151
1.42	7, 29	2.35	7	3.20	18, 34, 121
1.43	22*, 29, 136	2.37	16	3.21	30, 57, 58, 88,
1.47ff.	133	2.38	29, 116		116, 117, 161
1.47-49	136	2.39	125	3.22f.	112
1.47/51	16	2.40	125	3.22	3, 57, 89*,
1.50	29, 159	2.42	60		109, 151
1.51	3, 29, 136, 166	2.43	18	3.23f.	76
1.53f.	3	2.44	27, 112	3.23	88
1.54	46	2.45	24	3.24	45, 46, 107, 109,
2.3	44, 90	2.46	19, 24, 26, 27		139, 166
2.4	99	2.47	18, 19*, 116	4.1	27
2.5	29, 34	2.48	3, 18	4.2	4, 24, 57, 58,
2.6	23, 34, 44	2.49	16, 18, 112		117
2.8	23, 57	2.50	3, 19, 87, 88	4.3	16, 20, 26, 30,
2.9	90	2.51	3*, 7		151
2.10	3, 82	2.52	3, 18, 41,	4.4	40
2.12	148		82, 87		

B. OTHER BIBLICAL BOOKS

C. APOCRYPHA